C000144307

Troubleshooting

Microsoft®

Excel Spreadsheets

Covers Excel 97 and Excel 2000

Laurie Ann Ulrich

PUBLISHED BY
Microsoft Press
A Division of Microsoft Corporation
One Microsoft Way
Redmond, Washington 98052-6399

Copyright © 2001 by Laurie Ann Ulrich

All rights reserved. No part of the contents of this book may be reproduced or transmitted in any form or by any means without the written permission of the publisher.

Library of Congress Cataloging-in-Publication Data
Ulrich, Laurie Ann.
    Troubleshooting Microsoft Excel Spreadsheets / Laurie Ann Ulrich.
        p. cm.
    "Covering both Excel 97 and Excel 2000, this book shows how to troubleshoot
worksheets, analyze data, share data over the Web, and more."--Introd.
    Includes index.
    ISBN 0-7356-1161-0
    1. Microsoft Excel for Windows.   2. Business--Computer programs.   3. Electronic
spreadsheets.   I. Title.

HF5548.4.M523 U43   2000
005.369--dc21   00-048712

Printed and bound in the United States of America.

1 2 3 4 5 6 7 8 9   QWT   6 5 4 3 2 1

Distributed in Canada by Penguin Books Canada Limited.

A CIP catalogue record for this book is available from the British Library.

Microsoft Press books are available through booksellers and distributors worldwide. For further information about international editions, contact your local Microsoft Corporation office or contact Microsoft Press International directly at fax (425) 936-7329. Visit our Web site at mspress.microsoft.com. Send comments to *mspinput@microsoft.com*.

Age of Empires, FrontPage, Microsoft, Microsoft Press, PivotTable, PowerPoint, Visual Basic, Windows, and Windows NT are either registered trademarks or trademarks of Microsoft Corporation in the United States and/or other countries. Other product and company names mentioned herein may be the trademarks of their respective owners.

Unless otherwise noted, the example companies, organizations, products, people, and events depicted herein are fictitious. No association with any real company, organization, product, person, or event is intended or should be inferred.

Acquisitions Editors: Christey Bahn, Alex Blanton
Project Editors: Jenny Moss Benson, John Pierce

Editorial & Production Services: Online Training Solutions, Inc. (OTSI)

Quick contents

Contents

Workspace customization

Acknowledgments

I'd like to thank Jenny Benson and John Pierce for their guidance and vision on this project. I'd also like to acknowledge the great job Joyce Cox (from Online Training Solutions) did in dealing with scheduling changes and keeping the editorial phase of the project running smoothly. In addition, the group of Microsoft Press editors who helped refine the Troubleshooting series in general, and this book specifically, did a great job. I appreciated their diligence, patience, and devotion to creating a truly helpful book. I am grateful to have been included in the development of what I'm sure will be a great new series for both Microsoft Press and its readers.

I'd also like to thank my friend and fellow trainer, Jim Moore, who helped me brainstorm and add to my list of common Excel problems. Both Jim and I have trained more people to use Excel (and the rest of the Office suite) than we could possibly count, and I knew I could rely on Jim to help me remember all the problems our students have experienced over the years, and the many enlightening questions they have raised.

Finally, I must thank my agent, Margot Maley. I don't know how I've survived as a writer without her!

About this book

Troubleshooting Microsoft Excel Spreadsheets presents a series of problems commonly experienced by Excel users and provides clear, concise, and effective solutions to those problems. Whether the problem is the source of a current crisis or just a nagging question you've always wanted answered, the comprehensive set of problems and problem-solving flowcharts presented in this book will turn you into a more confident, well-informed Excel user.

Which version?

Troubleshooting Microsoft Excel Spreadsheets covers both Excel 97 and Excel 2000. Differences between the versions are noted in either the source of the problem or the solution steps. Most of the illustrations show dialog boxes and other elements of Excel 2000. Readers who are using Excel 97 might see some differences in appearance, but the steps and explanations are the same unless otherwise noted.

How to use this book

This book is designed to be read on an as-needed basis—the problem occurs, you look it up using the index or table of contents, you read the solution, and voilà! Problem solved. You'll also learn a lot about Excel by poking around and reading up on features you haven't used before—think of it as preventative medicine to ward off problems before they happen. To make it easier to find your problem or topic of interest, we've grouped the problems you're most likely to have into chapters that are listed alphabetically; the chapter titles are kept simple so that you know at a glance what kinds of topics the chapter contains. Each chapter is broken down into two specific elements: the flowchart and the solutions.

Flowcharts

The first thing you'll see when you go to a chapter is a dynamic, easy-to-use flowchart. It starts by asking you a broad question and then takes you through simple, yes-or-no questions to help you diagnose your problem. If the solution to your problem is a simple one involving only a step or two, you'll be given a quick fix right there on the flowchart.

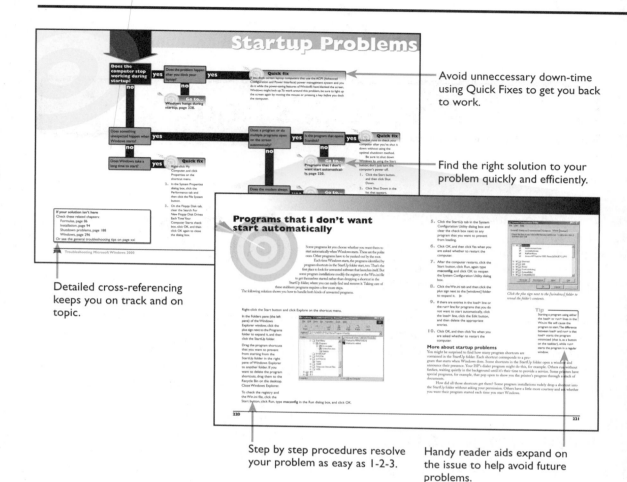

Avoid unneccessary down-time using Quick Fixes to get you back to work.

Find the right solution to your problem quickly and efficiently.

Detailed cross-referencing keeps you on track and on topic.

Step by step procedures resolve your problem as easy as 1-2-3.

Handy reader aids expand on the issue to help avoid future problems.

Your problem will be solved and you'll be back to work (or play). If your problem requires a little more explanation and a few more steps, you'll be directed to the page number of the relevant solution. And if your problem isn't addressed on the flowchart, you can consult the list of related chapters where your problem might be addressed.

Solutions

The solutions are where the real troubleshooting takes place. Each solution provides you with the source of the problem you're experiencing and then tells you how to fix it with clear, step-by-step instructions. The solutions contain plenty of screen shots that show you what you should be seeing as you move through the steps. While the goal is to give you just the facts so that you can be on your way, the solutions also provide some background information of interest for a deeper understanding of why you might have encountered your problem and how to avoid it in the future. Tips contain related material you might find interesting, and warnings indicate what you should or shouldn't do before you begin.

Troubleshooting tips

To troubleshoot, as defined by the *Microsoft Computer Dictionary*, is to "isolate the source of a problem in a program, computer system, or network and remedy it." But how do you go about isolating the source of the problem in the first place? Generally, if you know the source of a problem, you're more than half way to solving it—or at least you know who you need to call to fix it. In reality, however, the source of a problem might not be obvious, might be a symptom masquerading as the source, or might reveal itself to be something other than you initially thought. Does this sound like the very act of troubleshooting is a problem unto itself? Perhaps, but don't let that idea take root. Excel provides some significant tools for you to employ as you troubleshoot problems with your workbooks and their content.

How to troubleshoot

The easiest way to isolate a problem is to start broad (Are you having trouble printing your worksheet?) and then narrow down the scope (Are you having trouble printing your entire worksheet on one page?) until you've reached a specific question you're not sure

how to answer (Have you used the Page Setup dialog box?). The questions help you view the problem objectively while they narrow down the solution.

As you take a fresh look at each problem, guided by the ever-narrowing questions, take note—literally—of the problem and its symptoms. When does it occur? What's happening at that time? Does it happen consistently or only when a specific set of circumstances exist? Effective troubleshooting is a skill, and one that takes some time to acquire. Hey, if everyone were good at it, who'd need a Troubleshooting book? Seriously, though, you can hone your troubleshooting skills by unleashing your powers of observation and as much objectivity as you can muster. The more you know about when a problem occurs, the surrounding circumstances, and how it affects your use of Excel, the closer you are to solving the problem.

Further, the process of observing the problem in action and identifying its source makes it much easier to take advantage of the solutions in this book. Take the time to go through the flowcharts and you'll not only find the solution to your problem, but you'll find a lot of related information as well that can help you with other problems you've had in the past or prevent problems in the future.

Help!

"Help!" need not be a plea for assistance, screamed into the void with no hope of response. Excel's Help files, accessed directly or with the help of any one of the Office Assistant characters, can be a great tool in your troubleshooting arsenal. Between the Index, Contents list, Answer Wizard, and Office Assistant, there are so many ways to pose your question or search for the cause of your problem. Usually, help that can refine your sense of the problem is close at hand.

Simply click the Microsoft Excel Help button, click Microsoft Excel Help on the Help menu, or click the Office Assistant and then type a question in the What Would You Like To Do box. The Office Assistant will then suggest that you click a topic, such as Troubleshoot Printing, to view the related Help topics; yours will most likely be among them. Not too shabby, huh?

If you're not sure how to word a question to the Office Assistant, or if you just don't want to deal with the Office Assistant at all, try typing the single word "Troubleshoot" in the Type Keywords box in the Help window. "Wait a minute," you say. "What Help window?" If all you can see is the Office Assistant, right-click him (or her, or it), and then click Options on the shortcut menu. In the Office Assistant dialog box, clear the Use The Office Assistant check box, and click OK. To access the Help window thereafter, click Microsoft Excel Help on the Help menu. If you click the Index tab, you can type keywords to search by to find the solution to your problem. Using either the Office Assistant or the Help window's Index results in the same choices for Help topics, so feel free to use whatever method works best for you. There are many roads to the same destination!

If you're still stuck

I've endeavored to anticipate the most common problems Excel users run into, but I can't possibly cover them all. I've taught Excel for ten years, and that decade of experience was helpful in determining which problems were the most common. But I'm sure you'll have at least one problem that I haven't solved in this book. If you run into a dead end, you can turn to Microsoft product support (you can find it on the web at *http://support.microsoft.com/support/excel/content/faq/default.asp*) or the Microsoft Office web site (*http://microsoft.com/office*). Another great site where you can get some assistance is *http://www.learnlots.com*. This site offers online tutorials in Excel and a wide variety of other applications. Use the site's search box to find all the tutorials that pertain to Excel.

Troubleshooting web site

With the purchase of this book, you now have access to the Microsoft Troubleshooting web site (*mspress.microsoft.com/troubleshooting*), which complements the book series by offering deeper, more extensive, and regularly updated troubleshooting information, posted monthly. So if you have a problem that wasn't addressed in this book, you can check this web site to see if it's addressed there. (Remember, the updates on the web site are free, but connect time charges might apply.) To access the site, you need this code: **MSE1733**. The Troubleshooting web site will be just as easy to navigate as the book, and keeps in mind the goals of helping you quickly locate your problem and its solution without going into too much detail.

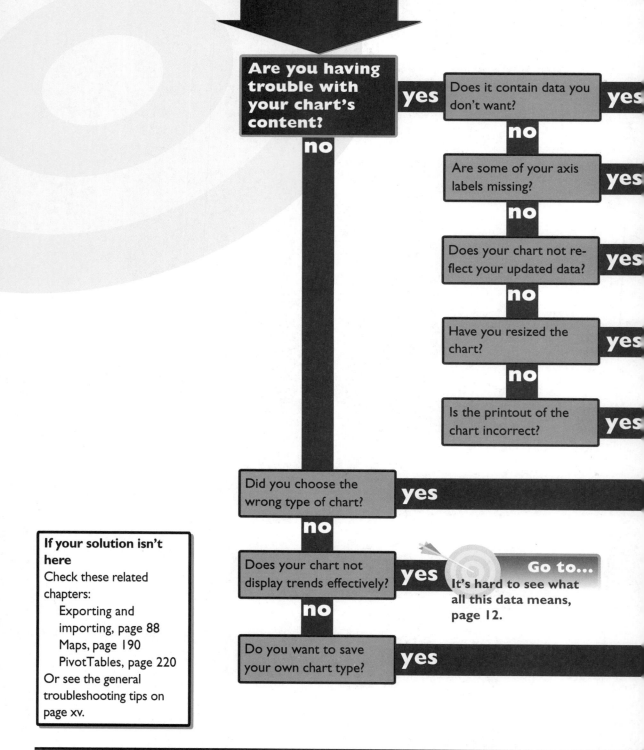

Are you having trouble with your chart's content?

yes — **Does it contain data you don't want?** yes

no

Are some of your axis labels missing? yes

no

Does your chart not reflect your updated data? yes

no

Have you resized the chart? yes

no

Is the printout of the chart incorrect? yes

no

Did you choose the wrong type of chart? yes

no

Does your chart not display trends effectively? yes

Go to...
It's hard to see what all this data means, page 12.

no

Do you want to save your own chart type? yes

If your solution isn't here
Check these related chapters:
  Exporting and
  importing, page 88
  Maps, page 190
  PivotTables, page 220
Or see the general
troubleshooting tips on
page xv.

Go to...
My chart includes data
I don't want, page 4.

Quick fix

This is probably due to your chart's size. Resize it to make it wider if the missing labels are along the horizontal category axis, or make it taller if the missing labels are on the vertical value axis. If resizing the chart isn't an option, try reducing the font size for your labels so that more of them fit on the chart. Click any one of the labels, click the Font Size arrow, and then click a smaller size in the list.

Go to...
My chart doesn't
change when I update
my worksheet, page 6.

Go to...
I've resized my chart,
and now it looks
jumbled, page 8.

Go to...
My chart doesn't look
the way I expect when
I print my worksheet,
page 10.

Quick fix

Click Chart on the Chart menu, and select an alternate chart type and sub-type to meet your needs. Don't forget to check out the Custom Types tab for some less common charting options.

Quick fix

1. Right-click the chart, and click Chart Type on the shortcut menu.

2. On the Custom Types tab, click the User-defined option, and click the Add button to create a new chart type.

3. Give the chart type a name, and click OK.

My chart includes data I don't want

Source of the problem

You know the saying, "It's all in the wrist"? Well, your unwanted data could simply be the result of selecting an extra
row or column—a slip of the mouse that grabbed too much
stuff, resulting in unwanted plotted points or pie slices.
If your mousing skills are beyond reproach, it could
just be that you made an error when selecting the cell range
you wanted to chart. Did you include the totals at the foot of a
series of rows or in the last column in the range? Normally, you
don't want to plot the totals, because they make it hard to visually inter-
pret the numbers that contributed to them. Did you simply select the wrong range of cells from the
wrong part of the worksheet? You're not alone—it's easy to do, and we've all done it. The good
news is that fixing the problem is nearly as easy as causing it was.

How to fix it

1. Right-click the chart in your worksheet, and
   click Source Data on the shortcut menu that
   appears.

2. On the Data Range tab of the Source Data
   dialog box, check the Data Range box. It contains a range statement, which includes the
   name of the sheet from which you selected
   the chart's data and the range of cells you
   selected within that sheet. ▶

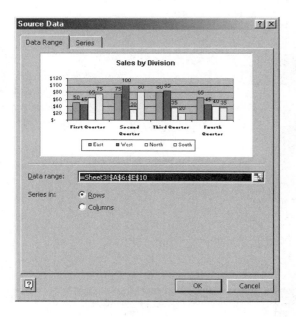

3. If the data you need to plot is on a different
   sheet, click that sheet's tab in the open workbook. If the desired data is within the active
   sheet, stay right where you are.

4. When you're on the sheet that contains the
   data to be plotted, click the first cell in the
   range you want to plot, and drag through
   the adjoining cells until only those that you
   want to plot in the chart are selected.

5. Click OK to redraw the chart using your
   revised range of cells.

Make the bad charts stop!

The secret to including only the data you want in your chart is obviously to select only the desired data in the first place. No surprise there. But what if you're not sure which data is the right data? Here are some pointers:

- Think about what you're charting. If you're charting sales, leave out the columns pertaining to expenses. If you're charting this year's productivity figures, omit the column that includes projections for the part of this year that hasn't happened yet. You'd be surprised how much time you save by stopping and taking a look at your data and imagining the resulting chart *before* you start selecting cells to chart.

- When charting a series of totaled columns and/or rows, include the column headings and row labels (which become your axis labels and legend text), but leave out the totals.

- Just because data appears in contiguous sections on your worksheet doesn't mean you have to include all of those sections on your chart. To select noncontiguous sections of a worksheet, use the Ctrl key when selecting the sections. For example, if you want to chart columns B, C, D, and F (not E), drag through the data in columns B, C, and D, and then release the mouse button. Press and hold down the Ctrl key, drag through the cells you want in column F, release the Ctrl key, and then release the mouse button. Your data range will include two sheet name references and two sets of cell ranges, but that's no problem—the second set of references and ranges resulted from your using the Ctrl key to add to an existing selection.

When all else fails

The Chart Wizard is such a simple tool to use that if your chart is totally wrong, you can just delete it and start over. For most charts it takes only a couple of minutes to complete the process. Yeah, we're usually taught not to take the easy way out. Well, in this case, it's OK.

> **Tip**
>
> Excel uses shorthand for referencing cell ranges. For example, A4:C10 indicates that all cells from the fourth row in column A to the tenth row in column C are included in the range. Some cell ranges include dollar signs before the column letters and row numbers in the cell references (for example, $A$4:$C$10). The dollar signs indicate absolute, or fixed, cell references that won't change if your worksheet changes. An exclamation point next to a sheet name in a cell reference means that the referenced cells are located in a worksheet other than the one in which you are working.

> **Tip**
>
> If your chart is on its own sheet and you want to delete it, delete the entire sheet. If the chart is an object within a sheet, click the chart's boundary to select the entire chart, and press the Delete key.

My chart doesn't change when I update my worksheet

Source of the problem

You've got a chart, you've got a worksheet, and when you change the worksheet data, you expect the chart to change with it—bars to get taller or shorter, pie slices to get thinner or fatter, lines to move up or down on the chart. Why don't they change? There are a couple of potential causes.

First you could be editing part of your worksheet that isn't linked to the chart. When you select worksheet data and then create a chart based on it, a link between the cells and the chart is created. If you then forget which part of your worksheet was plotted in the chart and edit the wrong part of the worksheet, the chart won't change. The fix for this is obvious—edit the right part of your worksheet, and the chart will be updated. Not sure which part is the right part? See "My chart includes data I don't want" on page 4. You need to check the data range for the chart by right-clicking the chart and clicking Source Data on the shortcut menu. You'll see that the current range in the Data Range box is selected, allowing you to simply type a new range to replace the highlighted selection. Once you know the range of cells that was included in your chart, you know which cells to edit if you want the chart to change.

If you've established that you are working with the correct data, you have to consider the second possibility: You might have inadvertently severed the link between the data and the chart. Is your chart based on data in your open worksheet (the one that contains the chart)? If not, perhaps the worksheet that contains the data was moved, renamed, or deleted. If the source data was removed, either from your computer or from the chart by severing the link, the chart will be blank. If the chart has data in it, the first problem is your most likely cause.

How to fix it

1. Confirm that the correct cells are linked to the chart by right-clicking the chart, clicking Source Data on the shortcut menu, and examining the selected range in the Data Range box on the Data Range tab. (The corresponding cell range is also indicated by a dashed rectangle on the source worksheet.)

2. If the correct cells are linked to the chart but the chart is blank, your source data is completely gone. You have to reenter it from whatever manual source (say, a written list of sales totals) or electronic source (such as another worksheet or a Microsoft Word table) that you used when you originally built your worksheet.

3. If the data is correct but not linked properly, you'll have to reestablish the link. If necessary, switch to the worksheet containing the chart. (If the worksheet is in a different workbook,

navigate to where the workbook is stored, open it, and then click the tab of the worksheet that contains the cells with which you want to establish a link.) Right-click the chart, and click Source Data on the shortcut menu that appears. Drag through the cells to be charted, and release the mouse button. ▶

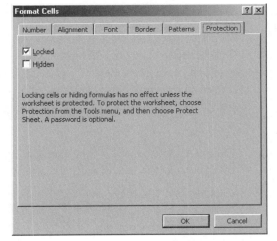

	A	B	C	D	E	F
1						
2						
3		Source Data - Data range:				?X
4		=Sheet3!$A$6:$C$11				
5						
6		First Quarter	Second Quarter	Third Quarter	Fourth Quarter	
7	East	50	75	80	65	
8	West	45	100	85	45	
9	North	65	30	35	40	
10	South	75	80	20	35	
11	TOTAL	235	285	220	185	
12				6R x 3C		

4. Click OK to close the Source Data dialog box and redraw the chart with the reestablished data.

Fool me once...

If other people have access to your worksheets, it's possible that they could make changes to the data that then prevent your charts from being updated. It's essential to treat your workbooks and worksheets carefully, protecting their contents from being accidentally deleted by you or by others who work with the same files. To keep your chart data from being deleted, protect it. Select the cells that contain the data that is linked to your chart (be they in the same or a different workbook), and click Cells on the Format menu. In the Format Cells dialog box, click the Protection tab, and make sure the Locked check box is selected. ▶

For this lock to take effect, you must then protect the entire sheet that contains the data. On the Tools menu, point to Protection, and then click Protect Sheet. In the Protect Sheet dialog box, type a password (if you want to be able to edit or delete the data yourself, but prevent others from doing so), and click OK. ▶

The worksheet will be protected, preventing changes to the locked range of cells and thus protecting the chart you have based on them. (Note that if you want to edit data on a protected sheet, you will have to unprotect the sheet using your password, make your changes, and then protect the sheet again.)

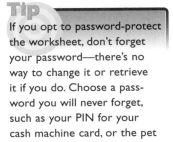

Tip
If you opt to password-protect the worksheet, don't forget your password—there's no way to change it or retrieve it if you do. Choose a password you will never forget, such as your PIN for your cash machine card, or the pet name of a loved one.

I've resized my chart, and now it looks jumbled

Source of the problem

You've done all this work to create a chart, and now you can't even read it! Don't worry—that's usually an easy fix. In many ways, a chart looks and acts like any other graphic object on your worksheet—you can drag it to move it, and you can use the handles on its sides and corners to resize it. If you resize a chart, however, you might get different results than if you resize a piece of clip art or shape you've drawn. Because the chart has content, resizing it affects that content, and in many cases, it can end up jumbled, causing words and numbers to overlap and become hard to read.

This is especially true when the chart's size is reduced, and when any of the chart elements—the legend, titles, or axis labels—have been reformatted before the chart was resized. If adding content and resizing your chart caused the problem, resizing the content and the chart itself can solve it.

How to fix it

1. Click outside your chart to deselect it. This makes certain that no individual element within your chart, such as the legend or chart area, is selected.

2. Click once in the background of the chart object. (The easiest way to select this background correctly is to click the chart object's boundary.) Handles will appear on the four corners and in the middle of the top, bottom, left, and right sides of the chart object.

3. Point to a corner handle until the mouse pointer changes to a two-headed arrow.

4. Drag diagonally away from the chart's center to adjust both your chart's width and height. (You can resize the chart proportionally by holding down the Shift key as you drag.) A dashed box appears and resizes to match your mouse movement. ▶

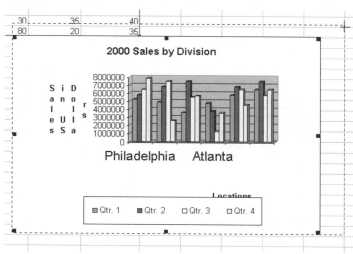

5. When the chart is the size you want it to be, release the mouse button.

6. If the chart's elements are still jumbled or just don't look right, resize the chart in small increments until the chart elements look OK again.

Other chart-mending techniques

If resizing the chart doesn't do a complete job of returning the chart to a visually tidy and legible state, try resizing individual elements of the chart. For example, you can quickly adjust text labels on your chart by selecting the axes, legend, or chart title—or the entire chart, if you want—and then selecting different font types and sizes from the Font and Font Size dropdown lists on the Formatting toolbar. Such changes can solve the "jumbled" problem, and in many cases, even give you more room to work in the chart itself.

A legend in your own mind

Repositioning your chart's legend can help distribute the chart elements more effectively. By default, the chart legend appears on the right side of the chart, with the legend items stacked in a list. Moving the legend so that the legend's color boxes and text appear in a horizontal string at the bottom of the chart gives you more room for the chart and its category axis by providing more room left to right within the chart.

To most precisely reposition the legend, click the legend once, and when handles appear around it, right-click it and click Format Legend on the shortcut menu that appears. In the resulting dialog box, click the Placement tab, and choose Bottom from the list of options. ▶

Click OK, and the legend is both resized and repositioned for you.

A further benefit of moving the legend from the right side of the chart to the bottom is that the chart resizes within the chart box and spreads out horizontally, which might resolve any problems with missing or jumbled axis labels and titles.

Tip

To select a chart's axis, click the axis label, and the axis itself becomes selected. To make sure you've selected the axis you want, hold the mouse pointer over the axis label, and check the ScreenTip. When you click the Format menu, you'll see a command reflecting the selected element, as in Selected Axis. Clicking the command displays a dialog box that allows you to change the patterns, scale, font, number format, and text alignment of the selected axis.

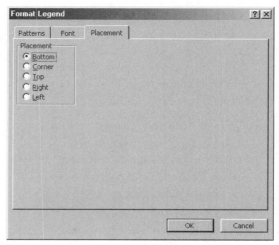

My chart doesn't look the way I expect when I print my worksheet

Source of the problem

Problems printing a chart are generally caused by one of two things: the position of the chart on the worksheet, or the size of the chart itself. In the case of the chart's position, if the chart falls over the edge of a worksheet print area— either one you have set manually or one imposed by the size of the page and its margins—part of the chart will be cut off when you print the worksheet. If the chart is too big to fit on a page or so small that it's illegible when you print it, how the chart was resized after it was created is the culprit.

How to fix it

If your chart is being partially cut off when you print it, follow these steps:

1. On the sheet containing the chart, click Page Break Preview on the View menu. (Make sure the chart isn't selected, or else the Page Break Preview command won't be on the menu.) In Page Break Preview, solid blue lines enclose the entire print area of the worksheet; any worksheet element that falls outside these lines and into the solid gray area will not be printed. Horizontal and vertical dashed blue lines indicate breaks between pages within the print area; any worksheet element that falls across these lines will be broken across printed pages. ▶

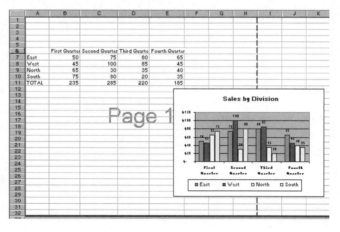

2. To make sure your chart is printed completely on one page, drag the chart so that it appears completely within both the solid and dashed blue lines of the page on which you want it to be printed.

3. On the Standard toolbar, click the Print Preview button, and confirm that your entire chart will now fit on a page. If it still doesn't fit, repeat the previous steps, moving the chart until it fits within the page.

If your chart is too big to fit on a page or is too small to read, follow these steps:

1. If necessary, switch to Normal view by clicking Normal on the View menu.

2. Click the chart to select it. Make sure the chart itself, and not one of its internal elements, is selected by clicking just within the chart's boundary.

3. Resize the chart by dragging the chart's corner handles. Make it larger (drag outward) if it's too small to read; make it smaller (drag toward the chart's center) if it's too large to fit on the page when you print it.

4. Make sure your chart will fit on the page by clicking the Print Preview button on the Standard toolbar. If your chart still overflows the page, continue to resize it until it fits.

Tip

If your chart is positioned so that it straddles a page break and you either don't want to or can't move it, try changing your page orientation so that the entire chart will fit on one page. On the File menu, click Page Setup, and on the Page tab, choose Landscape orientation. Through Print Preview, you'll be able to tell if this solved the problem.

Other chart printing problems and solutions

It's rare that you won't be able to print your chart or that you'll be able to print it only partially. This is usually the result of problems with your printer—your printer does not have enough memory to handle the amount of information being sent to it, or the driver (the file that tells your printer and computer how to communicate) has gone bad or was never right from the start.

A good procedure for any printing problem is to cancel the print job and turn off the printer. Wait a few seconds, turn the printer back on, and then try to print your chart again. If you still can't print the chart, try quitting Excel and restarting Windows. Reopen Excel and the worksheet containing your chart, and attempt the print job again.

If you still can't print the chart, try reinstalling your printer. Click the Start button, point to Settings, and then click Printers. In the Printers window, double-click the Add Printer icon. A series of dialog boxes will step you though the process of selecting your printer from a list of manufacturers and models. (You might need to insert the original CD-ROM from which you installed the software.) If this also fails to solve the problem, you might need to install a new printer driver. You can probably download one from your printer manufacturer's web site.

Tip

For more information on printing your worksheets and controlling their size and layout when you print them, see "Printing" on page 234.

It's hard to see what all this data means

Source of the problem

Charts are created to convey a graphical message about numeric data. That message generally tells one of three stories: a trend (usually told with line charts), a comparison (shown by bar, column, and pie charts), or the frequency of events (shown with a scatter chart). Bar and column charts can also show a trend, assuming the bars or columns represent, for example, sales over a series of months, quarters, or years. The trend is evident, but may not be obvious. The goal of any chart is to convey the numeric message quickly, and if someone has to ponder the chart and refer to the data in order to get the message, the chart has failed.

If the chart type you've selected doesn't tell the whole story, you can try switching to a different chart type. (See the "Quick fix" on page 3.) But for complex data or a story that includes, for example, both a trend and comparisons, this might not solve the problem. You'll want to combine both bars and columns that show comparisons and a line that shows a trend over time. To better illustrate the story you want to convey, add a trendline to your chart.

How to fix it

1. Click your chart's boundary to select the entire chart.

2. On the Chart menu, click Add Trendline.

3. In the Add Trendline dialog box, click the Trend type, and choose which series within your data the line should follow.

4. If you want to give the trendline a new name, click the Options tab, and type the name in the Custom box.

5. Click OK to apply the line to your chart. ▶

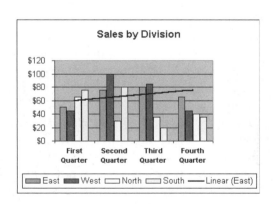

But what about pie charts?

A pie chart can show only one data series, whereas bar, line, and column charts can show several series in the same chart. So pies show only comparisons and are rarely used to show trends.

Other ways to add to the chart's message

To control the message conveyed by a trendline, you can use the Drawing toolbar's Line or Arrow tools to manually draw a line that skims the tops of your bars or just tracks the columns in one data series rather than in the entire chart. If the plotted data series follow a span of time, they're already showing a trend by themselves. Adding the line emphasizes the trend so that no one misses the point.

You can draw two kinds of lines: straight, and "multi-jointed." To add a straight line, click the Drawing button on the Standard toolbar (if the toolbar isn't already visible). Then click the Line or Arrow button on the Drawing toolbar, move the mouse pointer to the worksheet, and hover over the part of your chart where you want the trendline to begin. Your mouse pointer will appear as a crosshair. Drag the mouse, following the tops of the bars to create a single, straight line. ▶

Sometimes your trend doesn't convey a simple "Sales are on the decline" message. If your numbers (and therefore the heights of the bars) go up and down across the width of the chart, your trendline should do the same. Use the AutoShapes Freeform line tool to draw a segmented line that changes its direction. Click the AutoShapes button, point to Lines, and then click the Freeform tool. Drag to draw the first segment of the line (the portion of the line before the trend changes). Then click and drag in a different direction to continue drawing at a new angle. ▶

Tip

You might notice the Set Intercept = check box on the Options tab of the Add Trendline dialog box. The intercept is where the trend-line you want to add should cross the value (or y) axis. By default, the trendline crosses at the zero point, which is normally the bottom of the axis. To start the trendline at any other point on the value axis, enter that value in the Set Intercept = box.

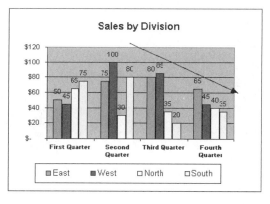

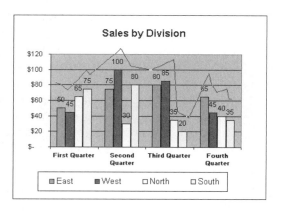

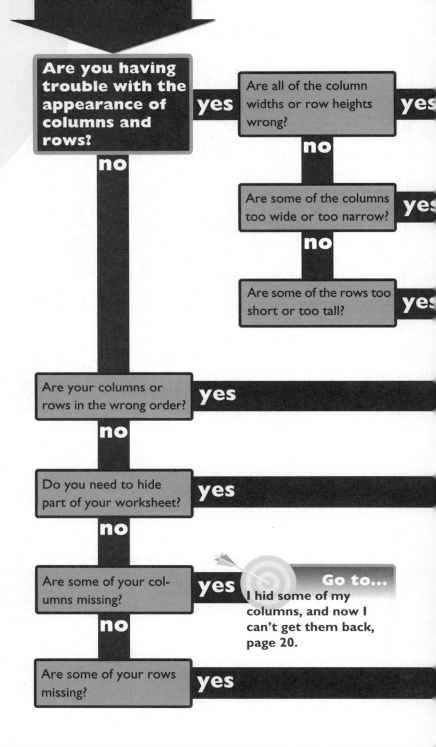

Are you having trouble with the appearance of columns and rows?

yes → Are all of the column widths or row heights wrong? **yes**

no

Are some of the columns too wide or too narrow? **yes**

no

Are some of the rows too short or too tall? **yes**

no ↓

Are your columns or rows in the wrong order? **yes**

no

Do you need to hide part of your worksheet? **yes**

no

Are some of your columns missing? **yes**

Go to...
I hid some of my columns, and now I can't get them back, page 20.

no

Are some of your rows missing? **yes**

Quick fix

1. Select your entire worksheet by pressing Ctrl+A.
2. Point to the seam between any pair of column letters or between any pair of row numbers.
3. Drag to the left or right to adjust the width of all the columns, or drag up or down to adjust the height of all the rows.

Quick fix

1. Point to the seam to the right of the column's letter.
2. Drag to the left to make the column narrower or drag to the right to make it wider.

Go to...

I adjusted my row heights, and now my new entries don't fit, page 16.

Go to...

Some of my columns and rows are out of order, page 18.

Quick fix

1. Select the columns or rows you want to hide, and right-click the selected range.
2. Click Hide on the shortcut menu, and the selected columns or rows will disappear.

Go to...

Rows are missing from my worksheet, page 22.

If your solution isn't here
Check these related chapters:
Formatting worksheets, page 136
Printing, page 234
Templates, page 292
Or see the general troubleshooting tips on page xv.

I adjusted my row heights, and now my new entries don't fit

Source of the problem

By default, Excel adjusts the height of rows for you if you increase the font size of your entries or make your content bold and therefore need the rows to be taller. Sounds like you'd never need to play with row heights on your own, right? Wrong. There are plenty of reasons to adjust row heights manually. To achieve a spread-out look with white space between row content is one of the most common reasons. Further, you might want to make your rows shorter to accommodate very small text, because Excel doesn't shrink rows below the default height of 12.75 even if you choose a tiny font size. Or you might want to turn a blank row into a border by shading the row and making it very short, thereby creating a thin, colored separation between sections of a worksheet.

These manual adjustments are where problems can arise. Suppose you made a row taller to accommodate big text, and now you need to reduce the size of that text. When you choose a smaller font size, the row will remain tall, leaving a lot of white space. Now imagine that you reduced a row's height, and later increased the content's size. Excel won't resize the row automatically once you've tinkered with the height manually, so you end up with a short row with tall text, with the tops of the letters cut off. ▶

Resolving these problems is easy, requiring only that you restore the row or rows in question to a size that meets the needs of the tallest text in the row.

	A	B	C	D	E
1	Sales by Division				
2					
3	Division	Q1	Q2	Q3	Q4
4	Philadelphia	5.25	6.3	6.42	7.15
5	New York	5.65	7.25	8.3	8.25
6	Chicago	7.24	8.25	3.45	5.5

How to fix it

1. Select the rows that are no longer sized appropriately. If you want to fix only one row, click a cell in the row you want to resize. To select a series of contiguous rows, drag through their row numbers. If the rows are noncontiguous, hold down the Ctrl key, click the row numbers for the rows you want, and then release the key when you've selected all the rows you need.

2. Point to the bottom seam of any of the row headings (the buttons with the row numbers on them) of the row or rows you want to fix, and then double-click. The row(s) are automatically resized to fit the tallest entry in each row. ▶

Here is the row height adjustment in progress.

More woes with rows

Rows start out just big enough to display 10-point or 12-point text, with a little room above and below the text. This can look a little cramped, and if you have many rows of similar content, it can be hard to read. Further, if you're printing your worksheet without the gridlines, you might read across the width of the sheet and have your eye accidentally stray up or down a row when the data is housed in that tight an arrangement.

To make more visual room on your worksheet, you can make some or all of your rows taller, even if you don't increase your fonts beyond the default 10-point size. ▶

Simply select the entire worksheet by pressing Ctrl+A, or select a specific range by dragging through the row numbers for the range of rows you want to resize. Using any seam between the row headings, drag down to make the rows taller. As you're dragging, a ScreenTip appears to show the adjusted row height.

Tip
Once you've reset the row heights to automatically accommodate the tallest entry, Excel will return to resizing those rows if you increase the font size again.

Tip
You can set a specific row height for one or more rows by selecting the rows you want to adjust and then right-clicking. When the shortcut menu appears, click Row Height, type a measurement in the Row Height dialog box, and then click OK. All your selected rows will be resized to the height you specified.

Some of my columns and rows are out of order

Source of the problem

First let's make it clear what "my columns are out of order" really means. It doesn't mean that Excel suddenly forgot the alphabet and row M is appearing before row G. Rather, "columns out of order" refers to column headings and content that are not in a logical order in relation to other headings and content in the worksheet. For example, if you're setting up a database, it's easy to forget a column (like one for Check Number in a database that stores customer order information) and then throw it in at the end, only to wish later that it were in a different place (like the seventh column, next to Date Paid, rather than the ninth column, after Amount Due). ▶

Now, hang on a minute. Does this mean *you* are the source of the problem? Well, yes. But don't feel bad; we've all done it, and we'll all do it again. The goal is to know how to fix the problem when it inevitably arises, and the solution is easy—you just have to move the columns around until they're in the order you want them.

	A	B	C	D	E	F	G	H	I
1				Customer Orders					
2									
3	First Name	Last Name	Date of Order	Order Total	Amount Paid	Paid By	Date Paid	Amount Due	Check Number
4	Smith	John	8/27/00	$153.78	$153.78	Visa	8/31/00		
5	Brown	Bill	8/15/00	$257.35	$250.00	Check	9/15/00		458

How to fix it

1. Select the column that you want to move, by clicking its column heading (the button with the column letter on it).

2. From anywhere in the range of selected cells, point to the left or right edge of the selected column. Your mouse pointer turns into a left-pointing white arrow. (If you point to the left or right seam of the column heading, the pointer becomes a black double arrow.)

3. Using the *right* mouse button, drag the column to the desired location among the other columns. Release the mouse button.

Tip

If the column you want to move contains a merged cell (perhaps you've applied the Merge And Center command to the title of the worksheet), you cannot drag the column to a new location. First remove the Merge formatting. Select the merged cell, and click Cells on the Format menu. On the Alignment tab, clear the Merge Cells check box, and click OK. Now you can move your column, and when it's properly placed, remerge the cell as desired.

4. On the shortcut menu, click Shift Right And Move. ▶

5. Check your column's new position. If you dropped it in the wrong spot, repeat steps 2 through 4 until the column is where you need it to be.

Move it AND lose it?

Be careful when you move worksheet content, be it entire columns or a block of cells. If you simply drag the text from place to place, you run the risk of replacing the content where you drop the text (and deleting the existing content in the process). Of course, a dialog box appears with a message asking if you want to replace the content at your destination. Be sure to read this message (and others like it) thoroughly, and click Cancel if you had intended to do something else. Be careful not to get into the habit of clicking OK without reading the message first! ▶

If you copy or cut content from one location and then paste it in another location using the Copy, Cut, and Paste commands or the corresponding toolbar buttons, no such prompt appears—the paste operation replaces anything that was already in place, no questions asked. A way around this? Always drag with your right mouse button. You'll then be able to choose the Shift And Move command from the shortcut menu, protecting existing content at the new location.

Rearranging rows

If your rows are out of order, meaning that you want the content in one row to be above another row rather than below it, you can drag that row's content into a new position in the same way you drag a column. Click the row heading to select the row, and then point to the bottom edge of the selected cells, not the seam of the row heading. Hold down the right mouse button, and drag the row up or down, releasing the mouse button when you've reached the appropriate spot. On the shortcut menu that appears, click Shift Down And Move.

Tip

If you need to move more than one consecutive column, select them by dragging through their column letters, and then point to an outer edge of the selected cells. When your mouse pointer becomes a left-pointing arrow, drag the columns with the right mouse button, and put them where you want them, clicking the Shift Right And Move command on the shortcut menu that appears when you release the mouse button.

I hid some of my columns, and now I can't get them back

Source of the problem

At some point, you might decide to hide some columns in your worksheet—perhaps to conserve space or to protect confidential data from being viewed by others. Later, you might want to bring the columns back so that you can work on them or use their cells in formulas—but you can't seem to make the columns reveal themselves. Being unable to bring the hidden columns back would certainly be a problem!

If you're thinking, "Then I won't ever hide my columns," imagine this: You have a worksheet for tracking employee information. It includes salary data in columns E and F, which you wisely chose to hide so that anyone viewing or printing the worksheet wouldn't get an eyeful of information that should remain confidential. ▶

	A	B	C	D	G	H
1			Employee Database			
2						
3	First Name	Last Name	Dept.	Date Hired	Insurance y/n	
4	John	Smith	Marketing	5/23/1998	Y	
5	Bill	Brown	Sales	12/15/1999	N	
6	Mary	Jones	Accounting	4/27/2000	Y	
7						

Good choice. But now you need to update the salary columns to reflect recent raises, so you need to bring the hidden columns back into view. Wait a minute, they won't come back!

When you attempt to drag a column back into view using the column headings (the buttons with the column letters on them), you end up only widening the adjoining columns. If you've hidden multiple columns, you might have trouble bringing one or all of them back. What to do? Well, you can drag column headings to reveal the hidden column or columns, or you can use the Unhide command. Essentially, you reverse the steps you took to hide the columns in the first place.

Tip

Dragging to widen the columns isn't always easy. Because you did such a good job hiding the columns, it's hard to tell whether you're dragging the seam to widen the column that's hidden or the column next to it! The trick is to select the columns both before and after the hidden column or columns. Point to the seam between the two columns, and then drag the double-headed arrow to widen the columns and expose the hidden ones. The width of the formerly hidden columns is equal to that of the two adjusted visible columns. After you do this, you might have to readjust column widths to your liking.

How to fix it

To reveal a hidden column by widening it, follow these steps:

1. Point to the seam between column headings, and be on the lookout for a special mouse pointer—a variation of a two-headed arrow. When a column is hidden, the two-headed arrow appears to be split down the middle. ▶

This two-headed arrow pointer is used to reveal hidden columns or rows.

2. When the split two-headed arrow appears, drag to the right to widen the hidden column. Once the hidden column is visible again, it appears in place in the worksheet, and you can adjust its width as needed to view the column's content.

To reveal a hidden column by using a menu command, follow these steps:

1. Select the columns on either side of the hidden column.

2. Right-click anywhere in the selected columns' cells.

3. Click Unhide on the shortcut menu. ▶

Come out, come out, wherever you are

If you have more than one hidden column, you can reveal all hidden columns in one fell swoop. (See the tip in "Rows are missing from my worksheet" on page 22.) Press Ctrl+A to select the entire worksheet, and then right-click any of the column headings. On the shortcut menu, click Unhide. Voilà! All your hidden columns are revealed. (If you want to unhide only specific columns using the shortcut menu, you need to select the column to the right of the hidden column or columns and click Unhide for each of the hidden columns.)

Tip

In case you're wondering how to hide multiple columns in the first place, it's easy. Select the columns you want to hide by dragging through their headings. (To select nonadjacent columns, hold down the Ctrl key while you click the headings for the columns you want to select.) Right-click anywhere on the selected cells, and click Hide on the shortcut menu.

Rows are missing from my worksheet

Source of the problem

At some point, you might be working in a worksheet and notice a gap in row numbers. Or you might look for data that you know exists, but you can't see it. Maybe you know the data still exists because there's a formula that refers to a cell in that row and the formula still works, so the data has got to be there. So what's going on? Just as you can hide columns (see "I hid some of my columns, and now I can't get them back" on page 20), you can hide rows on a worksheet. You can hide them by selecting the row or rows, right-clicking any of the selected cells, and clicking Hide on the shortcut menu. You can also hide them by reducing their height to zero, just as you can accidentally reduce a column's width to nothing. This technique is often inadvertently applied. For example, you might attempt to select a series of rows to format them. Instead of just clicking the row headings (the buttons with the row numbers on them) to select the rows, you click the seam between the rows and drag, thereby resizing the rows. Or you might attempt to resize a row, and accidentally hide the row altogether. ▶

	A	B	C	D
1			**Employee Database**	
2				
3	First Name	Last Name	Dept.	Date Hired
4	John	Smith	Marketing	5/23/1998
7				
8				

Rows 5 and 6 are hidden accidentally.

Because it happens accidentally, you might not notice the problem right away. What to do? You can employ one of two methods: dragging to reveal the hidden rows, or utilizing the Hide command's companion, Unhide.

How to fix it

To reveal a hidden row by making it taller, follow these steps:

1. Point to the seam between row numbers, and a two-headed arrow that looks split down the middle will appear. (If multiple rows are hidden, you must select the row before and after the hidden rows to reveal them all using the dragging process.)

2. Drag down to make the hidden row appear.

3. Adjust the height of the rows as needed.

To reveal a hidden row using a menu command, follow these steps:

1. Select the row above and below the hidden row or rows.

2. Right-click any of the cells in the selected rows.

3. Click Unhide on the shortcut menu. ▶

To reveal all hidden rows at once, press Ctrl+A to select the entire worksheet, right-click anywhere on the worksheet, and click Unhide on the shortcut menu.

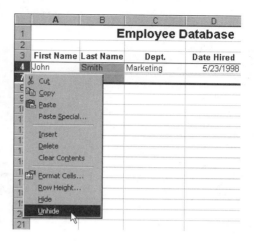

Tip

Another quick way to reveal all your hidden rows—or columns, for that matter—is to select your entire worksheet (press Ctrl+A), point to any seam between row or column headings (your mouse pointer will appear as a two-headed arrow), and double-click. This technique is normally used for resizing rows or columns to fit their largest entry, and in so doing, you return any zero-height rows or zero-width columns to the default size, which is 12.75 for rows, and 8.43 for columns.

Risky row revelations

If you're keeping a list of records in your worksheet, be careful when hiding rows within the list. If you hide rows, sorting those rows might not appear to work, and if you filter for data that's contained in the hidden row(s), you won't be able to see the data. Before doing any sorting or filtering of your data, reveal all your hidden rows by pressing Ctrl+A, right-clicking a row heading, and clicking Unhide on the shortcut menu. With all your rows visible, use the Data menu's Sort and Filter commands as needed.

Comments

Do you want to control the appearance of your comments? → **yes**

no ↓

Are you having trouble hiding your comments? → **yes**

no ↓

Are your comments missing from your worksheet printout? → **yes**

no ↓

Are some of your comments no longer needed? → **yes**

no ↓

Are you having trouble tracking the changes made to your worksheet? → **yes**

no ↓

Do you want to veto some of the changes others have made to your worksheet? → **yes**

Go to...

I don't want to keep some of the changes made since Track Changes was turned on, page 32.

Go to...
I don't want my name to appear in the comment box, page 28.

Go to...
Comments and track-change comments pop up on the screen, and I don't want them to, page 26.

Quick fix
1. On the File menu, click Page Setup.

2. On the Sheets tab of the Page Setup dialog box, click the Comments drop-down arrow, and click At End Of Sheet or As Displayed On Sheet to indicate where in your printout the comments should appear.

Quick fix
Right-click the cell with the comment (look for the red triangle in the cell's upper right corner), and click Delete Comment on the shortcut menu.

Go to...
Other people make changes to my worksheet, and I want to keep track of those changes, page 30.

If your solution isn't here
Check these related chapters:
Drawing shapes and lines, page 66
Hyperlinks, page 170
Printing, page 234
Or see the general troubleshooting tips on page xv.

Comments and track-change comments pop up on the screen, and I don't want them to

Source of the problem

If the worksheet you're working in includes comments and change notes, you might find that boxes pop up right when you're trying to get work done. To solve this problem, you need to understand what these boxes are and where they come from.

You can add comments to a worksheet to annotate its content. For example, you can remind yourself or others who might be using the worksheet to do something or where supporting information can be found. You can also use Track Changes to have Excel insert track-change comments whenever someone edits a cell in the worksheet. The history of the edit—who made it, what the edit was, and when it was made—is stored as a comment in the cell.

Comments are indicated by red triangles in a cell's upper right corner. Track-change comments are indicated by blue triangles in a cell's upper left corner and are outlined in blue. (Cells can have both comments and track-change comments.) The triangles tell you that a cell has a comment and/or has been edited, without your having to look at the comments all the time. ▶

Many users become aggravated when comment boxes pop up all over the place as they edit their worksheets. It can seem as though every time you move your mouse pointer, a little box pops up to distract you! ▶

The solution lies in telling Excel what you want to see on the screen. You can tell Excel to not display red triangles and comments, or if you are working with Track Changes turned on, you can turn off on-screen highlighting of edited cells. This will prevent Excel from displaying blue triangles and comments that describe the edits that have occurred.

A comment triangle indicates that a cell has a comment.

Track Changes is on, and this cell was edited.

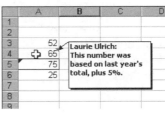

Laurie Ulrich:
This number was based on last year's total, plus 5%.

Tip

Inserting a comment is easy—simply right-click the cell where you want to insert the comment, and click Insert Comment on the shortcut menu. A text box appears, into which you can type your comment. After you enter the comment, click outside the box to complete the process. A small red triangle appears in the cell's upper right corner.

How to fix it

To keep comments from popping up on your worksheet, follow these steps:

1. On the Tools menu, click Options, and in the Options dialog box, click the View tab.

2. In the Comments section, click None. This won't delete your comments, but it will prevent the red triangles from being displayed while you're working, and the comment boxes won't appear as your mouse pointer moves over commented cells. ▶

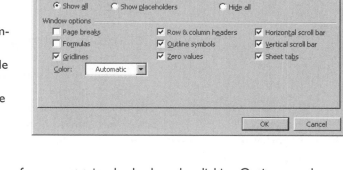

3. After you've finished working in a worksheet, you can turn the display of comment triangles back on by clicking Options on the Tools menu, and on the View tab, resetting the Comments option to Comment Indicator Only.

To prevent blue triangles and comments from appearing when Track Changes is turned on, follow these steps:

1. On the Tools menu, point to Track Changes, and then click Highlight Changes.

2. In the lower left corner of the Highlight Changes dialog box, clear the Highlight Changes On Screen check box. ▶

3. Click OK to close the dialog box, and continue working in your worksheet. Track Changes will still be turned on, but you won't see the track-changes comments, and blue triangles will not appear in the upper left corner of any edited cells.

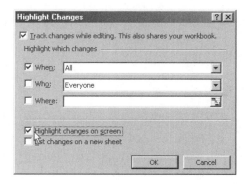

> **Tip**
> If Track Changes is turned on but the on-screen display of changes is turned off, remember to turn the display back on before anyone else edits or views your worksheet. Without the blue triangles displayed on the screen, other users won't know that Track Changes is on, and they might not realize that their edits will be tracked. On the Tools menu, point to Track Changes, click Highlight Changes, and select the Highlight Changes On Screen check box to redisplay blue triangles and comments.

I don't want my name to appear in the comment box

Source of the problem

When you insert a comment in your worksheet or make an edit while working with Track Changes turned on, your name is included in the comment box. Comments, indicated by a red triangle in the upper right corner of a cell, are a tool that you can use to insert notes to yourself or others who might use a worksheet. Track Changes is a tool that monitors changes to a particular worksheet, including who has made those changes and when they were made. Cells edited while Track Changes is turned on are indicated by a small blue triangle in the upper left corner of a cell. It makes sense to have the name of a comment's author in the comment box so that if others are viewing comments and perhaps even adding their own comments to the worksheet, it's clear who said what. ▶

You might, however, prefer to keep your name out of it—perhaps you're editing a worksheet on behalf of someone else, or you want your comments to be anonymous so that any suggestions or questions posed are not given more or less credence because of their author. You can remove names from existing comments by editing comments manually. You can also remove a name association from a workbook and see to it that names are not included in a particular workbook in the future.

How to fix it

To remove names from existing comments, follow these steps:

1. Point to a cell that contains a comment (any cell with a red triangle in the upper right corner), and when the comment is displayed, right-click the cell.

2. Click Edit Comment on the shortcut menu. The comment box remains on the screen with the insertion point active within the box.

3. Select the displayed name in the comment box, and press Delete. You can press Delete again to pull the comment text up one line, as needed.

Tip

If you're working with a group of people who are editing the same workbook, you can have all users change their User Name setting to a different made-up name: User1, User2, and so on. You can also ask each person to come up with a unique name or nickname and enter that in the User Name box.

To eliminate names from future comments in the active workbook, follow these steps:

1. On the Tools menu, click Options.

2. In the Options dialog box, click the General tab, and look at the User Name box. The name in this box will appear on all comments. ▶

3. Edit the name. You can't simply delete it, because the box requires an entry. If you want to use a made-up name, such as "User 1," type that in the box. If you want no name whatsoever to appear, type a period or a dash—some character to satisfy the box's content requirement.

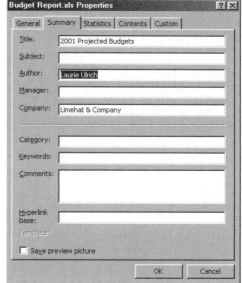

My identity? No comment

Excel derives the name that appears in the comment box from the user information entered when the software was installed. If you don't want any of your work—workbooks, comments, edits made while Track Changes is turned on—to bear your name, you have to edit this user information. On the File menu, click Properties, and click the Summary tab. (The name in the Author box is the name Excel will associate with any workbook created on your computer.) ▶

You can edit or delete the author name. If you completely remove the author name from your current workbook and any workbooks you later create, an ellipsis (…) will appear in the Author box because the box requires an entry. Unless you are working on an administrator's computer (such as a Windows 2000 Advanced Server computer), the user name assigned to a particular workbook will override the name that appears in the Properties dialog box.

Note that your old workbooks will still show your name in their Properties dialog boxes, so if you want to change them, you'll have to open them individually and edit the dialog box for each one. The Properties dialog box can be viewed by anyone who opens your workbook—whether they open it from an e-mail message, over your network, or from a floppy disk—so bear that in mind as you make your changes to the Author box and other boxes, such as Company and Manager.

Other people make changes to my worksheet, and I want to keep track of those changes

Source of the problem

So, you've set up a worksheet, and you've entered the data. Someone else comes along and makes changes to the layout (column headings, row labels) or the data. You open the worksheet the next day, and you have no idea who made the changes or why. This can be disconcerting, especially if you didn't know other people would be editing your worksheet. Even if you were aware that others would be making changes, you probably want to know exactly which cells were changed and who made the changes. That's where Excel's Track Changes feature comes in. By turning Track Changes on, you can keep track of which cells have been changed, what they used to contain, what they contain now, who made the change, and when. ▶

3	52650	45675	
4	65872	65520	
5	75268	Laurie Ulrich, 8/11/2000 1:34 AM:	
6	25340	Changed cell A6 from '25' to '25340'.	
7			
8			
9			

Despite the Big Brother sound of all that, you'll find that Track Changes can be a significant tool for any worksheet edited by more than one person, or even a worksheet that only you use—no one can remember everything, and you might need a reminder as to which cells you've edited.

When Track Changes is turned on, by default the entire worksheet will be tracked for any changes or additions by any user. You can edit these settings, however, by using the When, Who, and Where boxes in the Highlight Changes dialog box.

How to fix it

1. On the Tools menu, point to Track Changes, and then click Highlight Changes.

2. Click the Track Changes While Editing check box.

3. To limit tracking to a specific time frame or specific people, select the check box next to When or Who, and then click the down arrow and select your preference.

4. To limit tracking to a specific cell or range, select the check box next to Where. Then click the Collapse button to the right of the box to temporarily shrink the Highlight Changes dialog box, and click the cell or drag through the range of cells in which you want to use Track Changes.

When you've made your range selection, click the Expand button to restore the dialog box to its full size, and you'll see the range selection displayed in the Where box. (If you want Track Changes to apply to the entire worksheet, leave the Where box blank.) ▶

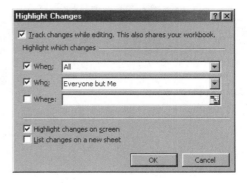

5. Choose whether or not you want to see the edits on-screen all the time. If you don't want to see them, clear the Highlight Changes On Screen check box.

6. Click OK to turn Track Changes on with the settings you specified.

I know what you did last time you edited the worksheet

When Track Changes is turned on, the cells that have been edited have a blue triangle in the upper left corner of the cell. When you click a cell bearing that triangle, a comment box appears, showing the name of the person who made the change or addition, the time and date that the cell was last edited, what the cell originally contained, and what the change was. (Comment boxes might also pop up when you move your mouse pointer over cells with a red triangle in the upper right corner. If any of these boxes get in your way, see "Comments and track-change comments pop up on the screen, and I don't want them to" on page 26.)

Track Changes can be turned off at any time, and at some point, you need to turn it off and accept or reject each of the changes made to the worksheet. The process for doing this is covered in "I don't want to keep some of the changes made since Track Changes was turned on" on page 32. If people have made changes you don't want to keep, you can throw them out and revert to the original worksheet content.

Covering one's tracks

Track Changes isn't foolproof. Other users can turn Track Changes off while they're working, thus hiding the fact that they've made changes. If you don't want to alert people to the fact that Track Changes is on, on the Tools menu, point to Track Changes, click Highlight Changes, and clear the Highlight Changes On Screen check box in the Highlight Changes dialog box. There will be no visible sign that Track Changes is turned on, and you can turn the screen highlighting back on when you're ready to inspect the worksheet. Of course if people need to know what others have done in order to make their own changes, you'll have to leave highlighting turned on and trust that in the spirit of teamwork, no one will turn Track Changes off.

I don't want to keep some of the changes made since Track Changes was turned on

Source of the problem

Actually, this is a good problem to have. The beauty of using Track Changes, in addition to being able to see who made the changes and when, is that you can go through the worksheet and choose which changes stay and which changes go.

When Track Changes is turned on, any edits you or others make to a worksheet are, well, tracked. You see the history of the changes in a comment box, and any cell that has been changed is indicated by a small blue triangle in its upper left corner. The very fact that you're working with Track Changes turned on means that you can easily find each change that's been made to your worksheet and choose whether or not to keep it. This includes actual changes as well as new information added to your worksheet. You can choose which person's edits to review (and to then accept or reject), which ranges of the worksheet to review, and which changes within those ranges to review. As long as Track Changes is on, you can turn back the clock and make it as though no one ever touched your worksheet.

How to fix it

1. On the Tools menu, point to Track Changes, and then click Accept Or Reject Changes to display the Select Changes To Accept Or Reject dialog box. ▶

2. To review changes made since a particular date, click the When down arrow, and click Since Date in the list. Today's date will appear in the box, and you can edit it by typing a past date.

3. To review only those changes that were made by a particular person, click the Who down arrow, and make a selection from the list. The list will include yourself, Everyone, Everyone But Me, and anyone else who edited your worksheet.

4. If you want to review only part of your worksheet, click the Collapse button at the end of the Where box, and specify a range of cells to review. The dialog box will shrink to expose the whole worksheet, and you can drag through the range of cells you want to review. Then click the Expand button. ▶

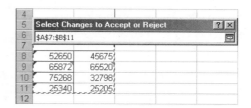

5. Once your review settings are in place, click OK to begin reviewing the changes that have been made. Each one will appear in the Accept Or Reject Changes dialog box, showing the name of the person who made the change, when it was made (date and time), and what the change was. ▶

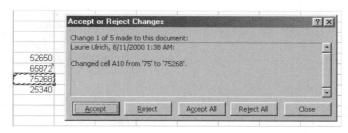

6. Click Reject to get rid of whatever change was made. The cell's entry reverts to what it was before Track Changes was turned on. Assuming you turned Track Changes on just before you made the worksheet available for use by others, and assuming none of them turned Track Changes off, you'll be able to return the worksheet to the way you left it before others got their hands on it!

7. As you click Reject (or Accept, if you run into any changes you want to keep), the dialog box shows you each change, one by one. When you have reviewed all of the changes, the dialog box closes, and you are returned to your worksheet.

Tip
You can click the Reject All button in the Accept Or Reject Changes dialog box if you want to get rid of all changes without having to review each one. On the Tools menu, point to Track Changes, and then click Accept Or Reject Changes. If necessary, save the workbook when prompted. When the Select Changes To Accept Or Reject dialog box appears, make sure the Where check box and text box are clear, and then click OK. In the Accept Or Reject Changes dialog box, click Reject All. When you're prompted to confirm your intention to reject all changes without reviewing them, click OK to proceed. (Likewise, you can click Accept All to accept all changes without reviewing them.)

Tip
Once you've rejected (or accepted) changes and the reviewing process is over, you cannot undo your rejection or acceptance of the edits. Other than saving the file with a different name before beginning the reviewing process and then going back to the original file, you cannot get the changes back once you've rejected them and the rejection/acceptance process is complete.

Do you need help setting up your conditional formats? → **yes**

no

Do you need to turn off conditional formatting? → **yes**

no

Do you need to set up multiple conditions? → **yes**

no

Are you having trouble getting conditional formatting to work? → **yes**

no

Is the Conditional Formatting command dimmed on the menu? → **yes**

no

Do your conditional formats fail to change when you update your data? → **yes**

Go to...
The conditional formats I set up aren't updated when I edit my worksheet, page 42.

no

Are you having trouble changing your conditional formats? → **yes**

Go to...

I'm not sure how to set up conditonal formatting, page 36.

Quick fix

1. Click Conditional Formatting on the Format menu, and click the Delete button. When the Delete Conditional Format dialog box appears, select the check box for each condition you want to delete.

2. Click OK twice to close the dialog boxes.

Go to...

I don't know how to set up multiple conditions, page 38.

Go to...

I applied conditional formatting, but it didn't work, page 40.

Quick fix

The Conditional Formatting command is unavailable if Excel is in Edit mode, if your worksheet is currently set to be shared, or if Track Changes is turned on.

Go to...

I'm not sure how to change my conditional formats, page 44.

If your solution isn't here

Check these related chapters:

Formatting numbers, page 114

Formatting text, page 124

Formatting worksheets, page 136

Or see the general troubleshooting tips on page xv.

I'm not sure how to set up conditional formatting

Source of the problem

The Conditional Formatting dialog box isn't terribly self-explanatory, so don't feel bad that you didn't yell, "Of course! I understand!" the first time you tried to use this feature. The concept is simple: show the cells in this range that are greater than some specified number or contain some certain value or formula. But setting up the criteria so that the conditional formatting is applied to the right cells is not always a snap.

To set up conditional formatting, it's important to know what you want the formatting to tell you. What is it you're looking for? Do you want to be alerted if any employee's "Remaining Sick Days" hits zero? Do you want to see all the sales figures that exceed a quota of $150,000? If you know what it is you want flagged, you're more than halfway there.

The second part of the process involves expressing a "say when" aspect to Excel, which means choosing an operator (Greater Than, Less Than, Equal To, and so on) and entering or selecting a value that Excel should compare with the cells in your selected range. After that, you just need to tell Excel what formatting it should use to flag the cells that meet the criteria you've established. It's important to set up formats that will stand out. Many people think a command didn't work, when in reality, they chose a subtle change—such as changing the color of the text from black to navy blue—that's easy to miss, especially when the worksheet is printed.

So, the problem can usually be fixed by thinking things through before you start setting up your criteria. With some prep work under your belt, you'll master conditional formatting in no time.

How to fix it

1. Select the range of cells you want to apply conditional formatting to. To select noncontiguous ranges, hold down the Ctrl key, click the noncontiguous ranges you want to include, release the mouse button, and then release the Ctrl key. ▶

	A	B	C	D	E	F	G
1							
2							
3		Qtr. 1	Qtr. 2	Qtr. 3	Qtr. 4	TOTALS	Qtr. 1
4	Philadelphia	5250678	5786452	6425642	7854251	$ 25,317,023	603
5	New York	4875986	6785428	7452987	2578456	$ 21,692,857	560
6	Chicago	3587452	7458976	5487653	5648752	$ 22,182,833	412
7	Atlanta	4789521	3789451	1258795	3567894	$ 13,405,661	550
8	Phoenix	5784236	6785497	6456781	4526781	$ 23,553,295	665
9	San Francisco	6452179	7425891	5784696	6457251	$ 26,120,217	742
10	TOTAL	$30,740,052.00	$38,031,695.00	$32,866,754.00	$30,633,385.00	$ 132,271,886	$ 35,351,
11							
12							
13							
14							

2. On the Format menu, click Conditional Formatting to display the Conditional Formatting dialog box.

3. In the Condition 1 section of the dialog box, leave the first box set to Cell Value Is if you want to apply conditional formatting to specific values. (If you want to apply conditional formatting to a specific formula, click Formula Is in the list, and then type the formula you want to format.)

4. Choose an operator from the box next to Cell Value Is. (If you've selected Formula Is instead of Cell Value Is, you won't need to choose an operator.)

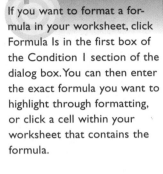
If you want to format a formula in your worksheet, click Formula Is in the first box of the Condition 1 section of the dialog box. You can then enter the exact formula you want to highlight through formatting, or click a cell within your worksheet that contains the formula.

5. In the next box or boxes (depending on which operator you chose), type a value or values, or select a cell in the worksheet that contains the value you want. ▶

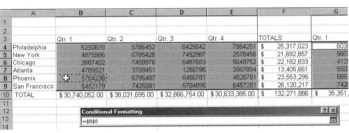

6. Click the Format button. The Format Cells dialog box appears, where you can choose font formatting and border and pattern settings to apply to the cells that meet your conditions. Click OK when you have finished setting the formats you want. ▶

7. In the Conditional Formatting dialog box, click OK to apply your formatting.

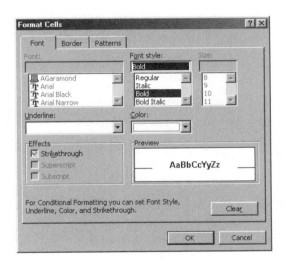

Tip

Be sure to choose formats that will stand out against whatever formatting is already in place in your worksheet. If, for example, your text is already bold or in a different color, the conditional formatting should not include a change to bold or that color.

I don't know how to set up multiple conditions

Source of the problem

Sometimes a simple "If any cell in this range is less than 1, change the background to blue" condition isn't enough. What if you also want to know if any cells contain a value greater than 5? If you want to know which employees have no sick days left *and* which haven't used any sick days at all, for example, you need a second set of conditions to format cells that meet this second criterion. There is no single operator within the Conditional Formatting dialog box that will cover cells that are both below 1 and more than 5.

To apply formatting to more than one set of conditions, you need to set up a second (and perhaps third) set of conditions to compare to your selected range of cells.

How to fix it

1. Select the range of cells to which you've already applied conditional formatting and to which you now want to add a second set of conditions. You can also select a range to which you have not applied any conditional formatting and apply a brand new set of conditions.

2. On the Format menu, click Conditional Formatting.

3. If necessary, in the first box of the Condition 1 section of the Conditional Formatting dialog box, click either Cell Value Is if you want to apply conditional formatting to specific values, or Formula Is if you want to apply conditional formatting to a specific formula.

4. Choose an operator from the box next to Cell Value Is. (If you've selected Formula Is instead of Cell Value Is, you won't need to choose an operator.)

5. In the next box or boxes (depending on which operator you chose), type a value or values, or select a cell in the worksheet that contains the value you want. ▶

6. Click the Format button. The Format Cells dialog box appears, where you can choose font formatting and border and pattern settings to apply to the cells that meet your conditions. Click OK when you have finished setting the formats you want.

7. Click the Add button. The dialog box expands to display a Condition 2 section. This isn't an "and" or an "or" addendum to the first condition, but a completely separate set of conditions.

8. Set up the Condition 2 criterion the same way you did the Condition 1 criterion. Then click the Format button, and specify the formatting. You can apply the same formats used for Condition 1 or apply a new set of formats. Click OK to return to the Conditional Formatting dialog box. ▶

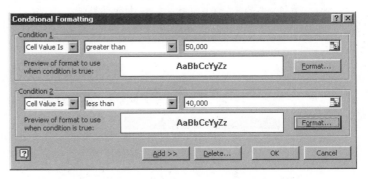

9. If you need a third set of conditions, click Add again, specify an operator and a value, or a formula, and then specify your formatting options. ▶

10. When you've established all the conditions, click OK to apply the conditional formatting to your worksheet.

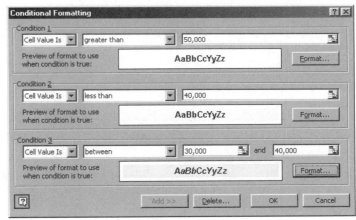

Tip

You can set multiple conditions to work like AND or OR criteria. Say you want to isolate people aged 20 through 25 from a long list. If you use the Between operator to set a single condition for the values between 20 and 25, the formatting will be applied only to 21, 22, 23, and 24. Instead, set Condition 1 to Greater Than Or Equal To 20 and Condition 2 to Less Than Or Equal To 25. If you apply the same formatting to both conditions, it appears as if only one condition is set, but you've included the comparison values of 20 and 25.

What did blue mean again?

It's a good idea to apply different formatting to each set of conditions so that you can tell one from another. Obviously the cells themselves will tell the story, but if your criterion for Condition 1 isn't glaringly different from Condition 2—for example, Condition 1 makes all cells over 50,000 blue, and Condition 2 makes all cells between 40,000 and 50,000 blue— you might not remember later if you had one condition for "anything over 40,000" or if you set two sets of criteria. Having all cells between 40,000 and 50,000 turn green instead of blue will show that two sets of conditions are at work.

I applied conditional formatting, but it didn't work

Source of the problem

As the name implies, conditional formatting is formatting that is applied only if certain criteria are met. How conditional formatting will work is determined by the range of cells that you select before clicking the Conditional Formatting command on the Format menu, the conditions you specify, and the formatting you choose to apply to content meeting those conditions. If any one of these elements is out of whack, the formats won't be applied, or they'll be applied to cells other than those you want to format. In short, the cause of this problem is a conflict in the way conditional formatting was set up.

Solving the problem requires you to retrace your steps—figure out which cells you specified for conditional formatting, what conditions you set (and if any of the selected data actually meets those conditions), and what formatting you chose to apply. This might sound like an instance where "Just forget it, do it again," is appropriate, but that's not the plan. What you need to do when conditional formatting appears to fail is to make sure you haven't applied it to the wrong cells, given it criteria that can't be met by the selected cells (such as numerical values when the cells contain text), or assigned formatting that doesn't make any visual difference in the worksheet appearance (maybe the numbers were *already* bold). If, after exploring all these possible holes in the setup, you still can't make it work, "Just forget it, and do it again!"

How to fix it

1. To determine which cells have been selected for conditional formatting, click Go To on the Edit menu.

2. In the Go To dialog box, click the Special button, and then click Conditional Formats in the Go To Special dialog box. (Don't worry if your buttons don't look the same as ours do.) ▶

3. Check that All is selected as the Data Validation option.

4. Click OK. The range of cells that was selected for conditional formatting is highlighted. (If you have set up multiple conditions, select a cell in the range you want to format, and repeat steps 1 through 3, selecting Same instead of All in the Go To dialog box.)

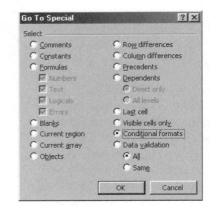

5. To determine what criteria were applied to your range of cells, click Conditional Formatting on the Format menu to display the Conditional Formatting dialog box. ▶

6. View the criteria in the Condition 1 section of the dialog box. (If you have set up multiple conditions, check the appropriate Condition section for the highlighted cells.) If need be, change the conditions, the operator, or both to meet the possible conditions within the selected range on the worksheet.

7. Click the Format button to check your formatting in the Format Cells dialog box. If you only made text bold or changed the text color, the format might already be in use in the selected range or be too subtle to notice. Make whatever formatting changes you want , and then click OK to close this dialog box.

8. In the Conditional Formatting dialog box, click OK to apply any changes you made to the selected range.

You can always start over

Conditional formatting is a very simple feature, but you have to really think about what data is within the range to which the formatting is applied. For example, suppose you use the Greater Than operator and type *5000000.00* in the value box (as opposed to clicking a cell that contains a value that you want to compare to all the other cells in the selected range). If there are no numbers over 50,000.00 in the worksheet, none of your cells will be formatted. A simple extra zero or two can be the culprit. If after checking everything you've done, the conditional formatting still doesn't work, click Conditional Formatting on the Format menu, and in the Conditional Formatting dialog box, click the Delete button. Select the check boxes for each of the conditions you want to delete (even all of them, if you want), and then click OK. You can then start over, being careful to establish criteria that will apply to at least one of the cells in the range you specify for conditional formatting.

Tip
One of the most common errors in setting up conditional formatting is failing to select the entire range of cells that should be checked for values meeting the conditional criteria. Many people forget to select a range before setting up their conditional formats and then wonder why they don't work. If you click Conditional Formatting on the Format menu with a single active cell selected, that's the one and only cell to which conditional formatting will be applied.

The conditional formats I set up aren't updated when I edit my worksheet

Source of the problem

Excel's Conditional Formatting feature doesn't tell you when you've set conditions that don't work or if the multiple conditions you set contradict one another. Nor does it tell you if your new entries don't meet the conditions that you set. It also doesn't tell you if you edited a portion of your worksheet that wasn't included in your conditional format settings, and therefore the edits don't have any impact on your conditional formatting.

This all sounds like more than one source of the problem, but it isn't. When your conditional formatting doesn't change even though you've edited the worksheet such that the cell values should either return to an unformatted state (because they no longer meet your conditions) or change to a different format (because they meet a different set of conditions now that they've been edited), you've probably edited a section of the worksheet that either has no conditional formatting set, or that has a different set of conditions applied than you're remembering.

In either case, the solution lies in reviewing your conditions for the edited cells and determining if what you expect to happen is possible given the conditions you've set for the cells in question.

> **Tip**
>
> If you selected or entered a particular cell's address as your value setting for one or more of your conditions, make sure that cell's contents haven't changed. If they have, your edited cells might not meet the condition's criteria because the new value isn't the same as it was when you originally established the conditional formatting.

How to fix it

1. First determine which cells have conditional formatting applied. On the Edit menu, click Go To, and then click the Special button in the Go To dialog box.

2. Click Conditional Formats in the list of options, and then click All under Data Validation. This will highlight any cells in your worksheet to which conditional formatting has been applied.

3. Click OK to see which cells are highlighted. ▶

4. If there are multiple conditional formats set throughout your worksheet, select a cell or range of cells to which conditional formatting has been applied. Then repeat steps 1 and 2, but choose Same from the Data Validation options in the Go To Special dialog box. This will show only the cells with the same conditional formatting as the cells currently selected in the worksheet.

	A	B	C	D	E	F	G
1							
2							
3		Qtr. 1	Qtr. 2	Qtr. 3	Qtr. 4	TOTALS	Qtr. 1
4	Philadelphia	5250678	5786452	6425642	7854251	$ 25,317,023	603
5	New York	4875986	6785428	7452987	2578456	$ 21,692,857	560
6	Chicago	3587452	7458976	5487653	5648752	$ 22,182,833	412
7	Atlanta	4789521	3789461	1258795	3567894	$ 13,405,661	550
8	Phoenix	5784236	6785497	6456781	4526781	$ 23,553,295	665
9	San Francisco	6452179	7425891	5784896	6457251	$ 26,120,217	742
10	TOTAL	$ 30,740,052.00	$ 38,031,695.00	$ 32,866,754.00	$ 30,633,385.00	$ 132,271,886	$ 35,351,
11							
12							
13							
14							

Tip
If you set two conditions for one section of the worksheet, and both of them could apply to the same cells, only the first condition's formatting will be applied.

5. If it turns out that you are editing cells to which conditional formatting is applied, you must find out if the new content in the cells conflicts with the conditions set, or if two or more conditions apply to the same cells. On the Format menu, click Conditional Formatting, and review the conditions you've set in the Conditional Formatting dialog box. Perhaps the new cell values are still within the conditions; in this case, no formatting change is warranted. However, if the new cell values now meet the criterion for Condition 2 as well as the criterion for Condition 1, only Condition 1's formats will be applied. To solve the problem of two or more conditions applying to the same cells, click Delete, select the check box for Condition 1, and then click OK twice.

I'm not sure how to change my conditional formats

Source of the problem

Change is a good thing, but only if you know how to make the change! If you're using someone else's workbook or you have no memory of how the conditional formatting that's in place was established, you might encounter a problem when you want to adjust the conditions or remove them altogether.

Changing or deleting conditional formats is easy, assuming you know to which cells conditional formats were applied, and how those conditions were set in the first place. This is really a two-phase solution: You start by revealing the cells to which conditions are applied, and then you go to the source of the conditional formats—the Conditional Formatting dialog box.

How to fix it

1. Unless you already know the full range of cells to which conditional formatting was applied, you must first identify the range. On the Edit menu, click Go To, and then click the Special button in the Go To dialog box.

2. Select Conditional Formats from the list of options, and then select All from the options under Data Validation. This will highlight any cells in your worksheet to which conditional formatting has been applied.

3. Click OK to view the worksheet and see which cells are highlighted. The cells might be in one contiguous range or scattered over much of the worksheet. ▶

	A	B	C	D	E	F	G
1							
2							
3		Qtr. 1	Qtr. 2	Qtr. 3	Qtr. 4	TOTALS	Qtr. 1
4	Philadelphia	5250678	5786452	6425642	7854251	$ 25,317,023	603
5	New York	4875986	6785428	7452987	2578456	$ 21,692,857	560
6	Chicago	3587452	7458976	5487653	5648752	$ 22,182,833	412
7	Atlanta	4789521	3789451	1258795	3567894	$ 13,405,661	550
8	Phoenix	5784236	6785497	6456781	4526781	$ 23,553,295	665
9	San Francisco	6452179	7425891	5784896	6457251	$ 26,120,217	742
10	TOTAL	$ 30,740,052.00	$ 38,031,695.00	$ 32,866,754.00	$ 30,633,385.00	$ 132,271,886	$ 35,351,
11							
12							
13							
14							

4. If there are multiple conditional formats set throughout your worksheet, select a cell

or range of cells to which conditional formatting has been applied, and then repeat steps 1 and 2, but choose Same from the Data Validation options. This will show only the cells with the same conditional formatting set as the cells currently selected in the worksheet.

5. With the cells highlighted, click Conditional Formatting on the Format menu.

6. In the resulting Conditional Formatting dialog box, look at the conditions set in Condition 1 (and perhaps Condition 2 and 3 if the range of selected cells includes second and third conditions).

Tip

If more than one condition can apply to the same cell or cells, only the first condition will be applied. If you remove Condition 1 but leave Condition 2, Condition 2's formats will take the place of the previous conditional formatting applied to the cells.

7. Make whatever changes you want to the operator (Greater Than, Less Than, and so on), the value (either a cell address containing a comparison value or a value typed manually into the dialog box), the formula, the formats, or all these criteria. ▶

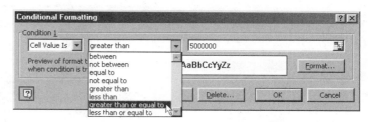

8. If you want to remove one or more of the conditions, click the Delete button, and in the Delete Conditional Formatting dialog box, select the check boxes for any or all of the conditions you want to remove. ▶

9. Click OK to return to the Conditional Formatting dialog box, and click OK again to put your changes into effect.

Are you having trouble applying the Currency format?

yes →

no ↓

Did you apply the Currency format by mistake?

yes → Go to...
I clicked the Currency Style button, but now I wish I hadn't, page 48.

no ↓

Is the euro formatting button missing from your toolbar?

yes → Go to...
I have no euro currency formatting button on my toolbar, page 50.

no ↓

Would you like to type a euro symbol manually?

yes →

no ↓

Do you need to apply a different kind of international formatting?

yes → Go to...
I'm not sure how to format my numbers as foreign currency, page 54.

Have your numbers turned into pound signs?

yes

Quick fix
Your numbers are too wide for the column. Double-click the seam to the right of the column heading.

no

Do your numbers have decimal places that you don't want?

yes

Quick fix
1. Select the cells containing numbers with unwanted decimal places.
2. Click the Decrease Decimal button on the Formatting toolbar until the decimal places are reduced as needed.

no

Has the number you entered changed since you applied the Currency format?

yes

Go to...
When I press Enter, the number I typed changes, page 52.

Quick fix
Press Alt+0128 on the numeric keypad to type a euro symbol.

If your solution isn't here
Check these related chapters:
Formatting numbers, page 114
Formulas, page 146
Functions, page 158
Or see the general troubleshooting tips on page xv.

I clicked the Currency Style button, but now I wish I hadn't

Source of the problem

It's easy to accidentally click the wrong button on a toolbar—there's not a lot of wiggle room between the buttons. Say you wanted to see the zeroes after the decimal point in a cell or range, and instead of clicking the Increase Decimal button, you clicked the Currency Style button. Or maybe you didn't click the wrong button at all—you might have *thought* you wanted to format the numbers as currency, and now you wish you hadn't. Whether the click was accidental or the result of a moment of impetuous formatting, it's often easy to resolve—simply click the Undo button.

But what if the click wasn't the last thing you did, and you don't want to undo the other stuff you've done to your worksheet since then? If that's the case, the resolution gets slightly more involved. Slightly. We're talking about opening a dialog box and making a selection, so your numbers will be back to non-currency status in no time at all!

How to fix it

1. If necessary, reselect the cells that were incorrectly formatted as currency.

2. Right-click the selection, and then click Format Cells on the shortcut menu. The Format Cells dialog box appears, with the Number tab displayed. ▶

3. To set the cells back to the default format, click General in the Category list.

4. Click OK to close the dialog box and change the formatting of the selected cells.

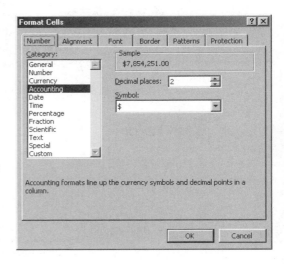

Who said Accounting?

When you go to the Format Cells dialog box to change the formatting back to General, you'll notice that Accounting is the format that's in force. You'd think it would be Currency, but that's not the case. You have to apply that format directly from the Format Cells dialog box—clicking the Currency Style button on the Formatting toolbar does not apply the Currency format.

Funny money

If you don't find a currency format that you like, you can create your own. Click Custom in the Category list of the Format Cells dialog box to see the Type section, which displays options for creating formats for currency, dates, times, and so forth. ▶

To create your custom format, use any of the following symbols or abbreviations to designate the parts of a number and how you want them displayed in your worksheet:

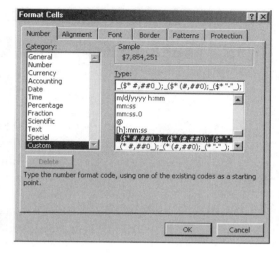

Symbol	Stands for
#	A number
?.?	Decimal numbers with the decimals aligned
?/?	Fractions with the division symbols aligned
$	A dollar sign to be added to the number
h:	Hours
mm:	Minutes
ss	Seconds
d	Days
m	Month
y	Year
@	Text after the number (for example, " units"@)

For example, if you select #,##0.00 from the Type list and change it in the Type box to #,###.00, your customized format will apply commas for numbers in the thousands, display two decimal places, and won't insert a zero if the number has no digits to the right of the decimal. Once you've created the format, it will be available from the Custom category list within the Format Cells dialog box.

Tip

If you find yourself hitting the Currency Style button a lot by accident, try dragging it to a new location on the toolbar—somewhere farther away from frequently used buttons. Hold down the Alt key, drag the toolbar button to a new location on either the Standard or Formatting toolbar, and then release the Alt key.

Tip

If you want to include decimal places for selected cells, click Number instead of General in the Category list of the Format Cells dialog box. In the Decimal Places box, specify the number of decimal places you want to display. If you want, choose a comma separator or negative number format in the section below the Decimal Places box, and then click OK.

I have no euro currency formatting button on my toolbar

Source of the problem

Excel 2000

If your version of Office isn't specifically for the European Union, you won't find the Euro button on the Formatting toolbar by default. The default installation of Excel 2000 does offer euro currency formatting on the Number tab of the Format Cells dialog box, but you need to select the Euro button from a list of add-ins before it will appear on the Formatting toolbar.

How to fix it

1. On the Tools menu, click Add-Ins to display the Add-Ins dialog box.

2. Scroll through the list of available add-ins, and select the Euro Currency Tools check box. ▶

3. Click OK. You might be prompted to insert the Office 2000 installation disk to make the Euro button available.

No Euro Currency Tools add-in?

If Euro Currency Tools is not on the Add-Ins Available list, you'll need to install it by using Add/Remove Programs in Control Panel. You'll be prompted to insert the Office installation CD-ROM, and a series of dialog boxes will take you through the process of installing the tools. Once the tools are installed, you'll see the Euro button on the Formatting toolbar.

> **Tip**
> Once you have the Euro button, chances are you'll want to use it. Do so with care! Using the Euro button to apply the euro format cannot be undone with the Undo button, and if you apply it in error, you must click Format Cells and select a different format from the Format Cells dialog box.

Excel 97 and the euro

Excel 97 doesn't have the Euro Currency Tools add-in, so if you use Excel 97, you might be wondering how you can apply euro formatting. Excel 97 can recognize the euro currency symbol, though there's a chance that your computer's operating system might not be able to support it.

In either Excel 97 or Excel 2000, you can easily use the American National Standards Institute (ANSI) shortcut key combination for manually inserting the euro symbol before numbers: Hold down the Alt key, and type 0128 on the numeric keypad to type the euro symbol.

If you are having difficulty inserting the euro symbol in your worksheet, your operating system might not support it directly. You might want to consult the Microsoft web site at *www.microsoft.com/technet/euro/ofc/ofc.asp* for more information.

Tip
If your printer cannot print the euro symbol, a box rather than the symbol will appear in your printout. If this happens, contact your printer manufacturer. You might be able to get the required fonts for your printer by downloading them from the printer company's web site, and then you'll be able to print the euro symbol.

Some fonts snub the euro

The euro can be printed only in certain fonts, so beware when changing the fonts for sections of your worksheet that are formatted with the Euro button. Following are some commonly used fonts that are euro-friendly:

- Arial
- Arial Black
- Comic Sans
- Courier New
- Impact
- MS Sans Serif
- Tahoma
- Times New Roman
- Verdana

When I press Enter, the number I typed changes

Source of the problem

You type a number in your worksheet, and when you press Enter or Tab to confirm your cell entry, the number changes! Is it magic? A trick to mess with your mind? Nope, it's actually supposed to happen, but if you weren't expecting it or don't want it to happen, it can be an unpleasant surprise.

This phenomenon most often occurs in worksheets that someone other than you developed, or worksheets that you created and formatted some time ago. Why? Because when a number changes in this way, it's the result of formatting, and you might not know (or remember) what formatting was applied to the cells you're working with. Specifically, cells formatted with the Currency, Number, or Accounting formats available in the Format Cells dialog box get rounded according to the dialog box's Decimal Places setting. For example, say you type *567.85* and as soon as you press Enter, the number changes to *568*. In this case, the cell is most likely formatted to display no decimal places. Consequently, the decimal number you typed is rounded to the nearest whole number.

The solution is simple—to have numbers appear the way you type them, you have to make sure the cells are formatted to accommodate the number of decimal places you are using. If you don't want to display decimal places but you don't want your entries to be rounded, remove the numbers to the right of the decimal (delete them from your entries) so that the number cannot be rounded.

Even when Excel doesn't *display* decimals in your worksheet, it does *store* decimal numbers in your worksheet. To make sure that a cell or cells are indeed being rounded, and to see what formatting is in place, click the affected cell, and take a look at the Formula bar. If the Formula bar displays the number you typed, decimals and all, your cells are formatted to display no decimals. As a result, the numbers you typed are being rounded. ▶

This is the displayed number.

This is the stored number.

= 6425645.78

B	C	D
Sales by Division		
	2000	
Qtr. 1	Qtr. 2	Qtr. 3
5250678	5786452	6,425,646
4875986	6785428	7,452,987
3587452	7458976	5,487,653
4789521	3789451	1,258,795
5784236	6785497	6,456,781
6452179	7425891	5,784,896
$30,740,052.00	$38,031,695.00	$32,866,757.78

How to fix it

1. Select the cell or cells in which your numbers are being rounded.

2. Right-click the selection, and click Format Cells on the shortcut menu.

3. On the Number tab, increase the decimal places to 2. ▶

4. Click OK.

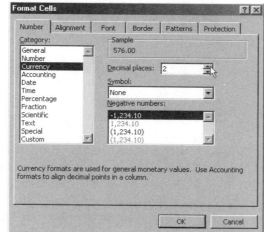

Format Cells ? ✕

| Number | Alignment | Font | Border | Patterns | Protection |

Category:
General
Number
Currency
Accounting
Date
Time
Percentage
Fraction
Scientific
Text
Special
Custom

Sample
576.00

Decimal places: 2

Symbol:
None

Negative numbers:
-1,234.10
1,234.10
(1,234.10)
(1,234.10)

Currency formats are used for general monetary values. Use Accounting formats to align decimal points in a column.

OK   Cancel

Tip
You can use the Increase Decimal button on the Formatting toolbar to add decimal places to selected cells. However, if you use it on a large range of cells (an entire column, for example), be sure that the top cells of the range contain numbers, and not blank space or letters. Otherwise, the button won't work. This applies to the Decrease Decimal button as well.

Well-rounded worksheets

When working with large currency amounts, it can be distracting to have cents (or their equivalents in other currencies) displayed, not to mention that columns have to be much wider to accommodate the additional numbers. For these reasons, people often don't want decimal places to appear. If you also don't want rounding to occur, you can refrain from entering decimal places at all, as previously suggested. If you want to enter them but don't want them to be displayed, you must use the rounding option. You can, however, alert the people reading or viewing the sheet to the rounding effect with a prominently placed text box or a comment (see "Comments and Track Changes" on page 24) inserted into the worksheet title indicating that the worksheet contains rounded numbers. ▶

Tip
To insert a text box, click the Drawing button on the Standard toolbar, and then click the Text Box button on the Drawing toolbar that appears. Use the crosshair pointer to draw a text box, and then start typing.

	A	B	C	D	E
1		Sales by Division			⊕	Laurie Ulrich:
2			2000			These dollar amounts are rounded, with the
3		Qtr. 1	Qtr. 2	Qtr. 3	Q	entered decimal places hidden.
4	Philadelphia	5250678	5786452	6,425,646	
5	New York	4875986	6785428	7,452,987	2578456	$
6	Chicago	3587452	7458976	5,487,653	5648752	$
7	Atlanta	4789521	3789451	1,258,795	3567894	$
8	Phoenix	5784236	6785497	6,456,781	4526781	$
9	San Francisco	6452179	7425891	5,784,896	6457251	$
10	TOTAL	$ 30,740,052.00	$ 38,031,695.00	$ 32,866,757.78	$ 30,633,385.00	$
11					
12			Sales figures are rounded up to the next		
13			dollar, with no cents displayed.		
14					

I'm not sure how to format my numbers as foreign currency

Source of the problem

When you click the Currency Style button or apply the Currency formatting, the currency formatting that is applied by default is based on the regional settings for your installation of Windows. If you live in the United States, your currency format is likely dollars and cents. If you often work with a different currency, this default won't be appropriate some or all of the time.

For example, currency in the United Kingdom uses periods where commas are used in U.S. currency (£1.000 is one thousand British pounds). With Excel, you can change the symbol in front of your currency amounts, but that's about it. So you can change a dollar sign to a pound sign, but that won't make Excel give up the commas for periods. To be able to apply foreign currency formats with the appropriate monetary symbols and use of commas and decimals for various national denominations, you need to change the Windows Regional Settings.

How to fix it

To change the currency symbol in Excel, follow these steps:

1. Select the cells that you want to format with a different national currency symbol.

2. Right-click the selection, and then click Format Cells on the shortcut menu.

3. In the Format Cells dialog box, click the Number tab if necessary.

4. In the Category list, click Currency if you don't need the currency symbols and decimal points to align, or click Accounting if you do.

5. Click the Symbol drop-down list.

6. Scroll through the list, and select a country name. (The country's currency symbol appears next to the country name.) ▶

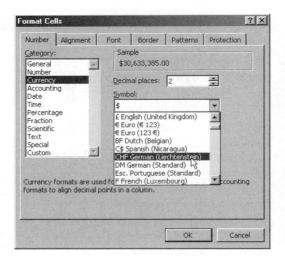

7. In the Decimal Places box, type or scroll to the number of decimal places you want to display.

8. If appropriate, click a format in the Negative Numbers list, and then click OK.

To change the Windows Regional Settings so that your currency is in a different format by default, follow these steps (your commands and dialog box names will differ slightly if you're working in Windows 2000 or Windows Me):

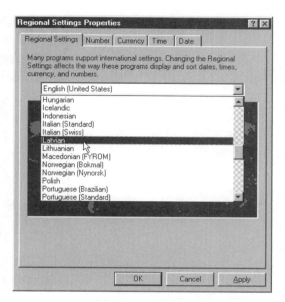

1. Click the Start button, point to Settings, click Control Panel, and then double-click Regional Settings.

2. On the Regional Settings tab of the Regional Settings Properties dialog box, select a country from the drop-down list above the world map. (Keep in mind that the country you choose will affect the way the time and date appear on the Windows taskbar; how dates, times, and currency symbols appear in other Microsoft Office applications; and how the default dictionary checks spelling.) ▶

3. Click the Currency tab, and view the options in the Currency Symbol, Decimal Symbol, and Digit Grouping Symbol drop-down lists. If more than one is available for the selected country, the alternative(s) will appear when you click the drop-down arrows. ▶

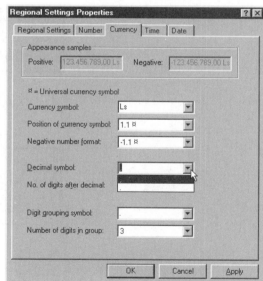

4. When your default settings are the way you want them to be, click OK. You'll be alerted that the changes won't take place until you restart your computer.

Tip

You can change your regional settings temporarily so that your worksheet formatting is appropriate for a particular currency. You might change them before creating a worksheet, save or print the worksheet so that you can distribute it to interested parties, and then restore the default regional settings for your version of Windows.

Tip

Be careful when changing your regional settings. Your outgoing e-mail will appear in the time format of the country you select, and this might be confusing for some of your e-mail recipients. If it's possible to get by with just changing the currency symbol and not adjusting your regional settings, you should consider taking this "path of least resistance."

Are you having trouble applying date formats?

yes

no

Does the date you inserted change into a number after you enter it?

yes

Go to...
When I enter a date, a number I don't recognize appears in the cell instead, page 58.

no

Do the month and day switch places after you enter the date?

yes

Go to...
The month and day I entered appear transposed in the date, page 60.

no

Do you need to apply a universal format to all your dates?

yes

Is the date format applied to the wrong cells? — **yes**

no

Quick fix

1. Select the cells that should not be formatted as dates, and on the Format menu, click Cells.

2. In the Format Cells dialog box, click the Number tab if necessary.

3. Click General to return the cells to a generic text/number status, or choose another format, such as Currency, as needed.

Do you need a date format that Excel doesn't offer? — **yes**

Go to...
The date format I need isn't provided by Excel, page 62.

no

Do you need to use four-digit years? — **yes**

Go to...
When I put Excel content into an Access database, I have trouble with cells formatted as dates, page 64.

Quick fix

1. Select all of the cells containing dates in your worksheet. (Hold down the Ctrl key while you select noncontiguous ranges.)

2. On the Format menu, click Cells.

3. On the Number tab, click Date, and choose the type you need from the list provided.

If your solution isn't here
Check these related chapters:
Entering data, page 78
Formatting numbers, page 114
Formatting worksheets, page 136
Or see the general troubleshooting tips on page xv.

When I enter a date, a number I don't recognize appears in the cell instead

Source of the problem

You enter *5/10* into a cell, and instead of *10–May* or *5/10* (or whatever date format you expect to see), you get *36656*. What's going on? If you type an accepted date format, such as *3/15, 3-15*, or *3/15/00*, into a cell that has been formatted with another numeric format, you won't see a date. For example, if the cell has the General or Number format, the date will be translated into an ordinary number. If it has the Currency or Accounting format, it will have a dollar sign. Other formats, such as Percentage or Scientific, will also result in glaringly obvious non-date numbers. ▶

Cell formatting is very easy to apply, so applying the wrong format can happen frequently. To solve the problem, there is no need to re-enter the dates—just change the format of the cells to Date.

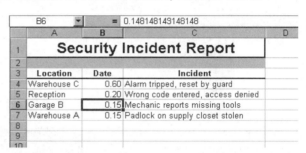

When the date 4/27 is entered in a cell with the Fraction format, the results are baffling.

How to fix it

1. Select the cells that aren't showing up as dates.

2. Right-click the selection, and then click Format Cells on the shortcut menu.

3. In the Format Cells dialog box, click the Number tab, if necessary. Click Date in the Category list, and then in the Type list, click the appropriate format for how you want the date to be stored and displayed. ▶

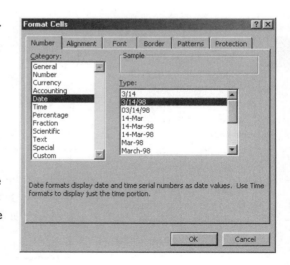

4. Click OK to apply the format you chose to the selected cells. (If Excel still doesn't recognize the numbers as dates, you might have to retype the dates to make them appear in the format you want.)

Keep it to yourself

Suppose all the dates you want to enter are in the current year, and displaying the year would be redundant. You can choose to enter the entire date (month, day, and year) but to display only the month and day. Select the cells in which you want to apply the format, right-click the selection, and click Format Cells on the shortcut menu. Click Date in the Category list, and in the Type list, click one of the formats that display only the month and day (such as *3/14* or *14-Mar*). Then click OK. Even if the dates you enter contain the year, they will appear in the cells as only the month and day. However, they will appear as you typed them (with years) in the Formula bar. ▶

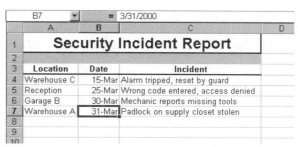

If necessary, you can always display the full date later by repeating the steps for displaying the Number tab of the Format Cells dialog box, and then choosing a date format that includes the year before clicking OK.

Although the year was entered for these dates, Excel displays the dates without the year.

Follow that format

Need to quickly include a list of dates in your worksheet, such as all the dates in a given month? Type the first two dates, such as *3/1* and *3/2*, and format those cells as you want all dates in the list to appear. Next select both cells, and using the AutoFill handle (the cross-shaped pointer that appears in the bottom right corner of the selected cells), drag downward through the adjoining cells in the column to fill in the remaining dates. Excel knows how many days are in each month, so when, for example, you drag past the cell containing *3/31*, the next cell will contain *4/1*. ▶

Tip
If you do not see the AutoFill handle in the bottom right corner of the selected cell or cells, you need to turn on drag-and-drop editing. On the Tools menu, click Options, and display the Edit tab. Select the Allow Cell Drag And Drop option, and click OK.

The month and day I entered appear transposed in the date

Source of the problem

Even if you format cells to store and display dates, there can still be some surprises. By default, when you type a date such as *March 15*, Excel displays it as *15-Mar*, with the day first, followed by the month. This differs from some preferred date formats, especially in the United States, where dates are commonly written or typed with the month first, followed by the day. ▶

Can you change this default? Well, no, you can't change the list of date formats Excel offers by default, but you can create a format that meets your needs for a month-day display, and make that format available for current and future cell formatting. Creating a new Number format requires specifying

B7	▼	= 3/15/2000	
	A	B	C	D
1		**Security Incident Report**		
2				
3	**Location**	**Date**	**Incident**	
4	Warehouse C	15-Mar	Alarm tripped, reset by guard	
5	Reception	25-Mar	Wrong code entered, access denied	
6	Garage B	30-Mar	Mechanic reports missing tools	
7	Warehouse A	15-Mar	Padlock on supply closet stolen	
8				
9				
10				

This date was entered as March 15, but is displayed as 15-Mar and is stored as 3/15/2000.

the structure for a cell entry, such as *mmm-dd* for a date that should appear as *Mar-15*. The *mmm* represents the first three letters of the month's name, and the *-dd* indicates that a dash and the day should follow the month.

How to fix it

1. Select the cells where the new date format should apply.

2. Right-click the selection, and then click Format Cells on the shortcut menu.

3. In the Format Cells dialog box, click the Number tab if necessary, and then click Custom in the Category list.

Tip

To apply the custom format to other cells after you've created it, select the cells that you want to format, right-click the selection, and then click Format Cells on the shortcut menu. In the Format Cells dialog box, make sure the Number tab is selected, and then click Custom in the Category list. In the Type list of custom formats, find the format you created, click the format to select it, and then click OK to apply it.

4. Type the format you want to create in the Type box. For example, if you want dates to be displayed as *Mar-15* when you enter *3/15*, *3-15*, or *March 15*, create the custom format *mmm-dd*. ▶

5. Click OK to apply the new date format to the selected cells.

As you like it

You can create date formats to suit any desired date display—*mmm-dd-yyyy, yyyy-mmm-dd*—any combination of month, day, and year will work. If you use two *m*s, the month is displayed as a number, and if you use three, it is displayed as text. The format *mm-dd-yyyy* will turn an entry of *3/15/2000* into *03-15-2000*, whereas *mmm-dd-yyyy* will turn *3/15/2000* into *Mar-15-2000*. If you type slashes instead of dashes in your custom format, you change the character that divides the sections of the date. If you don't want any divisional characters to appear, you can type the format as *mmm dd yyyy* with a single space between the date sections, and the entered date will appear as *Mar 15 2000*. ▶

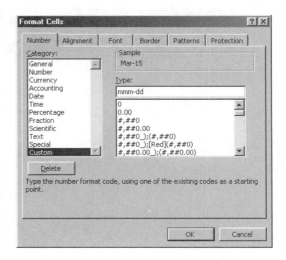

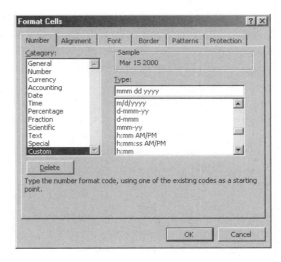

Tip
If you want the entire name of the month to appear, such as *December* instead of *Dec*, type *m* four times in the Type box when you create a custom date format. Excel recognizes the four *m*s as the month's full name, no matter how long or short the name actually is. For example, the format *mmmm dd yyyy* will result in a date such as *December 15 2000*, or even *May 03 2000*.

Tip
Want to see the day of the week as well? Create a formula that begins with four *d*s, as in *dddd, mmmm dd, yyyy* to see *Wednesday, August 23, 2000* displayed in your worksheet.

The date format I need isn't provided by Excel

Source of the problem

Excel offers the most frequently used date formats, and for most users and their worksheets, these formats are more than adequate. However, some people work with date formats from various countries or need to accommodate some other set of circumstances. If you fall in this group, the default offerings in Excel might not be sufficient.

A common problem is an inconsistency between the date that's entered and the date that Excel perceives based on that entry. This is especially apparent if you cite the day before the month. For example, if you enter dates with single-digit days—such as *2/3* for *2 March*, *7/3* for *7 March*, and *9/3* for *9 March*—Excel will interpret the entries as dates, but not those you intend—*February 3*, *July 3*, and *September 3*. If you enter *15 March, 2000* as *15/3/2000*, Excel will enter *15/3/2000* in left-aligned General format instead of right-aligned Date format. ▶

If this or similar situations occur when you use Excel, don't worry—you aren't stuck with forcing your data into an inappropriate format. You can create your own date formats and apply them to existing and future worksheets.

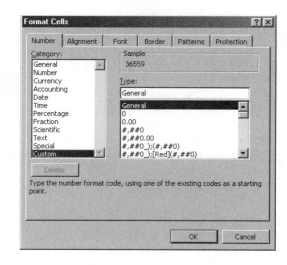

How to fix it

1. To create your own date format, select the cells to which the new format should apply, right-click the selection, and click Format Cells on the shortcut menu.

2. In the Format Cells dialog box, click the Number tab, if necessary.

3. In the Category list, click Custom. A list of existing custom formats appears in the Type list on the right side of the dialog box, along with a box into which you can type a new format. ▶

4. If necessary, select and delete the contents of the Type box, and type your own new format. For a European date format, type a format such as *dd/mm/yyyy*. This format tells Excel that the first two digits entered represent the day, the second two digits represent the month, and the last four represent the year. If you prefer that the month be spelled out, increase the number of month characters to three.

5. Click OK to apply the new format. The format is saved for future use, and can be found in the Type list the next time you need to apply it. If you have dates already entered in the cells you selected, you might have to retype the dates in the standard month-day-year format recognized by Excel so that the dates will appear with the new custom format in the worksheet.

Tip

If you've applied a custom format to any cells in a worksheet that others will use, it's a good idea to add a comment to one of the cells describing the format and how it displays and stores entries. (See "Comments and Track Changes" on page 24.)

Tip

Using four *m*'s in your date format will tell Excel to display the entire name of the month, even if there are more than four letters in the month.

Does anybody know what time it is?

If you want to enter the time along with the date, Excel offers a variety of date and time combinations in the Format Cells dialog box. You can customize these formats as needed by clicking Custom in the Category list, and then typing a custom date and time format in the Type box. (You can also modify an existing format by scrolling through the Type list, clicking the closest match, and then adding or changing elements as needed in the Type box.) Click OK to implement your new format. ▶

When devising a date and time format, remember that an *m* represents the month as long as it accompanies a *d* (for day) or a *y* (for year). If the *m* is accompanied by an *h* (for hours) or an *s* (for seconds), Excel recognizes the *m* as minutes. The format *mmmm dd, yyyy / hh:mm:ss*, for example, will display an entry typed as *3/15/2000 08:25:50* as March 15, 2000 / 08:25:50.

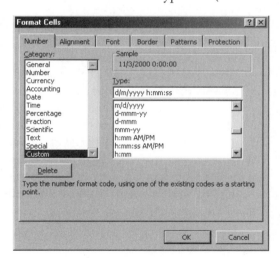

When I put Excel content into an Access database, I have trouble with cells formatted as dates

Source of the problem

Thank goodness all that year 2000 panic is over. For most of us, the new millennium arrived without any type of date-oriented disaster. Still, it's important to store electronic dates with four digits, even if you're using year 2000–friendly software. If you're importing or pasting your Excel worksheet's data into an Access database that stores all four digits of the year, it's essential that your worksheet follow suit.

By default, Excel turns a two-digit year entry into a four-digit entry, whether you're working in Excel 97 or Excel 2000. For example, if you type *3/15/00* into a cell, it is stored as 3/15/2000. If you check the Formula bar (where the entry is displayed), the full four-digit year appears there, too. ▶

So what's the problem? If a format that displays only two digits for the year has been applied to cells that will contain dates, you might find that the data imported or pasted into your Access database has two-digit years instead of the four digits required. The solution is simple—make sure your dates are set to store and display four-digit years if you will use the worksheet information to fill in a database outside of your current worksheet or beyond the Excel application itself.

B4		=	3/15/2000	
	A	B	C	D
1	\multicolumn{3}{c}{**Security Incident Report**}		
2				
3	Location	Date	Incident	
4	Warehouse C	3/15/00	Alarm tripped, reset by guard	
5	Reception	3/25/00	Wrong code entered, access denied	
6	Garage B	3/30/00	Mechanic reports missing tools	
7	Warehouse A	3/31/00	Padlock on supply closet stolen	
8				
9				
10				

How to fix it

1. To format all the dates in your worksheet so that the year is stored and displayed with four digits, select all of the date-bearing cells. You can select nonsequential ranges by holding down the Ctrl key as you drag through blocks of cells or click individual cells.

Tip
To quickly check the format applied to any cell, right-click the cell, and then click Format Cells on the shortcut menu. The Format Cells dialog box appears with the currently applied format selected. If you are truly just checking, press Esc to exit the dialog box without making any changes.

2. Right-click the selection, and then click Format Cells on the shortcut menu.

3. If necessary, click the Number tab, and then click Date in the Category list.

4. Scroll through the date formats in the Type list, and click a format with a four-digit year, such as *3/14/1998*. ▶

5. Click OK to apply the selected format and close the dialog box.

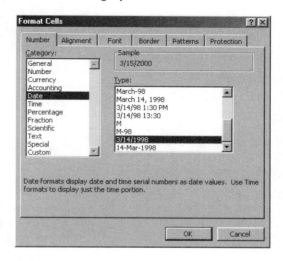

Don't touch my yyyyears, please

If other people use your worksheet, and you don't want to risk two-digit years being entered or displayed, protect the cells that contain dates.

To apply protection and to control which cells are protected (rather than protecting the whole sheet), select cells that *can* be edited (the cells that *don't* contain dates). Right-click the selection, and then click Format Cells on the shortcut menu. On the Protection tab, turn off the Locked option, and click OK. On the Tools menu, point to Protection, and then click Protect Sheet. You can apply a password and then distribute that password to people you want to be able to edit the protected cells. ▶

Once the protection is turned on, the date cells in the active worksheet will be protected from any changes. Attempts to change, delete, or add content to the protected date cells will result in an error message indicating that the cells are read-only.

Do you need help displaying the Drawing toolbar? **yes**

Quick fix

1. Right-click any visible toolbar or menu bar.
2. Click Drawing on the shortcut menu.

no

Are you having trouble applying formats to your AutoShapes and lines? **yes**

no

Do you need a consistent AutoShape format throughout your drawings? **yes**

Quick fix

Format an existing AutoShape, then right-click the shape, and click Set AutoShape Defaults to apply the settings to all new shapes you draw.

no

Is the Group command dimmed on the Draw menu? **yes**

Go to...

The Group command isn't available on the Draw menu, page 68.

no

Are you having trouble moving AutoShapes or lines? **yes**

Go to...

When I move my AutoShape, it changes size, page 70.

no

Do you need to adjust the direction of lines or callout connectors? **yes**

Go to...

My callouts aren't pointing to the right items, page 72.

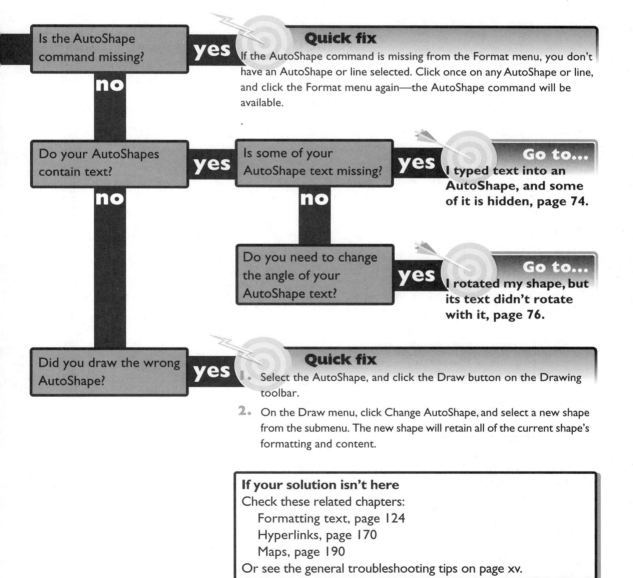

Is the AutoShape command missing?

yes → **Quick fix**
If the AutoShape command is missing from the Format menu, you don't have an AutoShape or line selected. Click once on any AutoShape or line, and click the Format menu again—the AutoShape command will be available.

no

Do your AutoShapes contain text?

yes → **Is some of your AutoShape text missing?**

yes → **Go to...**
I typed text into an AutoShape, and some of it is hidden, page 74.

no

Do you need to change the angle of your AutoShape text?

yes → **Go to...**
I rotated my shape, but its text didn't rotate with it, page 76.

no

Did you draw the wrong AutoShape?

yes → **Quick fix**
1. Select the AutoShape, and click the Draw button on the Drawing toolbar.
2. On the Draw menu, click Change AutoShape, and select a new shape from the submenu. The new shape will retain all of the current shape's formatting and content.

If your solution isn't here
Check these related chapters:
Formatting text, page 124
Hyperlinks, page 170
Maps, page 190
Or see the general troubleshooting tips on page xv.

The Group command isn't available on the Draw menu

Source of the problem

If you've spent several minutes aligning or positioning two or more objects on your worksheet, and you don't want to accidentally move them, you can group the objects to protect their relative positions. Grouping drawn objects—AutoShapes, WordArt objects, lines, arrows, text boxes—is a great way to lock their current positions. Grouping objects is easy—simply click the Draw button on the Drawing toolbar, and then click Group on the menu that appears. But wait! The Group command is dimmed on the Draw menu, so what can you do? ▶

The answer is simple. Because by definition a group is two or more objects, you need to have two or more objects selected when you click the Draw menu.

How to fix it

1. To select multiple objects on your worksheet, click the Select Objects button (the arrow next to the Draw button) on the Drawing toolbar, and then click and drag to draw a dotted-line rectangle that completely encompasses the objects you want to select. ▶

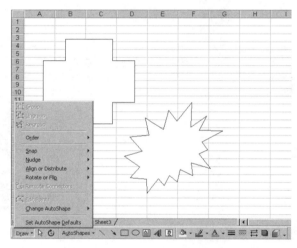

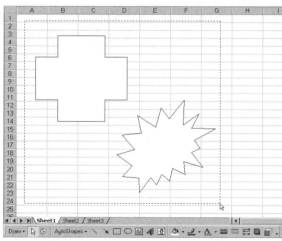

Tip

If the objects you want to group are not close to each other or there are objects between them, hold down the Shift key as you click each of the objects you want to select. After you have selected all the objects you want, release the shift key.

2. Release the mouse button when you have surrounded the objects you want; you'll see handles around each one of the objects, indicating that the objects are selected.

3. Click the Draw button, and then click Group to group the individual objects. ▶

Tip

If you want to sever the relationship between members of a group of objects, select the group, click the Draw button, and then click Ungroup on the Draw menu.

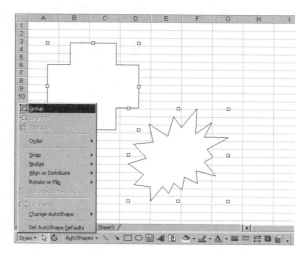

Groups of groups of groups

You can group groups of objects as well as individual objects. Suppose you've already created a group of objects such as AutoShapes, WordArt, lines, arrows, or text boxes on your worksheet, and now you want to add another object or another group to that group. Click the Select Objects button on the Drawing toolbar, and then drag to surround both the existing group and the new group or object with a dotted-line rectangle. ▶

Once the existing group and the new group or object are all selected, click the Draw button, and then click Group.

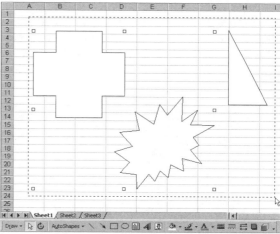

The existing group is selected, and a new object is being added to the selection.

Safety in numbers

Grouping objects doesn't just protect related graphics from being accidentally repositioned; it allows you to do things to the entire group rather than having to operate on each member of the group individually.

For example, if you want to make all the objects in the group a little larger or smaller, simply select the group, and then drag one of the handles (a corner handle if you want the objects to retain their horizontal and vertical proportions). Drag outward to make all the objects larger, or drag toward the group's center to make the objects smaller.

When I move my AutoShape, it changes size

Source of the problem

Oops! You wanted to move that AutoShape from the left side of your worksheet to the right, but when you did, all of a sudden the shape got much bigger. What happened? The answer lies with your mouse pointer. Of all the programs in the Office suite, Excel has the greatest variety of mouse pointers. It has pointers for entering content into cells, editing cell content, pasting cells from one place to another, copying cells, drawing objects, selecting objects, resizing objects—the list can seem endless. So the reason your AutoShape got bigger rather than moved is that you probably didn't notice that the mouse pointer had changed form. You simply missed the fact that when you wanted to move your AutoShape, your mouse pointer was in resize mode and not in move mode. ▶

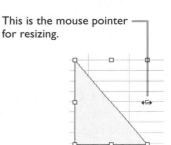

This is the mouse pointer for resizing.

How to fix it

1. If necessary, click Undo to reverse the erroneous resizing of your AutoShape.

2. Select the object that you want to move, and then point to the center of the object, staying clear of the object's handles. Your mouse pointer will turn into a four-headed arrow. ▶

3. Hold down the mouse button, drag the object to the desired location, and then release the mouse button.

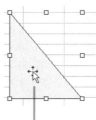

This is the mouse pointer for moving.

Tip

If you want to leave your object where it is and create a duplicate in a new location on your worksheet, drag the object while holding down the right mouse button. The original object remains in place, and a "ghost" of the object follows your mouse pointer. When you release the mouse button at the desired location for the new object, click Copy Here on the shortcut menu.

Nudge, nudge

As an alternative to dragging your objects to move them, try using the arrow keys. Click once on the object (or group), and when its handles appear, press the arrow keys on your keyboard to move up, down, left, or right. Each press of the key nudges the object one pixel at a time.

This nudging technique does more than eliminate your need to identify a move vs. a resize mouse pointer; it also allows you to move an object in one direction at a time. If you use the mouse pointer to move an object, you might end up moving it in more than one direction, simply because you're a human and not a robot. For example, if you try to drag your object down, you'll probably end up moving it a little to the right or left as well, whether or not you realize it when you're dragging. ▶

Another benefit is that you can nudge two ungrouped objects exactly the same distance. For example, if you have two circles, and they both need to be moved up a hair, select one of them, and then press the Up arrow key, counting the number of times you press it. Then select the second circle, and press the Up arrow key the same number of times. Voilà! You've nudged both objects the same amount.

Tip

You can nudge your selected object or group by pointing to Nudge on the Draw menu, and then clicking Up, Down, Left, or Right on the Nudge submenu.

Tip

To base nudging increments on the grid rather than on pixels, turn on Snap To Grid. Click the Draw button, point to Snap on the Draw menu, and then click To Grid. Each press of the arrow keys will then nudge your selected object one grid point.

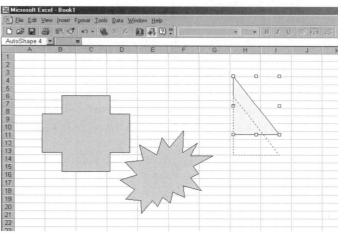

Nudging with the arrow keys is a quick way to move an object in only one direction.

My callouts aren't pointing to the right items

Source of the problem

You can annotate parts of your worksheet, charts, or even drawn objects by using callouts with descriptive information. Callouts—boxes, circles, or cartoon bubble-like shapes that contain text—are visually linked to data or graphical content by a connecting line that stretches from the callout box. The line should point to the subject of the callout, but if you move the subject of a callout by cutting or moving content or repositioning a chart or graphic, the callout will no longer point to that subject.

Another possible reason for a misdirected callout is that the callout itself was repositioned or resized. Often in an attempt to move a callout or to make a callout box bigger, the connecting line is redirected.

Solving the problem requires understanding the parts of a callout and manually redirecting its connecting line so that it points to the desired content or object.

> **Tip**
>
> Don't confuse callouts with comments. Callouts are drawn on top of the worksheet and are not attached to the worksheet's data. Comments are visible only if you point to the cell the comment is attached to. See "Comments and Track Changes" on page 24 for information about comments.

How to fix it

1. Click once on the edge of the callout box to select the box, its content, and the line pointing from the callout to the callout's subject. ▶

2. Point to the diamond at the end of the callout line, and wait for the mouse pointer to change to a small white arrowhead.

Proposed Increase	Projected Rate
0.015	0.203
0.02	0.357
0.01	0.02525
0.015	0.406
0.022	0.05621
0.0125	0.0354375
0.005	0.0201
0.012	0.0253
0.008	0.03024
0.0035	0.050175
0.0123	0.12087125

Increase as suggested by at least 50% of current vendors.

3. Drag the handle until the line is pointing to the intended subject of the callout. ▶

4. If necessary, reposition the callout box so that it is a reasonable distance from the subject. To do this, click away from the callout, and then reselect it by clicking the callout box. When the mouse pointer turns into a four-headed arrow, move the box (not the line) so that the line stays where you just put it.

Proposed Increase	Projected Rate
0.015	0.203
0.02	0.357
0.01	0.02525
0.015	0.406
0.022	0.05621
0.0125	0.0353475
0.005	0.0201
0.012	0.0253
0.008	0.03024
0.0035	0.050175
0.0123	**0.12087125**

Increase as suggested by at least 50% of current vendors

They went that-a-way...

If you want your callout line to have an arrowhead at the end of it, click the callout line to select it. When yellow diamonds appear on the line (indicating that the line and callout are selected), click the Arrow Style button on the Drawing toolbar, and then click a style on the menu. For example, to get a single arrowhead pointing away from the callout and toward the callout's subject, click the left-pointing arrow in the list of arrow styles. ▶

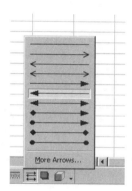

Tip
You can change the color of the callout border and connecting line by using the Line Color button on the Drawing toolbar. Select the callout, click the drop-down arrow to the right of the button, and then click a color on the palette.

I typed text into an AutoShape, and some of it is hidden

Source of the problem

A lot of people think that to have text appear in an AutoShape, you must place a text box on top of the shape and type the text into that box. But it's really much simpler to add text to an AutoShape itself. With your AutoShape selected, simply begin typing. The text you type appears within the shape, and in the case of paragraph text (more than a word or two), the text wraps within the confines of the shape.

Sounds good, eh? Well, normally it is, but you can run into a problem if you type more text into the shape than can appear within the shape's current size. The text that goes beyond the "window" within the shape's borders is then hidden from view. ▶

The solution to this problem requires you to make a change—resizing the shape, reducing the font size, editing the text to convey the basic information in fewer words, or a combination of these possibilities.

Carrier Code	Monthly Cost per Person	
A-45	$	175.00
A-72	$	200.00
B-36	$	185.00
B-58	$	225.00
C-75	$	500.00
D-63	$	550.00

with projected increases for the year 2001.

How to fix it

To increase the size of the AutoShape so that all of your text fits within it, follow these steps:

1. Click the edge of the shape to select it and display its handles.

2. Drag any of the corner handles diagonally away from the center of the shape to make the shape larger but retain the object's current vertical and horizontal proportions. ▶

Carrier Code	Monthly Cost per Person	
A-45	$	175.00
A-72	$	200.00
B-36	$	185.00
B-58	$	225.00
C-75	$	500.00
D-63	$	550.00

Vendors supplied their 2000 costs with projected

To make the text smaller so that more of it appears in the shape, follow these steps:

1. Click the AutoShape's border to select both the shape and its text.

2. Right-click the selected shape, and then click Format AutoShape on the shortcut menu.

3. Click the Font tab if necessary, and then make changes to the font, size, and style of the text so that all the text can fit in the shape. (If you're working in Excel 97, don't worry that your Format Shapes dialog box doesn't have a Web tab—you won't need it to troubleshoot this problem.) ▶

4. When you are finished making adjustments, click OK to view the results.

And if your text still doesn't fit...

Sometimes your text won't fit within the AutoShape even after you resize the shape or reformat the text. And sometimes you won't be able to resize the shape, but you still need all of the text to fit. At these times, you can reformat the margins of the shape so that it can hold more text.

Use the Margins tab of the Format Auto-Shape dialog box to adjust the margins within a selected AutoShape. Select the AutoShape, right-click it, and click Format AutoShape on the shortcut menu. Click the Margins tab if necessary, adjust the margins in the Left, Right, Top, and Bottom boxes as needed, and then click OK.

Remember that these margins are much smaller than page margins, so to allow the most amount of room inside the shape without the text touching the borders of the shape, set the margins to .1" or .2"—a tenth or a fifth of an inch. ▶

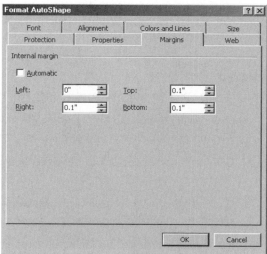

Tip
You can also use the Formatting toolbar's Font and Font Size buttons to adjust the appearance of your AutoShape text.

I rotated my shape, but its text didn't rotate with it

Source of the problem

By default, even if you rotate your AutoShape, Excel leaves the text in the AutoShape at a 0° angle, running at the same angle as the text and numbers typed into your worksheet cells. ▶

There are times, however, when you want to place your AutoShape text at an angle—perhaps the same angle as the rotation of the shape itself, or maybe just rotated slightly to make the text stand out against worksheet content or to better fit within the shape.

Depending on your text rotation goals, you have two possible solutions. The first solution offers you the most flexibility in rotating your text and objects, but it involves placing a WordArt object on top of the AutoShape and rotating the WordArt to the same degree as the shape. The second solution is less flexible in that it offers limited text rotation capabilities, but with this solution, you don't have to insert an additional object into your worksheet—you simply change the alignment applied to the AutoShape text.

5784236	6785497	6,456,781	4526781	$	23,553,295
6452179	7425891	5,784,896	6457251	$	26,120,217
,740,052.00	$ 38,031,695.00	$ 32,866,757.78	$ 30,633,385.00	$	132,271,890

Meet our
Sales
Stars!

The star has been rotated, but the text stayed in place.

How to fix it

To rotate the text within your AutoShape to the same degree as that of the shape, follow these steps:

1. Leave your AutoShape empty, or delete any existing text by right-clicking the shape, clicking Edit Text on the shortcut menu, and pressing the Delete key.

2. Click any worksheet cell to deselect the AutoShape. (Don't worry about choosing a spot for your WordArt right away; you can move the object where you want it later.)

3. Click the WordArt button on the Drawing toolbar to display the WordArt Gallery dialog box, select the WordArt style that you want to use by clicking the sample, and then click OK.

4. In the Edit WordArt Text dialog box, replace the instructional text with the text you want to rotate on top of your AutoShape. If you want, change the font, font size, and formatting, and then click OK.

5. Move the mouse pointer over the center of the WordArt object. When the pointer changes to a four-headed arrow, move the WordArt object until it is positioned on top of the AutoShape. (With the WordArt object selected, you can resize and adjust its shape as needed, by dragging the object's handles.)

6. Click the Free Rotate button on the WordArt toolbar. When the mouse pointer changes to a circular arrow and the WordArt object's corners become marked with small green circles, click and drag a corner's circle to spin the WordArt text to match the rotation angle of your AutoShape. ▶

7. Click any cell in the worksheet to deselect the WordArt object and hide the WordArt toolbar.

8. Group your WordArt and AutoShape objects. First select them both by clicking one object and then holding down the Shift key as you click the second object. Then with both objects selected, click the Draw button on the Drawing toolbar, and click Group on the menu.

> **Tip**
>
> When you rotate objects with the Free Rotate tool, you're using your eye to achieve what *looks* like matching angles. To make sure your AutoShape and WordArt objects are rotated to the exact same angle, first ungroup the objects. Click the grouped objects, click the Draw button on the Drawing toolbar, and then click Ungroup. Then right-click the AutoShape, and click Format AutoShape on the shortcut menu. On the Size tab, note the measurement in the Rotation box. Next right-click the WordArt object, and click Format WordArt on the shortcut menu. Click the Size tab, and in the WordArt object's Rotation box, enter the same measurement you noted for the rotation of the AutoShape. You can then group the two objects again.

To change the alignment of your AutoShape text without adding a WordArt object, follow these steps:

1. Select the AutoShape containing text, right-click it, and then click Format AutoShape on the shortcut menu.

2. On the Alignment tab, click the desired text alignment settings in the Horizontal or Vertical Text drop-down lists—or both if you want. As needed, select a 90-degree text setting in the Orientation section.

3. Click OK to apply the new alignment and orientation to your AutoShape's text.

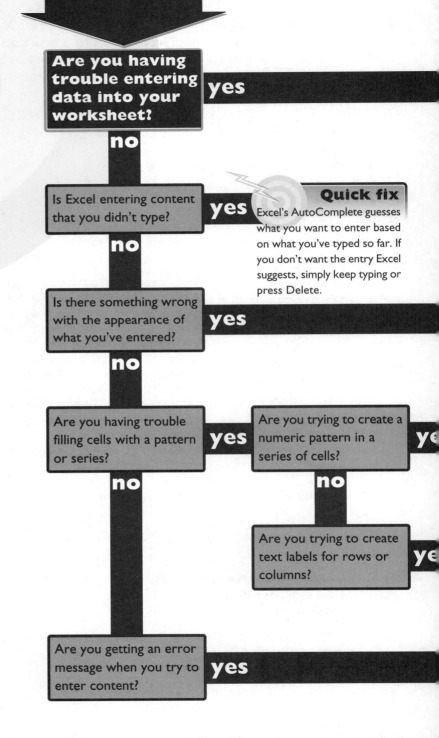

Are you having trouble entering data into your worksheet?

yes →

no ↓

Is Excel entering content that you didn't type?

yes →

Quick fix

Excel's AutoComplete guesses what you want to enter based on what you've typed so far. If you don't want the entry Excel suggests, simply keep typing or press Delete.

no ↓

Is there something wrong with the appearance of what you've entered?

yes →

no ↓

Are you having trouble filling cells with a pattern or series?

yes →

Are you trying to create a numeric pattern in a series of cells?

ye[s] →

no ↓

no ↓

Are you trying to create text labels for rows or columns?

ye[s] →

Are you getting an error message when you try to enter content?

yes →

Entering data

Do you need to enter content into a specific range of cells? — **yes**

Quick fix

1. Select the range of cells, and then begin typing in the first cell.

2. Press Enter to move from cell to cell within the selected range.

3. When you've finished entering content within that range, click outside of it to deselect it.

no

Does the active cell reject your entry? — **yes**

Go to...
When I type in the active cell, nothing happens, page 80.

Is some of your content cut off? — **yes**

Go to...
Text that I typed in a cell looks cut off by adjoining cells, page 82.

Quick fix

1. Type the first two numbers of the pattern into adjoining cells, and then select those two cells.

2. Using the fill handle in the second cell, drag through the remaining cells in the range to complete the pattern.

Go to...
I'm tired of entering the same series of labels in my worksheets, page 84.

Go to...
I can't get my data validation rules to work, page 86.

If your solution isn't here
Check these related chapters:
  Columns and rows, page 14
  Formatting text, page 124
  Formulas, page 146
Or see the general troubleshooting tips on page xv.

When I type in the active cell, nothing happens

Source of the problem

The operative word in this situation is "active." Even people with a reasonable amount of Excel experience will make the mistake of attempting to enter data into a cell other than the active cell. The active cell is the cell that has a thick, black border around it, and its address appears in the Name box to the left of the Formula bar. It's very easy to start typing and wonder why the cell you think should change doesn't. Then you discover that another cell was active when you started to type and that content is being added in a way you don't want.

Why might you become confused as to which cell is active? If you've applied thick, black borders to any cells, if you've changed your cell shading to black (in which case the active cell will have a thick, white border), or if you're concentrating on the particular cell where you intend to make an entry and forget to click it (leaving a previously clicked cell as the active cell), you might have trouble determining which cell is active. The latter situation, forgetting to click the right cell, results in an additional problem—whatever you type ends up in the wrong cell, and if the active cell contained content when you started to type, you overwrite it when you type the new content! To determine which cell is active, you need to take only a few steps.

How to fix it

1. Check the Name box, and note the address of the active cell. ▶

The Name box displays the address of the active cell.

2. If the address appearing in the Name box does not represent the cell in which you want to work, press Esc to undo any changes you might have accidentally made to existing material in that cell.

3. Click the cell in which you want to work, and then do what you need to do.

Watch that mouse

Pressing Enter or Tab after working in a cell is a good habit to get into. Using the mouse button to click another cell after making or modifying an entry confirms cell entries in a manner similar to pressing Enter or Tab, but be aware that you run the risk of leaving a cell active when you're really finished working with it, thereby making it vulnerable to unintended edits when you're trying to work in another cell. If you use the mouse to scroll to another part of your worksheet and then forget to click another cell to make it active, you might overwrite material in the cell in which you were just working without knowing it!

If you get into the habit of clicking another cell—or, better yet, pressing Enter or Tab—immediately after you add or modify a cell entry, you'll be more confident that your entries will stay intact—in the cells where you want them to be!

Tip
Need to get back to the beginning of the worksheet quickly? Press Ctrl+Home. You'll exit the cell you're in (confirming your most recent edit) and go back to cell A1 in one fell swoop.

Tip
When you press Esc, you lose whatever's just been entered into the active cell, leaving the cell with the content that existed before the last attempt to edit it, or returning the cell to a blank state if no material previously existed in that cell.

Tip
If your insertion point is blinking in any cell, you must press either Enter or Tab to confirm the cell's entry, or Esc to abandon any changes just made to the entry in the active cell. When a cell contains a blinking insertion point, any formatting you apply using menus, toolbar buttons, or keyboard shortcuts will affect any content you enter after the insertion point, but until you press Enter or Esc. If you apply formatting with cells or content selected, the formatting will apply to the selected text.

Text that I typed in a cell looks cut off by adjoining cells

Source of the problem

You've typed your text in a cell, and you've pressed Enter or Tab. You look at the cell you just finished editing, and the end of the word or phrase is missing—cut off at the right end of the cell. What's going on?

If the cell to the right has content, there's your culprit. If you type more numbers than will fit in a column, Excel either expands the column to accommodate the numeric entry, or turns the numbers you typed into pound signs (########) to signify that there

isn't room for the entire entry. In contrast, if text you type in a cell overruns that cell's column width, the text that doesn't fit will be obscured, or *truncated*, by the cell to the right if that cell has content. ▶

If the cell to the right is empty, a portion of the overflow text will appear to spill into that cell's space, though it won't actually

The text in cell A3 is truncated.

fill the cell itself. (This is good for worksheet titles that normally appear in cell A1. Cell B1 is usually empty, so long titles just flow over any adjoining cells as needed.) Generally, however, you want cell content to fit in the cell it was intended for, and so you need to make your columns wide enough to accommodate a worksheet's content. If you have already entered content and it's been truncated, you need to widen the column that contains the cell with the overrun text.

How to fix it

To widen a column to accommodate a particular entry, follow these steps:

1. Hold the mouse pointer over the right seam of the heading of the column you want to widen. (Note that you don't have to actually select the column to widen it.)

2. When the pointer changes to a double-headed arrow, hold down the mouse button and drag the seam to the right. ▶

3. Release the mouse button when the column is wide enough to fit the entry.

Column A is being widened to reveal the entire entry in cell A3.

To widen a column so that none of its entries is truncated by entries in an adjacent column, follow these steps:

1. Point to the column heading's right seam. (You don't have to select a column to widen it.)

2. When the pointer changes to a double-headed arrow, double-click the right seam of the column's heading to widen the column to fit its widest entry.

Don't widen, be happy

Just as it saves time and effort to format a word processing document after the entire document's typed (rather than stopping to format as you type), you can adopt a similar relaxed attitude about your worksheet's appearance while you're in the process of building the worksheet's content. Wait until all of your content is entered, ignoring any text that doesn't quite fit in the cells, and then press Ctrl+A to select the entire worksheet. Hold your mouse pointer between the seam of two columns, and when the pointer changes to a double-headed arrow, double-click the seam to adjust the entire worksheet so that each column accommodates its widest entry. ▶

When the entire worksheet is selected, widening one column widens them all.

Alternatively, you can select the entire worksheet, right-click any column's heading, and then click Column Width on the shortcut menu. In the Column Width dialog box, type a numeric column width that should apply to all of your worksheet's columns, and then click OK. The number you type should equal the maximum number of characters you want to appear across the column width; for example, if you type 20, then the column width will be adjusted to accommodate 20 characters, including spaces. Be sure you enter a number that will keep the worksheet from looking too cramped or too spread out. After you adjust the columns in the entire worksheet, you might need to adjust individual columns with entries that are larger or smaller than the global column width you set.

> **Tip**
> If you have a large worksheet with many cells that fall outside the visible portion of your worksheet, double-clicking the seam of a column heading to widen the column might have unexpected results. The widest entry might not be the truncated entry you can see and were trying to fix—another cell above or below the visible portion of the worksheet might contain entries that are even longer, and the column could become much wider than you intend. It's safest to scroll through the worksheet to find such entries, and if they're longer than the column width you had in mind, either shorten them or use the Wrap Text feature to make the text wrap onto multiple lines. Select the cells in which you want to wrap text (or press Ctrl+A to select the entire worksheet), and then press Ctrl+1 to display the Format Cells dialog box. Click the Alignment tab, select the Wrap Text check box, and then click OK.

I'm tired of entering the same series of labels in my worksheets

Source of the problem

It can be a real drag to build worksheets that have content similar to other worksheets. You know you've typed these exact words before—a list of locations, names, or products—and it aggravates you to know you're repeating your efforts and leaving yourself vulnerable to typos and other errors. Well, repeat yourself no more!

You might be aware that Excel completes lists automatically. For example, if you enter Quarter 1 in a cell and then use the fill handle to drag that entry through the adjoining cells, Excel fills those cells with Quarter 2, Quarter 3, and Quarter 4. If you keep going, Excel starts all over again with Quarter 1. You can also complete lists of months or days of the week this way. ▶

But what if you need a list of items that Excel doesn't know the order of, such as the list of your company's remote offices (Philadelphia, New York, Atlanta, Phoenix, San Francisco, and so on) or a list of products you track every month in a sales worksheet (A578-3B, A578-4B, A578-7C, B345-4E)? Excel lets you create a custom list that you can flesh out simply by typing any item in the list in an individual cell. You can base a custom list on existing content (in a worksheet where you've already typed a whole series of entries), or build a custom list from scratch.

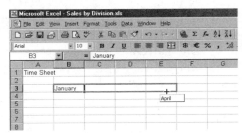

To fill adjacent cells with a list of months, use the fill handle.

How to fix it

To create a custom list from existing content, follow these steps:

1. Select the cells in your worksheet that contain the row or column labels that you want to turn into a custom list.

2. On the Tools menu, click Options.

3. In the Options dialog box, click the Custom Lists tab.

4. Click the Import button to bring in the content of the cell range listed in the Import List From Cells box. (This is the range you selected in step 1.) ▶

5. If you need to change a list entry, click next to the entry in the List Entries box, and then edit the entry's text as needed.

6. Click OK to close the dialog box.

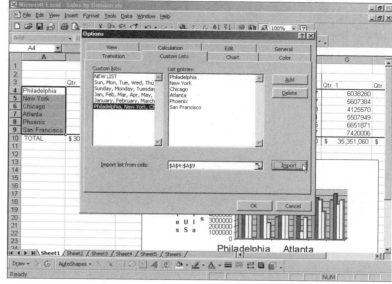

To create a custom list from scratch, follow these steps:

1. With any worksheet open, click Options on the Tools menu.

2. In the Options dialog box, click the Custom Lists tab.

3. With NEW LIST selected in the Custom Lists box, click in the List Entries box.

4. Type the list, pressing Enter after each item.

5. When your list is complete, click the Add button. Your list will appear in the box on the left side of the dialog box, with each item in the list separated by a comma.

6. Click OK to close the dialog box.

Once you've created your custom list, you can use it in any new or existing worksheet. Enter any item from the list in a cell, use that cell's fill handle to drag through the adjoining cells (in either the row or column), and release the mouse button to enter the remaining list items. The items will appear in the adjoining cells in the order you entered them in the list. If you drag through more cells than there are items in the custom list, the series will begin again with the first of the list items.

Tip

You can create as many custom lists as you need, and you can edit any list you've created. (Be aware that you can't edit the lists that are installed with Excel, such as months of the year or days of the week.) To edit one of your lists, click Options on the Tools menu, click the Custom Lists tab, and select the custom list you want to edit in the Custom Lists box. Click in the List Entries box, make edits as you need to, and then click OK. To remove a list completely, select the list in the Custom Lists box, click Delete, click OK to confirm the deletion, and then click OK a second time to close the Options dialog box.

I can't get my data validation rules to work

Source of the problem

Suppose your Excel database requires specific entries in some of the fields, such as complete department names in an employee list (to prevent the use of both "Mktg." and "Marketing" or "Acctg." and "Accounting," which can make filtering and sorting difficult) or only numeric content in an employee number field. To restrict the data that can be entered, you have set up rules, called *data validation* rules, but they aren't working! Now your database is at risk for inaccurate or inappropriate entries, especially if you're not the only one making entries in the worksheet. What happened?

Two possible scenarios that can prevent data validation rules from working are:

- The cell material wasn't typed directly into the cells, but was copied or cut and then pasted in them.

- You've made an entry in a cell for which no rules were established.

The solution to the first possibility is simple—don't allow anyone to paste content into cells in which data validation rules apply. For the latter possibility, you need to figure out which cells have rules applied to them, and then check and correct the rules that are in place, if any corrections are needed.

Tip

Why can't you just put a comment or text box on the worksheet to advise users what kind of data you want them to enter? Sometimes people ignore such advisories, and without data validation rules in place, Excel can't prevent entries that could result from ignored advisories. Excel will accept anything you type—text, numbers, symbols inserted with keyboard shortcuts—and doesn't make so much as a peep if you type something that doesn't make sense or that isn't appropriate for the cell where you've entered it.

How to fix it

To check for data validation rules, follow these steps:

1. On the Edit menu, click Go To.

2. In the Go To dialog box, click Special.

3. In the Go To Special dialog box, click the Data Validation option, and leave the All default setting in place. ▶

4. Click OK to have Excel select all cells with data validation rules applied to them.

Once you've determined which cells have rules applied to them, check the rules for omissions or errors by following these steps:

1. With the cells with data validation rules still selected, click one of these cells, and then click Go To on the Edit menu.

2. Click Special, click the Data Validation option, and then click Same below it. Click OK to select the cells where the active cell's data validation rules are also applied.

3. On the Data menu, click Validation.

4. In the Data Validation dialog box, examine the Allow box and all other applicable settings in the Validation Criteria section, to make sure the settings are correct. ▶

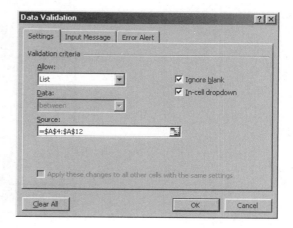

Rules are meant to be broken...sort of

Data Validation rules control what you can enter into selected cells, and that's a great thing when you're trying to keep people from entering erroneous or inappropriate data in a worksheet. You might encounter a problem with creating lists of acceptable entries, however. When you select the Source cell range in the Data Validation dialog box, the cells you designate as containing the acceptable entries are not protected by the rule, even if they're within the range of cells to which the rule applies. For example, if you're applying a rule to cells B1 through B25 and cells B1 through B6 are the Source range—meaning they contain the handful of entries that are acceptable for use in cells B1 through B25—the entries you make in cells B1 through B6 will (a) be allowed to violate the rule, and (b) become part of the list of acceptable entries for the range to which the rule is applied, no matter what you enter in those cells. Why is this? Search me. I don't imagine it was an intended part of the feature, because it can certainly blow holes in your validation rules. To eliminate this problem, make your Source range a block of cells that are away from the working part of your worksheet—squirrel them away in some obscure place in the workbook, where no one will possibly make any entries after the rule is created.

Tip

In the Data Validation dialog box, examine the Error Alert tab, and make sure the Show Error Alert After Invalid Data Is Entered check box is selected. If this check box is clear, Excel won't display a prompt indicating that the validation rules have been violated, and that alone could lead you to believe that the rules aren't working properly. If you need to, select this check box, click a type of error message symbol in the Style list, type appropriate messages in the Title and Error Message boxes, and then click OK.

Are you having trouble exporting Excel content to other applications? — **yes**

no

Are you having trouble importing content from your Word document into Excel? — **yes**

Go to...
When I paste a Word table into my worksheet, the table's content appears in the wrong cells, page 92.

no

Do you receive an error message when you try to edit an object that you imported into Excel? — **yes**

Quick fix
A lack of memory is the usual culprit. Close other applications that are open, or save your work and restart your computer to free up system resources.

no

Are you unable to insert an object in your worksheet? — **yes**

Go to...
The object type I want isn't listed in the Object dialog box, page 90.

no

Are people who use older versions of Excel unable to open the workbooks that you send them? — **yes**

Quick fix
When saving your Excel 97 or 2000 workbook for use by someone using an older version of Excel, use the Save As Type list in the Save As dialog box to select the version of Excel that they use.

Are you having trouble exporting worksheet cells to Word?

yes

Go to...
When I paste Excel cells into a Word table, the content appears in the wrong cells, page 94.

no

Are you having trouble exporting a chart to Word?

yes

Go to...
The chart I pasted into a Word document doesn't change when I update the Excel data, page 98.

no

Is your Excel chart changing unexpectedly after you paste it into a PowerPoint slide?

yes

Quick fix
If the Excel chart you pasted into your PowerPoint presentation changes whenever you edit your Excel data, there's a link between the chart and the slide. Simply delete the chart and re-paste it, being certain to click Paste on the Edit menu—no link will be established, and the chart will not change.

no

Is your Excel data appearing in the wrong place when you export it to Access?

yes

Go to...
When I paste Excel data into an Access table, column headings appear as the first record, page 102.

If your solution isn't here
Check these related chapters:
  Charts, page 2
  Hyperlinks, page 170
  Saving, page 244
Or see the general troubleshooting tips on page xv.

The object type I want isn't listed in the Object dialog box

Source of the problem

Your worksheet needs something—an editable graphic, a document, a movie, a sound—and you click Object on the Insert menu in the hope of selecting one of these items. To your surprise, however, the object you want to insert isn't in the Object Type list in the Object dialog box. How can that be?

The list of objects in the Object dialog box is based on the software installed on your computer. Any Office-compatible software that's properly installed will appear in the list. If the object you want isn't in the list, either the software that produces such an object isn't installed on your computer, or the software isn't compatible with Windows, or Office, or both.

To solve the problem, first make sure the software you need (such as sound-recording or editing software if you want to insert a .wav file object) is actually installed on your computer. If it's not, install it. If the software is installed, and you believe it is compatible with Windows and Office, try uninstalling and then reinstalling the software, so that if it is compatible, you'll be confident that the installation was complete. Plus, you'll have given Office a chance to recognize the software and offer the software's objects as insertable object types in Excel's Object Type list. ▶

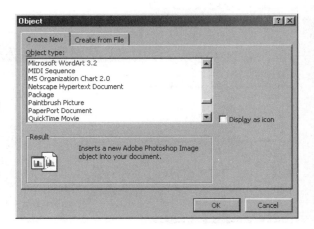

How to fix it

To verify that your computer contains the software that supports the object type you want, try one of these methods:

- Check the Programs list on the Start menu. Look for the software you believe supports the object type you want to insert. If you find the software listed on the Programs menu, click the item in the menu to see if the software runs properly. A menu item for deleted software often remains on the Start menu, unless a thorough uninstall operation was performed, usually with the Add/Remove Programs feature in Control Panel.

- Open Windows Explorer or My Computer, and then examine the Program Files folder. When software is installed, Windows normally creates a folder for the software as a subfolder of the Program Files folder. If you find a folder for the software, examine the folder and its own subfolders for an executable file (normally ending in an .exe extension) that starts the program. When you find the executable file, try double-clicking it to see if the program runs.

- If you know the name of the program, click Start, point to Find, click Files Or Folders, and then enter search criteria, such as the program name or a portion of it, as needed in the Find: All Files dialog box. (The command names might vary slightly in Windows 2000 or Windows Me, but the process is basically the same.) ▶

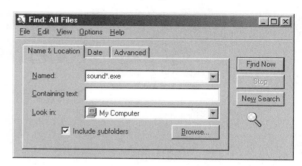

Pleased to meetcha

If you find the software through one of these methods, but the type of object is definitely not in the list of those that you can insert in your Excel worksheet (double-check the Object dialog box list, just to be sure), uninstall the software and reinstall it. Doing so should make Office "see" that the software is there and available.

To uninstall the software, don't just select its folder in the Windows Explorer or My Computer window and press Delete. No! This will remove the core programs, but won't thoroughly remove all the files that were planted throughout other folders in your system when the software was installed. Open Control Panel by clicking Start, pointing to Settings, and clicking Control Panel, and then double-click the Add/Remove Programs icon.

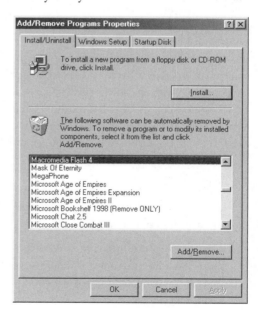

In the Add/Remove Programs Properties dialog box, check the list of programs that can be uninstalled. (Software must come with an uninstall utility in order to be uninstalled properly.) When you find the software you want to uninstall, select it, and click the Add/Remove button. Windows will prompt you to confirm your intention to uninstall the selected software. (Again, the command names might vary slightly if you're using Windows 2000 or Windows Me.) ▶

Once you've uninstalled the software, install the software again from the original CD-ROM or floppy disks. Office should be able to recognize the software and include its objects in the list of those that you can insert in all Office applications.

When I paste a Word table into my worksheet, the table's content appears in the wrong cells

Source of the problem

You might think a Word table and an Excel worksheet would be so similar that they'd work together seamlessly. In most cases, you'd be correct. However, sometimes you'll find that when you paste a Word table into your Excel worksheet, the columns and rows you neatly arranged and filled in Word look like a big mess in the worksheet. ▶

When your Word table becomes an Excel puzzle, it's generally the result of cells that were either split in the Word table, or drawn with the Draw Table feature (used to create cells with random widths and heights) in conjunction with the Insert Table tool or on its own. Often, the appearance of a mess in Excel is just the result of changes in row heights and column widths that occur when you force the table material into the structure of an Excel worksheet. With a little tidying up, you can make the worksheet table a near twin of the Word table. If the table's material is in the wrong place, you might need to move some of the text around by dragging it from one cell to another until all of the table's material is where you want it.

	A	B	C	D	E	F	G	H	I
1									
2									
3									
4		Invoice Number	Date			Amount			
5		B-35781		8/15/2000		$357.93			
6		B-52389		8/16/2000		$250.65			
7		C-35692		8/20/2000		$135.97			
8			TOTAL	$744.55					
9									
10									

How to fix it

1. To resize a column, point to the right seam of the column's heading, and then drag the seam to resize the column as you want.

2. To resize a row, point to the bottom seam of the row's heading, and then drag the seam to resize the row as needed. (Generally, row heights need to be adjusted only if the Word table was drawn by hand, or if more than one line of text is typed into a cell in Word, causing the row to become taller as the text wraps in the cell.)

3. Using drag-and-drop editing, move misplaced content from one cell to another by selecting the cell or cells containing the misplaced content, pointing to the edge of the cell or cells, and when your mouse pointer turns to a left-pointing arrow, dragging the content to the cell or cells in which you want it to appear. ▶

4. Repeat these steps until all of your content is where you want it.

	A	B	C	D	E	F	G	H	I
1									
2									
3									
4		Invoice Number	Date			Amount	F4:F7		
5		B-35781		8/15/2000		$357.93			
6		B-52389		8/16/2000		$250.65			
7		C-35692		8/20/2000		$135.97			
8				TOTAL	$744.55				
9									
10									

Imitation is the sincerest form of worksheet formatting

Excel looks at the formatting applied to the Word table and applies its closest match. For example, if you split a cell in one row but didn't split the cell directly below it in the next row, Excel will apply the Merge And Center command to the cell that wasn't split, allowing it to span two worksheet cells. If you typed a paragraph of text into your table cell and the text wrapped, Excel will turn on the Wrap Text setting for that cell in the worksheet. Border and cell shading applied in Word will be applied in Excel as well; as a result, you'll notice that cells with borders that are cut or copied from Word have a printable hairline border on them in Excel. ▶

A border applied in Word also appears in Excel.

	A	B	C	D	E	F	G
1							
2							
3							
4			Invoice Number	Date	Amount		
5			B-35781	8/15/2000	$357.93		
6			B-52389	8/16/2000	$250.65		
7			C-35692	8/20/2000	$135.97		
8				TOTAL	$744.55		
9							
10							

If you want to remove or edit any of the formats Excel applies based on how you've formatted the Word table, select the cells involved, right-click the selection, and then click Format Cells on the shortcut menu. In the Format Cells dialog box, adjust the formatting as needed, and then click OK.

TIP When measuring the space that the text takes up, try to remember that 72-point text takes up roughly 1 square inch per character. Therefore, 10-point text (the Excel default point size) is roughly 1/10th of an inch per character. So, for example, if the column in your Excel table has to be 1 inch wide to match the size you set in Word, you can fit seven 10-point characters across it. This basic equation should help you "do the math" to match Excel column widths to the equivalent Word settings.

When I paste Excel cells into a Word table, the content appears in the wrong cells

Source of the problem

Word and Excel are both part of the Microsoft Office suite of applications, so one assumes, and justifiably so, that the two applications and their files can play well together. Most of the time, you can paste Word content into an Excel worksheet—and, conversely, Excel worksheet content into a Word document.

However, sometimes the worksheet cells that contain the material you need to transfer to a Word table do not weather the trip to Word intact. If you cut or copy worksheet cells to the Clipboard and then paste the material into a Word table, you might find that the pasted cells erroneously move or reorder the existing table cells in a way that you don't want. The cause? Not providing the appropriate landing strip—in other words, a clean, empty part of the Word

document—on which the Excel content can land. The cells you pasted into the table shove Word's table cells over, and the table structure you took the time to set up to house your Excel content is completely messed up. ▶

You can generally paste a Word table into an Excel worksheet with little hassle. (See "When I paste a Word table into my worksheet, the table's content appears in the wrong cells" on

page 92.) So you might assume that, when pasting Excel worksheet content into a Word document, you'd have to paste the worksheet cells into an existing table. After all, because Excel's worksheet structure follows the pattern of a table, Excel provides a compatible environment for Word tables. It makes sense that you'd want Word to return the favor. The problem is that when you paste Excel content into Word, Word creates a separate table for the Excel material. Therefore, if you paste the Excel cells into an existing table, the cells form a table nested within the Word table, and the columns and rows you set up become extra baggage. You can take one of three different approaches to solving the problem of Excel content messing up your existing Word table.

Tip

By default, cut or copied Excel worksheet content usually appears in your Word document as a table with no borders, unless borders were applied to the original cells in Excel. If you want to apply borders to the new table in Word, you can either use the Tables And Borders toolbar buttons, or click Borders And Shading on the Format menu to access the Borders And Shading dialog box.

How to fix it

If pasting the Excel material into a Word document was the last action you did, you can undo the action and paste the material in a more appropriate place by following these steps:

1. Press Ctrl+Z to undo the paste.

2. Click an insertion point outside the table, on a blank line.

3. Press Ctrl+V to paste the table outside the existing Word table.

If it has been a while since the Excel material was pasted in the Word document, you can cut the Excel material, and then paste it in a more appropriate place by following these steps:

1. In Word, select the nested table that contains the Excel content, and then press Ctrl+X to cut the table to the Clipboard.

2. Delete the Word table, or if you want to keep it for another purpose, press Enter before or after the table to insert a few blank lines.

3. Paste the previously nested Excel table onto a blank line as a separate entity.

This solution is continued on the next page.

When I paste Excel cells into a Word table, the content appears in the wrong cells

(continued from page 95)

If you want to leave the pasted Excel content where it is and just get rid of the extra columns and rows in the Word table, follow these steps:

1. Using the mouse pointer, select the rows of the table you created before pasting. (Be sure not to select the row containing the nested table.) ▶

2. Delete the rows by pointing to Delete on the Table menu and then clicking Rows.

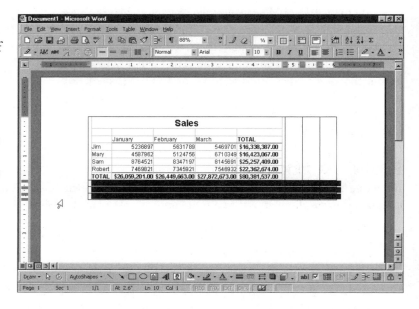

3. Repeat steps 1 and 2, selecting the extraneous table columns and clicking Delete and then Columns on the Table menu to get rid of the extra columns.

Just the words, ma'am

What if you want just the content inside the cells of an Excel worksheet, but not the cells themselves, to appear in a Word table? Imagine you have a cell in an Excel worksheet that contains a sentence, paragraph, or large number that you'd rather not retype—all you want to do is grab the text from the cells and paste it into your Word document without worrying about the Excel cells coming along for the ride. Can it be done? Yep. Just double-click the Excel cell that contains the text, and then select the text you want to copy. ▶

After you've made your selection, press Ctrl+C to copy the material to the Clipboard, and in your Word document, position the insertion point where you want the copied material to appear, and then press Ctrl+V to paste the copied text.

Thou shalt be converted

When you paste cells from an Excel worksheet into a Word document, the worksheet cells are quickly converted into Word table elements. If you want, you can just as quickly convert the Word table into non-table text. To select the table, click it, point to Select on the Table menu, and then click Table. On the Table menu again, point to Convert, and then click Table To Text (or click Convert Table To Text on the Table menu if you're working in Word 97). In the Convert Table To Text dialog box, click the Tabs option in the Separate Text With section, and then click OK to convert the table into a tabular list.

Tip
If you convert a table to text and choose tabs, commas, or some other character as the separator between the cells' content, you can use Word's Find And Replace feature to seek out the characters and replace each of them with a space. Click Replace on the Edit menu to access the Find And Replace dialog box.

The chart I pasted into a Word document doesn't change when I update the Excel data

Source of the problem

It's great that you can paste content, such as a chart, from an Excel worksheet into a Word document (or into a PowerPoint presentation slide, for that matter), and whenever you edit the worksheet, the chart you pasted into the Word file updates to reflect those changes. Wait—you mean that's not happening? Oops.

Automatic updates, such as the one that's supposed to be happening in your chart, occur through a link between the *target* (the Word document in which you pasted the chart) and the *source* (the Excel worksheet from which you copied the chart in the first place). Normally, your Excel chart is updated in the Word document whenever you edit the Excel material used to build the chart because the pasted content is linked to the source. If the source and target aren't connected, the pasted content exists in isolation—no updates will occur, and the most you can do is edit the pasted chart by double-clicking it in the Word document. Excel's menus and toolbars will appear on the screen, and you can edit the chart as you normally would in Excel. However, the edits you make to the chart in the Word document will not effect the original chart in the source worksheet.

What can you do? Well, if you've already pasted the chart using only the Paste command on the Word Edit menu (or its equivalent toolbar button or keyboard shortcut), delete the chart and paste it again, this time using the Paste Special command. With the Paste Special feature, you can establish the links you need to update the chart in the target Word document whenever you make changes to the chart in the source Excel workbook.

> **Warning**
>
> If you cut an Excel chart from its original worksheet—or if you rename, move, or delete the workbook file entirely—the chart you pasted into the Word document won't get updated when you change your source data. For the connection between the source and the target to be established and maintained, both files have to remain intact, with their original file locations and original names as they existed at the time you pasted the Excel chart into the Word document.

How to fix it

1. In the Excel worksheet, select the chart you want to paste into Word.

2. On the Edit menu, click Copy to move a copy of the chart onto the Clipboard.

3. Switch to or open the target Word document, and position your insertion point where you want the chart to appear.

4. On the Edit menu in Word, click Paste Special. (Be sure to click Paste Special, not Paste.)

5. In the Paste Special dialog box, make sure that Microsoft Excel Chart Object is selected in the As list, and then click the Paste Link option to create a connection between the source and target files. ▶

6. Click OK to complete pasting the chart into the Word document.

You can test your link by editing the source file, and then checking the chart in the target file. Within a few seconds, depending on your computer's memory and processor speed, the changes will appear in the linked chart. ▶

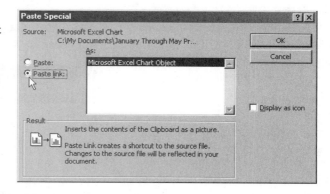

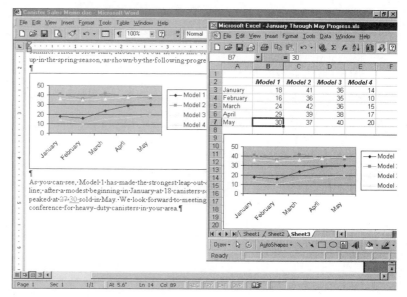

This solution is continued on the next page.

The chart I pasted into a Word document doesn't change when I update the Excel data

(continued from page 99)

Links like the Sphinx?
The link between your Excel chart and Word document will remain in place forever. Well, almost. The link will survive until and unless you sever it by clicking Links on the Edit menu in the Word document, and then clicking the Break Link button. (Click Yes when you are prompted to confirm the break.) ▶

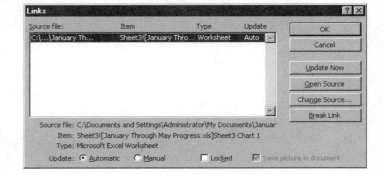

However, you might discover that you've also broken this link by accident. If you find that the chart you pasted from Excel no longer updates in Word, you might have done the following without realizing it:

- You might have accidentally deleted the source file.

- You might have moved either the source file or the target file to another directory or disk.

- You might have renamed either the source or target file.

If you've deleted the source file containing the Excel chart, you can delete the linked chart in Word, re-create the chart in a new Excel workbook, and use the Paste Special feature in Word to link the new chart to the Word document.

If you've moved or renamed the Excel workbook that contains the linked chart, don't worry; you can edit the link in Word. In the Word document containing the Excel chart, click Links on the Edit menu, and then click Change Source in the Links dialog box to display the Change Source dialog box. ▶

In the Change Source dialog box, locate the moved or renamed source file, select it, and then click Item. Excel displays the Set Item dialog box. ▶

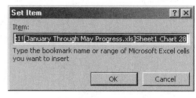

In the Set Item dialog box, select the old source file name in brackets, type over the selection, and make sure the sheet and chart numbers are correct. Click OK, click Open to confirm the new link, and then click OK to close the Links dialog box.

In the Links dialog box, you can choose how the link will update—automatically (the default), manually, or never (by choosing the Locked option). If you want to control when the target is updated, choose Manually. This will require you to click Links on the Edit menu when you open the target file, and then click the Update Now button to update the file with any changes made back at the source.

When I paste Excel data into an Access table, column headings appear as the first record

Source of the problem

A lot of Excel users are also Access users, maintaining the same or similar data in both applications. Often, Excel houses simple list type databases that users maintain daily; users import the worksheets into Access to flesh out a larger database on a weekly or monthly basis. However, you might encounter a problem when you're importing your Excel worksheet into Access for the first time, or if someone else converted an Excel worksheet to Access and missed the step in the Link Spreadsheet Wizard that converts Excel column headings to Access field names. Your column labels from the Excel worksheet appear as the first record in the converted Access table. ▶

This problem is the result of a misstep while working in the Link Spreadsheet Wizard that appears whenever you open an Excel workbook in Access. If the First Row Contains Column Headings check box in the first step of this wizard is not selected, Access treats every row in your Excel worksheet equally, and consequently doesn't recognize that the first row in the original Excel worksheet really represents the field names and not the data. It's easy to fix, requiring some minor table editing in Access, and then you're on your way.

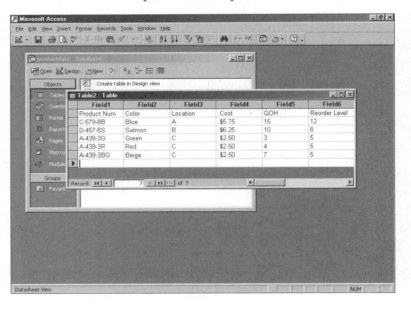

One way to fix this problem is to not cause it in the first place. This requires setting up an Access table to house your Excel content, and having the field names already set up in the Access table. The Access field names don't have to match your Excel column labels exactly, but for clarity's sake, they should be similar.

How to fix it

1. If you've already created your Access table, enter field names that match the names you're using in your Excel worksheet, open that table, and leave it open awaiting the Excel content.

2. Switch to or open your Excel worksheet, and select the cells containing the data you want to add to the Access table. Do *not* include the row of the worksheet that contains your column labels.

3. On the Edit menu, click Copy to place the Excel data on the Clipboard.

4. Switch back to the Access table, and click the first cell of the first row of the table.

5. On the Edit menu, click Paste Append. The Excel data appears in the table. Click Yes to confirm pasting the records.

Your Excel data will fill the rows of the Access table, and fill the same number of columns in the table as you pasted from Excel. This might or might not populate all of the columns (fields) in the Access table, as some of them might not have been mirrored in the structure of your Excel worksheet. ▶

Product#	ProdColor	Warehouse	Cost	QtyOnHand	ReorderLev	Vendor
C-579-8B	Blue	A	$5.75	15	12	
D-457-8S	Salmon	B	$6.25	10	8	
A-439-3G	Green	C	$2.50	3	5	
A-439-3R	Red	C	$2.50	4	5	
A-439-3BG	Beige	C	$2.50	7	5	

Recycle your Excel column labels

If your Access table was new and had no field names yet, you can use the Excel column labels to create them. Instead of selecting all of your Excel data except the row containing column labels, include that row in your selection. On the Edit menu, click Copy, and then switch to your new Access table. Click the first cell of the first row (under Field1). On the Edit menu, click Paste Append, and then click Yes to confirm pasting the records.

Your first record in the table will now be the field names from your Excel worksheet—and these names must be transferred to the field names at the top of each column in the Access table. To do this, double-click the first Access field name, and while the Field1 text is highlighted, type the field name you see in the first record. Move on to Field2, and repeat the process, continuing until all of the field names have been replaced by the column labels from your Excel data.

The last step of recycling column labels is to delete the first record—simply click the record number to the left of the row, and press Delete. The row will disappear, and you'll be prompted to confirm your intention to delete the record by clicking Yes.

Are you having trouble filtering your list? **yes**

no

Is the accuracy and consistency of your data in question? **yes**

Go to...
I don't know how to find and fix errors and inconsistencies in my data, page 110.

no

Are you having trouble entering records because you can't see your column headings? **yes**

Quick fix
To keep your column headings (field names) on the screen no matter how far down the list you scroll, click the row beneath your headings, and then click Freeze Panes on the Window menu. The headings row will be frozen until you click Unfreeze Panes on the Window menu.

Filtering records

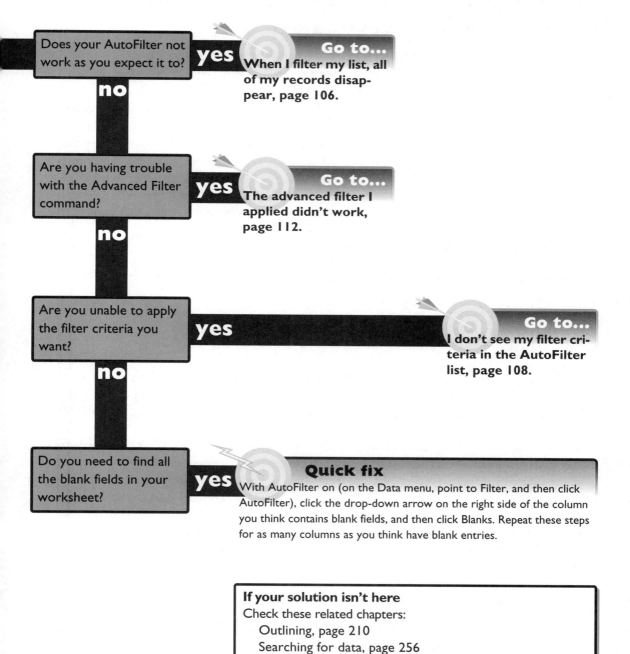

Does your AutoFilter not work as you expect it to?

yes

Go to...
When I filter my list, all of my records disappear, page 106.

no

Are you having trouble with the Advanced Filter command?

yes

Go to...
The advanced filter I applied didn't work, page 112.

no

Are you unable to apply the filter criteria you want?

yes

Go to...
I don't see my filter criteria in the AutoFilter list, page 108.

no

Do you need to find all the blank fields in your worksheet?

yes

Quick fix
With AutoFilter on (on the Data menu, point to Filter, and then click AutoFilter), click the drop-down arrow on the right side of the column you think contains blank fields, and then click Blanks. Repeat these steps for as many columns as you think have blank entries.

If your solution isn't here
Check these related chapters:
Outlining, page 210
Searching for data, page 256
Sorting data, page 266
Or see the general troubleshooting tips on page xv.

When I filter my list, all of my records disappear

Source of the problem

Well, that's not what you expected to happen, eh? But don't worry—it's actually a common problem, especially if you are working with a large data list—also called a *database*—that contains hundreds of rows of information— also called *records*. It's easy to establish AutoFilter criteria that either exclude all records in a database, or refine the list to include no records. You'll normally see these effects when you filter the list and subsequently apply criteria that none of the records that are currently displayed can meet. ▶

What normally causes this problem is using the Custom AutoFilter feature. With the Custom option in any field's AutoFilter list, you can set a filter criterion

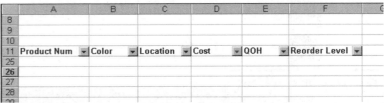

None of the records in this list meet the specified criteria.

such as Is Greater Than, Is Less Than, or Contains, and compare this criterion to an entry you type in the Custom AutoFilter dialog box. For example, you can set up a custom filter that looks for all products that cost more than $10.00, or for all products with product numbers beginning with "B."

If the database contains no products that cost more than $10.00, or if you've already filtered the list down to products that all cost less than $10.00, applying the custom filter you set will result in all the currently displayed records disappearing. They're not deleted, but hidden because they don't meet the criterion. It's easy to set the criterion to a value that doesn't exist in the database, by either introducing a typo or not being fully aware of all the data stored in the database. If you're working with someone else's list, the latter cause is probably the culprit. Regardless of why no records are displayed, solving the problem involves resetting one or more filter criteria to display the records you need to see.

How to fix it

1. Check your database for drop-down arrows that are blue. Blue drop-down arrows in a filtered database indicate columns—also called *fields*—to which filters are applied.

2. In any field with a blue drop-down arrow, click the arrow, and then click All in the drop-down list. This will remove the criterion applied only to this field and bring back any records that the criterion caused to be hidden. ▶

3. Repeat step 2 for as many fields as needed, until you have displayed all the records you want.

	A	B	C	D	E	F	
8							
9							
10							
11	Product Num ▾	Color ▾	Location ▾	Cost ▾	QOH ▾	Reorder Level ▾	
25					(All)		
26					(Top 10...)		
27					(Custom...)		
28							
29							

Start big, end small

When applying filters to your database, the process can be easy. For example, imagine that you want to refine the list by a single field—saying, in effect, "Show me all the products in warehouse B." This requires that only the Location field be filtered. On the other hand, if you need to see all the products in warehouse B that cost more than $10.00 and for which less than five items are in stock, you'll need to filter three fields: Location, Cost, and Quantity On Hand (QOH).

When filtering more than one field, you should filter the fields in the appropriate sequence. Be sure not to eliminate some of the records you want to end up with by filtering an out-of-sequence field first. Using the Warehouse B, Costs More Than $10.00, and Less Than 5 In Stock criteria in the previous example, you would want to filter the Location field, then the Cost field, and then the Quantity On Hand (QOH) field. Filtering in any other order could remove items that are in warehouse B, that have less than 5 items in inventory, or that cost more than $10.00. If you aren't familiar with the database (or the data stored in it), you might not realize that products in the database that meet your criteria are presented in an order that you don't intend.

Tip

You can redisplay all the records in one fell swoop and still keep the AutoFilter feature active by removing all filters. Click any field in your database. On the Data menu, point to Filter, and then click Show All.

Tip

When filtering a list, it's a good rule of thumb to start with the field that has the most duplicate entries, and end with a field that has few or no duplicates. For example, in an employee list, you might want to filter for all the employees in a specific department who earn more than a certain salary per year, and who were hired before a certain date. If the Department field has a lot of duplicates, you'll probably end up with more possible entries on which to use filters for the Salary and Date Hired fields, which would most likely have fewer duplicates in their columns.

I don't see my filter criteria in the AutoFilter list

Source of the problem

The AutoFilter list for any column, or *field*, shows all of the entries for that field, whether you are working with a list of information, or *database*, that contains 10 rows or 1000. If you choose an entry from a field's AutoFilter list, the only rows, or *records*, that will be displayed are those that match that specific entry in that specific field. So if you go to make a selection in the AutoFilter list and you don't see the entry that you want to filter on, you will know that the entry was not designated properly in the selected field in any of the records.

What could be the cause of this? There are several possible explanations for a missing AutoFilter entry:

- A skipped row. A row might have accidentally been inserted or skipped in the database you want to filter. Because AutoFilter recognizes only continuous and contiguous entries in a database, all you have to do in this case is delete the empty row. After you delete the empty row, the missing entry will appear in the AutoFilter drop-down list. ▶

	B26	▼	=	Navy Blue		
	A	B	C	D	E	F
10						
11	Product Num ▼	Color ▼	Location ▼	Cost ▼	QOH ▼	Reorder Level ▼
12	D-457-8S	(All)	B	$ 6.25	10	8
13	A-439-3G	(Top 10…)	B	$ 2.50	3	5
14	A-439-3BG	(Custom…)	C	$ 2.50	4	5
15	B-573-7R	Blue	C	$ 4.25	7	5
16	C-752-8C	Brown	A	$ 3.65	8	10
17	F-34903Y	Charcoal	B	$ 7.25	10	12
		Green				
18	V-912-5P	Purple	A	$ 9.50	32	25
19	G-239-5G	Red	C	$ 1.75	55	50
20	N-425-6B	Salmon	A	$ 3.50	60	45
21	G-334-6Z	Yellow	B	$ 7.75	50	15
		Charcoal				
22	G-427-7Z	Purple	D	$ 8.75	50	15
23	B-573-7R	Blue	B	$ 5.75	15	12
24	Z-975-3R	Brown	C	$ 6.25	10	17
25						
26	V-912-5P	Navy Blue	A	$ 3.50	40	10
27						

- Typos. If you're looking for the name Smythe, and if someone typed Smithe or Smyth instead when entering data in the database, you won't see Smythe in the AutoFilter list. If you suspect a typo is at the root of your missing entry problem, look for spellings that are similar to the entry you're looking for. (Don't forget misspellings!)

- Other fields have already been filtered. If other fields have been filtered, thus reducing the displayed records, any new filter will apply to only those reduced number of records. For example, if your database contains 1000 records but has been filtered down to 20 records, and if you then filter another field, 20 or fewer entries will be available in the AutoFilter list. The one record you are looking for might be hidden by the previously applied filters. If previous filters are the suspected cause, you have to remove them, and then search for your record from the complete list of records in the database.

● Entries in the wrong field. Be sure to carefully examine the columns on either side of the field that you're filtering to make sure the entry you're looking for wasn't typed by accident into either column. For example, a zip code entry might have been typed into the phone number field, or a city entry could have been typed into the street address field. ▶

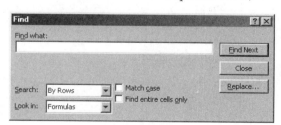

	D19 ▼	= 7.25					
	A	B	C	D	E	F	
8							
9							
10							
11	Product Num	Color	Location	Alt Location	Cost	QOH	Reorder
12	C-579-8B	Blue	B	C	$ 5.75	15	
13	D-457-8S	Salmon	B	C	$ 6.25	10	
14	A-439-3G	Green	B	A	$ 2.50	3	
15	A-439-3R	Red	C	A	$ 2.50	4	
16	A-439-3BG	Beige	C	B	$ 2.50	7	
17	B-573-7R	Red	A	B	$ 4.25	3	
18	C-752-8C	Charcoal	B	A	$ 3.65	8	
19	F-34903Y	Yellow	A	7.25			

How to fix it

1. Click any cell other than one containing a heading.

2. On the Data menu, point to AutoFilter, and then click Show All. All filters will be removed, although AutoFilter will remain in effect.

3. Click the drop-down arrow for the field containing the entry you need. Assuming none of the other potential causes of hard-to-find records are at work, the entry you're looking for should appear in the AutoFilter list.

Tip
If you're searching for a single letter or number (such as "A" or "3"), make sure the Find Entire Cells Only check box is selected. Otherwise, Excel will find every instance of that letter or number, even when it is part of larger words or numbers.

Seek and ye shall find

If you have used AutoFilter to look for a record and been unsuccessful, another way to look is to use Excel's Find command. Using Find, you can search the entire worksheet for a specific word, number, or even a single character. You can search all contents, formulas, or comments that have been added to annotate your worksheet.

To search the entire worksheet, press Ctrl+A, and then press Ctrl+F to display the Find dialog box. ▶

In the Find What box, type what you want to find, and then click the Find Next button until Excel finds the data you need.

Find	? ×
Find what:	
	Find Next
	Close
Search: By Rows	Replace...
☐ Match case	
Look in: Formulas	☐ Find entire cells only

I don't know how to find and fix errors and inconsistencies in my data

Source of the problem

From a filtering standpoint, consistency is important for finding and filtering records in any database. If, for example, you have a Department field in an employee database, it won't do to enter "Accounting" for one record, and "Acctg." for another. Why would variations on the spelling or abbreviation of a word be a problem? Because if you later want to filter for all people in the Accounting department, none of the people in the Acctg. department will meet the filter criterion, despite the fact that they, too, are in the Accounting department. You would have to filter twice to find all the people in this one department. ▶

Finding these inconsistencies is simple; fixing them is just a matter of entering the correct data after you've found the inconsistencies you want to eliminate.

	A	B	C	D	E	F
	First Name ▾	Last Name ▾	Department ▾	Date Hired ▾	Salary ▾	Bonus % ▾
2	Jim	Brown	(All)	6/30/1992	$ 73,250.00	7%
3	Dewey	Cheatham	(Top 10...) (Custom...)	11/10/1992	$ 75,250.00	8%
4	Stan	DeMan	Accounting	9/15/1999	$ 35,500.00	4%
5	Denton	Fender	Acctg.	2/27/1995	$ 62,500.00	7%
6	Bob	Frapples	Marketing	12/20/1997	$ 42,550.00	6%
7	Sam	Jones	Operations Sales	7/25/1990	$ 65,750.00	8%
8	Leva	Malone	Operations	5/25/1993	$ 48,350.00	8%
9	Mary	Smith	Accounting	5/15/1998	$ 52,500.00	5%

(Cell reference box: D12 =)

How to fix it

1. To make sure you can see all entries, including ones that are inconsistently spelled, abbreviated, or numbered, point to Filter on the Data menu, and then click Show All. (If this command is unavailable on the Filter submenu, you are already seeing all entries.)

2. Click the drop-down arrow on the right side of the column that has inconsistent entries. Examine the drop-down AutoFilter lists to find both the correct entry you want to retain and the alternate entry causing the inconsistency. Make a note of both entries' exact spellings.

3. Press Ctrl+H to display the Replace dialog box.

> **Tip**
> Don't forget to save your database after each round of edits, and be sure to save more frequently if the edits are numerous. Especially if you do have to make a lot of edits, you wouldn't want to repeat them! Commit the keyboard shortcut Ctrl+S to memory— you're much more likely to save if you don't have to first stop typing.

4. In the Find What box, type the entry that causes the inconsistency. In the Replace With box, type the entry you want to retain. ▶

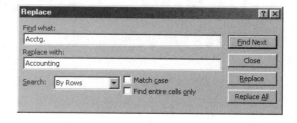

5. Click Find Next to locate the first instance of the erroneous entry, and then click Replace to replace the entry with the spelling or numbering you prefer. Continue clicking Find Next and then Replace to correct each instance individually, and then click OK when a message box notifying you that no more matches are found appears. (You can also simply keep clicking Replace, which will take you to the next instance of the Find text and replace it. If you are sure that replacing all specified entries at once will not cause conflicts with similar data, click Replace All to replace every instance of the offending entry with one fell swoop.)

6. Repeat steps 2 through 5 for additional inconsistent entries as needed.

An ounce of prevention is worth hours of editing

Unless you like to search for errors and edit them—perhaps hundreds of them, considering that each worksheet can contain as many as 65,000 records—you'd be wise to set up your database worksheet so that only certain entries will be accepted. Wouldn't it be great if users attempting to enter "Acctg." for the Department field received an error message that informed them that only certain department names are accepted in the field? You can create such error messages through Excel's Data Validation feature.

To apply data validation, select the column that you want to control. On the Data menu, click Validation. In the Data Validation dialog box, make sure the Settings tab appears, and then click List in the Allow drop-down list. In the Source text box, type the acceptable entries, separating each with a comma. ▶

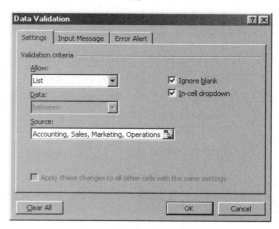

On the Input Message tab, you can create your own input messages to advise users which entries are acceptable for the cells in which they're working. On the Error Alert tab, you can create your own error messages to inform users that they've typed entries that don't meet the data validation rules you've applied. These alerts will appear as needed, when the user works in the selected column's cells.

(If you have any trouble with this feature, see "I can't get my data validation rules to work" on page 86.)

The advanced filter I applied didn't work

Source of the problem

Excel's Advanced Filter feature might not seem like the most intuitive tool on the planet, so don't feel bad if you get an error message or if the filter just plain doesn't work. Once you understand exactly how this particular filter operates, however, you'll find it helpful as an alternative to the more limited capabilities of the AutoFilter command.

Using the Advanced Filter feature, you can set one or more criteria for filtering your data list, or *database*, and then either reduce the database to the rows, or *records*, that meet the criteria or copy the records that meet the criteria to a separate place in the workbook—on the same sheet or on a different sheet.

So the problem is that you applied a filter and nothing happened, or you got the wrong records, or Excel threw an error message up on the screen to taunt you. ▶

What could have gone wrong? Any of the following could be the culprit:

- The range you selected in the Copy To box in the Advanced Filter dialog box does not contain enough room for the filtered records to be copied.

- You could have accidentally made an error selecting the criteria range.

- The criteria you set don't match any of your records.

With these potential causes for problems, it's understandable that your first (or second, or third) attempt to use Advanced Filter has run aground. The solution is usually simple, albeit enigmatic. Repeating the Advanced Filter command with a greater understanding of what the feature can do is usually the best approach.

How to fix it

1. Set up a range for the criteria you want in the rows above the database you want to filter. (You might have to insert several blank rows above your column headings to prepare for the actual Advanced Filter process.)

2. Select the column headings, or *field names*, for the columns, or *fields*, you want to filter, and copy them to the first row of the criteria range.

3. Type the entries you want to filter for under the copied column headings. ▶

4. With your criteria range set up and your criteria entered, click inside the database list, point to Filter on the Data menu, and then click Advanced Filter.

5. In the Advanced Filter dialog box, choose how Excel will display the results of the filter. Click either Filter The List In-Place (which reduces the displayed list to the records that meet the criteria), or Copy To Another Location (which displays the records that meet the criteria in another place on the same worksheet or in another worksheet in the open workbook).

6. Verify the cells that appear in the List Range box. Excel should select all of the rows and columns included in the range to be filtered; however, you can select the cells you want to filter by clicking outside the Advanced Filter dialog box and then selecting the range you want. The Advanced Filter dialog box temporarily shrinks so that you can see the range you're selecting. When you release the mouse button, the dialog box displays the range you've selected.

7. In the Criteria Range box, select the field headings and entries you set up earlier.

8. If you click the Copy To Another Location option, specify a range of cells into which Excel should copy the records that meet your filter criteria in the Copy To box.

9. Click OK to apply the filter. ▶

Tip

If you want to create a report based on the records that meet your criteria, it's a good idea to click the Copy To Another Location option in the Advanced Filter dialog box. This approach also keeps your advanced filter list intact in case you want to use the AutoFilter or Sort features on the original list.

H15 =

	A	B	C	D	E	F
1			Department		Salary	
2			Accounting		>50,000	
3			Sales			
4						
5						
6						
7						
8						
9						
10	First Name	Last Name	Department	Date Hired	Salary	Bonus %
11	Jim	Brown	Acctg.	6/30/1992	$ 73,250.00	7%
12	Dewey	Cheatham	Sales	11/10/1992	$ 75,250.00	8%
13	Stan	DeMan	Operations	9/15/1999	$ 35,500.00	4%
14	Denton	Fender	Sales	2/27/1995	$ 62,500.00	7%
15	Bob	Frapples	Marketing	12/20/1997	$ 42,550.00	6%
16	Sam	Jones	Marketing	7/25/1990	$ 65,750.00	8%
17	Leva	Malone	Operations	5/25/1993	$ 48,350.00	8%
18	Mary	Smith	Accounting	5/15/1998	$ 52,500.00	5%

H9 =

	A	B	C	D	E	F
1			Department		Salary	
2			Accounting		>50,000	
3			Sales			
4						
5	First Name	Last Name	Department	Date Hired	Salary	Bonus %
6	Dewey	Cheatham	Sales	11/10/1992	$ 75,250.00	8%
7	Denton	Fender	Sales	2/27/1995	$ 62,500.00	7%
8	Mary	Smith	Accounting	5/15/1998	$ 52,500.00	5%
9						
10						
11	First Name	Last Name	Department	Date Hired	Salary	Bonus %
12	Jim	Brown	Acctg.	6/30/1992	$ 73,250.00	7%
13	Dewey	Cheatham	Sales	11/10/1992	$ 75,250.00	8%
14	Stan	DeMan	Operations	9/15/1999	$ 35,500.00	4%
15	Denton	Fender	Sales	2/27/1995	$ 62,500.00	7%
16	Bob	Frapples	Marketing	12/20/1997	$ 42,550.00	6%
17	Sam	Jones	Marketing	7/25/1990	$ 65,750.00	8%
18	Leva	Malone	Operations	5/25/1993	$ 48,350.00	8%
19	Mary	Smith	Accounting	5/15/1998	$ 52,500.00	5%

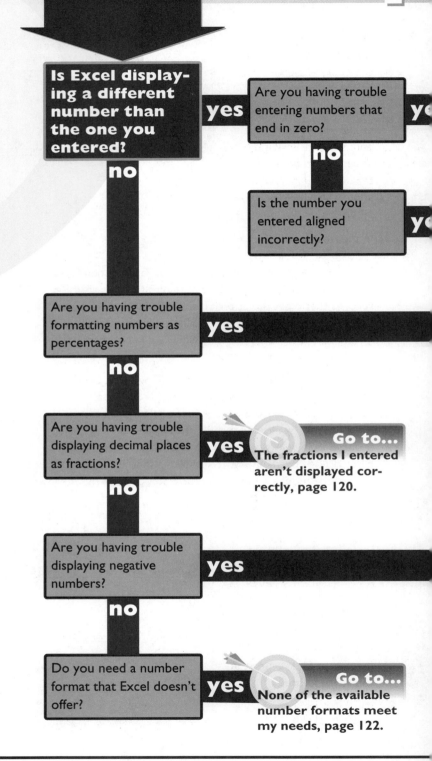

Is Excel displaying a different number than the one you entered?

yes → Are you having trouble entering numbers that end in zero?

no ↓

Is the number you entered aligned incorrectly?

no ↓

Are you having trouble formatting numbers as percentages?

yes →

no ↓

Are you having trouble displaying decimal places as fractions?

yes → **Go to...** The fractions I entered aren't displayed correctly, page 120.

no ↓

Are you having trouble displaying negative numbers?

yes →

no ↓

Do you need a number format that Excel doesn't offer?

yes → **Go to...** None of the available number formats meet my needs, page 122.

Go to...
When I type a decimal ending in zero, the zero disappears, page 116.

Go to...
I typed a number, but it's not right-aligned, page 118.

Quick fix

To turn a number into a percentage, select it, and click the Percentage Style button. (This feature works best with numbers that are actually the result of a formula that calculates a percentage—such as 10 divided by 50, which equals .2, or 20%.)

Quick fix

If you can't tell your negative and positive numbers apart, right-click any cell, and click Format Cells. In either the Numbers or Currency category, click a format in the Negative Numbers list.

If your solution isn't here

Check these related chapters:
Currency, page 46
Formatting text, page 124
Formatting worksheets, page 136
Or see the general troubleshooting tips on page xv.

When I type a decimal ending in zero, the zero disappears

Source of the problem

As you're zipping along entering your data, you enter a number, say 3.50, and as soon as you press Enter, the zero disappears, leaving you with 3.5 in the cell. Not really a major disappointment, but if the cell is in the Price column for a list of products, a price of 3.5 doesn't make sense. "Format it as currency!" you say. Well, maybe not. Not all numbers that represent money have to be formatted as currency—a simple two-decimal number format will do just fine.

So what's the problem? Why is Excel dropping your zero? Because by default all cells are formatted as General content, and that particular format drops the zero for decimals ending in zero. When the General format sees numbers, it right aligns them, drops the zero, and that's it. Yes, its handling of decimals can be a pain, but no, you aren't stuck with it.

Solving the problem requires either a proactive plan, or a reactive one. You can either format the Price column (or your version thereof) for two decimal places before you enter any content, or you can format it after you've entered your content, restoring all those zeroes to visibility in the worksheet. Either way, the steps are the same.

Tip

Should you be proactive or reactive? It's really a matter of preference—neither approach is better than the other, nor more labor-intensive. If you never want to see your zeroes disappear, format the columns that will contain price-like numbers ahead of time; if you don't mind seeing them disappear for a while (until you've finished making your entries), bring them back later by formatting after the fact.

How to fix it

1. As you build the headings and layout of your worksheet, select the column(s) or range(s) that you want to be formatted as numbers with two decimal places displayed.

2. On the Format menu, click Cells.

3. In the Format Cells dialog box, make sure the Number tab is visible. The General format is selected by default unless you are working with a blank worksheet or you have applied another format to cells within your worksheet.

4. Click the Number category and view the options on the right side of the dialog box. Using the Decimal Places box, you can specify how many decimal places you want to display. If 2, the default setting, does not appear in the Decimal Places box, return the setting to 2 by clicking the up or down arrows. ▶

5. Click OK to apply the format and close the dialog box.

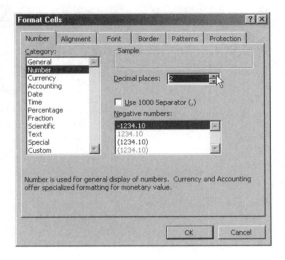

All at the click of a button

Instead of opening the Format Cells dialog box, you can also adjust the decimal settings for any selected cell or range by using the Increase Decimal button on the Formatting toolbar. Of course, you can also use the Decrease Decimal button if more than two decimal places are displayed. Select the cell or range (including whole columns and rows) to be reformatted. Be sure that only numeric content appears in the selected range. If the column heading is already typed, drag through the cells that contain numbers—the decimal formatting buttons don't work if the selected range contains anything other than numbers. Click the Increase Decimal button once to increase the setting from one decimal place to two places, and then click a cell outside the range to deselect the cells you just formatted.

Do as I do, not as I say

If you don't want to wait until all of your numeric entries are made to use the Increase Decimal button, enter one of your numbers, select the cell containing it, and then click the Increase Decimal button until the desired number of decimals are displayed. With that cell still selected, click the Format Painter button, which copies the formatting of the selected cell, and then drag through the remaining empty cells in the range. They'll then be ready to accept your entries, including those with decimals ending in zero, and the zeroes will be displayed.

Tip
You can't use the Increase Decimal or Decrease Decimal buttons on blank cells, so this approach is a reactive one. If you think the toolbar buttons are the way to go, wait to use them until all of your entries are made.

I typed a number, but it's not right-aligned

Source of the problem

By default, numeric content is right-aligned. As you type a number in a cell, the number builds from the left side of the cell. When you press Enter, however, the number moves to the right side of the cell. This is the case whether the cells where you're typing are formatted as General, Number, Currency, or Accounting (the category list options in the Format Cells dialog box). Dates and times are also right-aligned, even though they contain text.

So what's going on when you type a number in a cell, press Enter, and the number remains on the left side of the cell? One of two things can be causing this phenomenon: how the cell is formatted, or a typo. How can this be?

Imagine these scenarios:

- The Align Left button was accidentally clicked while the cell was selected.

- Left alignment was applied through the Format Cells dialog box.

- You typed some non-numeric character when entering the number in the cell—a period instead of a comma (to separate thousands), a space, the letter O instead of zero (0), or additional symbols that would normally be accepted as numeric content—an extra decimal point, two slashes, two dashes, or two commas typed together.

Should any of these situations occur, your numeric entry will be left-aligned. In the case of the accidental use of the Align Left button, Excel still thinks the entry is numeric, but thinks you want it left-aligned. In the case of typos, the addition of non-numeric content convinces Excel that you're entering the equivalent of text.

The solution to this problem is to determine the cause (formatting or typo), and either reformat or edit the cell.

> **Tip**
> Don't forget the Center button—this can be accidentally applied just as easily as the Align Left button. If your number moves to dead center in the cell after you press Enter, formatting is your culprit—no typo will result in a centered number.

> **Tip**
> Your cell could be set to left alignment as the result of formatting applied to previous content. If you've done some renovations in your worksheet, taking stuff from here and putting it there, you might be entering numbers into what was a column or row formatted for text, with left alignment previously applied.

How to fix it

To change formatting from left to right alignment using toolbar buttons, follow these steps:

1. Select the cell or range for which you want to change the alignment formatting.

2. Click the Align Right button. The numeric content will move to the right side of the selected cells.

To change formatting from left to right alignment by editing text, follow these steps:

1. Select the cell that contains a typo or a non-numeric character.

2. Make whatever changes are necessary to the entry in the Formula bar to edit the cell, moving or removing whatever's wrong with the entry. ▶

	A	B	C	D	E
	B10 ▾ X ✓ = 26.120,217				
1					
2	REGION SUMMARIES				
3					
4	Total Sales	$132,271,889.78	Percentage of Total		
5	Philadelphia	$25,317,026.78	19%		
6	New York	$21,692,857.00	16%		
7	Chicago	$22,182,833.00	17%		
8	Atlanta	$13,405,661.00	10%		
9	Phoenix	$23,553,295.00	18%		
10	San Francisco	26.120,217	20%		
11					
12					

With only the best indentions

Another cause of seemingly odd alignments is the use of Excel's Indent feature, which can be applied (accidentally or on purpose) from the toolbar or in the Format Cells dialog box.

Why would someone indent in a worksheet? To create a simple visual distinction between content in vertically adjoining cells, or to show hierarchy between entries, such as a total at the top level, and the numbers that created it beneath. ▶

	A	B	C	D	E
	B4 ▾ = =SUM(B5:B10)				
1					
2	REGION SUMMARIES				
3					
4	Total Sales	$132,271,889.78	Percentage of Total		
5	Philadelphia	$25,317,026.78	19%		
6	New York	$21,692,857.00	16%		
7	Chicago	$22,182,833.00	17%		
8	Atlanta	$13,405,661.00	10%		
9	Phoenix	$23,553,295.00	18%		
10	San Francisco	$26,120,217.00	20%		
11					
12					

To apply or remove an indent, click a cell or select a range of cells, and click the Increase Indent or Decrease Indent button on the Formatting toolbar. You can also click Cells on the Format menu, and on the Alignment tab of the Format Cells dialog box, use the up and down arrows of the Indent spin box to increase or decrease the indent currently set. (The default is zero.)

> **Tip**
> If your entry is numeric, clicking the Increase Indent button when the entry is selected left-aligns the number no matter how it was previously aligned. Be careful when you use the Increase Indent button, or you might have to reapply right alignment or centering to numeric content that you want to keep that way!

The fractions I entered aren't displayed correctly

Source of the problem

While the stock market might be abandoning fractions for decimals, many people still like fractions. They don't want to hear that four out of five dentists surveyed recommend something, they want to see that 4/5 (four-fifths) of all dentists agree.

Of course, Excel's default treatment of a typed fraction is to turn it into a date. If you type 4/5 into a cell to which no special formatting has been applied, it becomes 5-Apr as soon as you press Enter (if you're working in a U.S. date format). If you typed your number as a decimal such as .80, you can turn that into a fraction (4/5) by applying any one of several Fraction formats to the cell in question. ▶

Whether you typed your fractions and they turned into dates, or you typed your entries as decimals and now you want to see them as fractions, the same solution is called for—apply Fraction formatting to the cell or range.

How to fix it

1. Select the cell or range that contains or will contain numbers that should be displayed as fractions.

2. Click Cells on the Format menu.

3. In the Format Cells dialog box, click the Number tab.

4. Click the Fraction category, and select the fraction format you want to apply from the Type list. You can control the number of digits in the fraction, or designate whether the fraction is expressed in halves, quarters, eighths, sixteenths, tenths, or hundredths. (You might have to retype the fractions after you've formatted the cells to get the results you want.) ▶

5. Click OK to apply the format and close the dialog box.

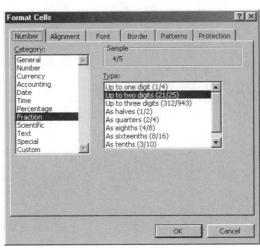

That's either a fraction or very high blood pressure

It's a good idea to annotate your worksheet with a comment or callout to indicate to other users that a given range of cells is formatted for fractions. This will prevent confusion when someone enters a number such as .786, and it turns into 393/500. To insert a comment, right-click the cell and click Insert Comment on the shortcut menu. In the text box that appears, type "This cell is formatted to store all entries as fractions" or something to that effect. To confirm your new comment, click any cell.

If you prefer to annotate a range of cells, use callouts. Click the AutoShapes button on the Drawing toolbar, point to Callouts, click one of the callout options, and drag to draw a callout with a line pointing to the cell where you started to drag. Then type the callout's text. (The callout can contain the same text you might enter in a comment.) You can also use the drawing tools on the Drawing toolbar to add an extra arrow pointing from the callout to the cells so that it's clear that the callout refers to a range of cells. ▶

Tip
The use of comments is covered in greater detail in "Comments and Track Changes" on page 24. You can find out more about using AutoShapes and callouts in "Drawing shapes and lines" on page 66.

Tip
When you make your fraction format selection from the Type list, choose carefully. Say, for example, your cell contains 3.5 now. If you apply the Fraction format and choose As Tenths (3/10) from the Types list, 3.5 becomes 3 5/10 (3 and 5 tenths). This might be confusing to people who expect 3.5 to turn into 3 1/2.

C4	▼	= 0.8			
A	B	C	D	E	F

1					
2	*Chemical Analysis*				
3					
4	Nitrogen	4/5		Data is stored as	
5	Lead	3/4		entered, but	
6	Chlorine	1/10		displayed as fractions.	
7					
8					
9					

None of the available number formats meet my needs

Source of the problem

Excel has nine different types of number formats that you can apply, and most of them have several variations—different ways to express negative numbers, different currency symbols, choices about how many decimals are displayed or how thousands are separated. There is also the Special format category, which offers formatting for Social Security numbers, phone numbers, and zip codes.

So how can the number format you need be missing? Easy. If your worksheet contains serial, credit card, bank routing, product, or identification numbers, or if it contains any number format that includes dashes, slashes, dots, or fixed-position letters or symbols, you'll need to create your own number format.

Why not just enter the number with all the extra trimmings? Because it wastes time. If you knew you could enter 34-A5-7891 and skip the dashes and the A, wouldn't you want to? Aside from saving time, entering just the numbers can help reduce the margin for typing errors.

So how do you tell Excel where to insert dashes, letters, and other symbols in your entry so that all you have to type is the numbers? You build a custom number format, that's how.

How to fix it

1. Select the range of cells that needs the custom format.

2. Click Cells on the Format menu.

3. In the Format Cells dialog box, make sure the Number tab is visible.

4. Select the Custom category, scroll through the list of existing custom formats and look at how they're expressed. (Note that the existing custom formats use pound signs to indicate numbers entered by the user and intervening characters, such as hyphens, to separate the numbers into segments.) Try to find a format that most closely matches the way in which you want to display numbers in the selected range, and then select it so that you can use it as a basis for the custom format you want to design. ▶

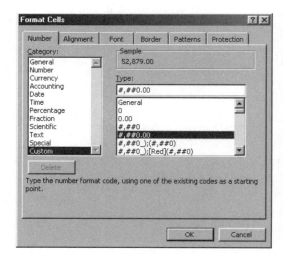

5. Delete any of the format's characters you don't want by highlighting them with your mouse pointer in the Type box and pressing the Backspace key. (Alternatively, you can simply highlight the entire string of characters in the Type box and enter your format—the characters you type will override the existing ones. Remember that you can break your number into only four or fewer sections through the use of intervening symbols.)

6. Click OK to apply the format and close the dialog box.

Tip
Your custom number format can have only four sections—for example, you can set up a format to build 123-45-67-89, but not 123-45-67-89-0. Your entry can have an unlimited number of numbers in it, but the groups created by the intervening symbols or letters are limited to four.

The sky's the limit, unfortunately...

Why "unfortunately"? Because while the custom format you create will control the placement of numbers that you type within the format, it won't control how many numbers you type. For example, if your worksheet contains product numbers such as 15379-A5-62, the creation of a format #####-A#-## will allow you to type 15379562, and have it all fall into place. There's nothing stopping you, however, from entering 153795625897126, which would result in 15379562587-A1-26. You could also enter too few numbers, such as 153795, and 153-A7-95 would result. Although the format inserts the symbols for you, it doesn't require that a certain number of numbers are entered.

How can you prevent people from entering too many or too few numbers? Set up validation rules for the range of cells in your worksheet that will be formatted with the custom number format. Select the range that will use the custom format you created, and click Validation on the Data menu. On the Settings tab of the Data Validation dialog box, select Text Length in the Allow box, select Equal To in the Data box, and type the number of digits you want people to type in the Length box. ▶

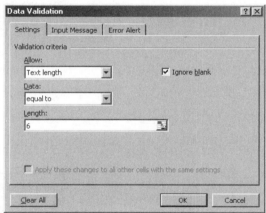

Click OK to set the validation rule and close the dialog box. If you want, you can also create custom input and error messages by clicking the Input Message and Error Alert tabs and following the instructions on each tab. Even if you don't create a custom error message, if anyone tries to enter more or fewer numbers than the validation rule specifies, a default error message appears, notifying users that the correct number of digits must be entered before the cell can be filled.

Tip
When entering the number of digits in the Length box, don't count the symbols or letters that the custom format will be inserting for you—just count the number of digits that the user will type.

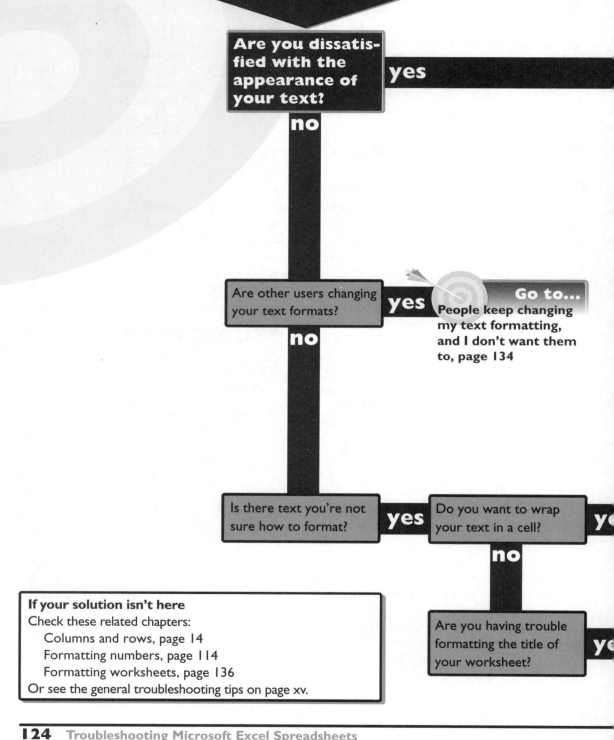

Are you dissatis-fied with the appearance of your text?

yes

no

Are other users changing your text formats?

yes

Go to...
People keep changing my text formatting, and I don't want them to, page 134

no

Is there text you're not sure how to format?

yes

Do you want to wrap your text in a cell?

y●

no

If your solution isn't here
Check these related chapters:
  Columns and rows, page 14
  Formatting numbers, page 114
  Formatting worksheets, page 136
Or see the general troubleshooting tips on page xv.

Are you having trouble formatting the title of your worksheet?

y●

Formatting text

Are you having trouble with the size of your text?

yes → **Go to...** My worksheet text is too small to read, page 126.

no

Does some of your text disappear after you press Enter?

yes → **Quick fix** Text that's too wide for a column will overflow on top of (not into) the cell to its right. If the cell to the right contains text, however, the overflow is hidden. Reduce the font size, or to widen the column, right-click the column heading, click Column Width, and enter a larger number in the Column Width dialog box.

no

Are you having trouble making your worksheet look uniform?

yes → **Go to...** The format of my text isn't consistent throughout my worksheet, page 128.

no

Are you unsure which fonts are the most professional looking?

yes → **Quick fix** Avoid using very ornate or artistic fonts, except for occasional use in titles. Fonts such as Arial (the default) and Times New Roman are the conventional fonts in business environments.

Go to... I'm not sure how to format paragraph text in my worksheet, page 130.

Go to... I can't center a title across the top row of my worksheet, page 132.

My worksheet text is too small to read

Source of the problem

By default, Excel applies the 10-point Arial font to all text and numeric content. For some people, that's just too small. A worksheet in 10-point Arial can seem rather cramped and difficult to read, especially if the content is crowded into narrow columns and rows.

The solution to this problem depends on whether you want to change only the view on your screen, or actually resize fonts in both displayed and printed worksheets. If you find it difficult to read your menus and toolbar buttons as well as your worksheet content, consider lowering your monitor resolution to 800 × 600 or 640 × 480. If you want larger text to appear in both displayed and printed worksheets, use a larger font size for some or all of your worksheet content.

> **Tip**
> Most monitors can display an 800 × 600 screen, but some older monitors cannot handle higher resolutions, such as 1024 × 768. To avoid problems, don't increase your screen resolution without checking the monitor's user guide to see what resolution it is capable of supporting.

How to fix it

To change the resolution of your monitor even if only for the time you're working in Excel, follow these steps:

1. Minimize all open windows to display the Windows desktop.

2. Right-click an empty spot on the desktop, and then click Properties on the shortcut menu.

3. In the Display Properties dialog box, click the Settings tab. ▶

4. In the Screen Area section, drag the slider to the left to reduce the resolution to either 640 × 480 or 800 × 600.

5. Click Apply. Windows tells you that your resolution will change and your screen might flicker. (You might even have to restart Windows for some of your applications to work properly.) Click OK.

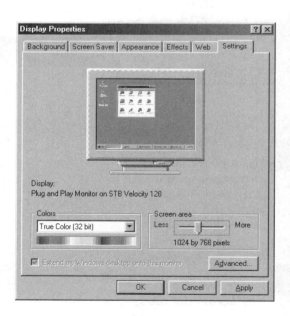

6. After approximately 15 seconds, your screen resolution will change to the new setting. If the screen is legible, click OK when prompted to confirm the new resolution.

To increase the font size in your worksheet, follow these steps:

1. Select the cells that you want to change to a larger font.

2. On the Formatting toolbar, click the Font Size drop-down arrow, and click a larger font size. ▶

Tip

If you want all of your text to be larger than 10 points on all worksheets, click Options on the Tools menu, and on the General tab, change the settings in the Standard Font and Size lists. Then click OK.

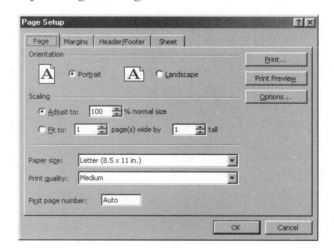

What you see is what you get...?

If your worksheet will be viewed on paper more often than on the screen, you might want to adjust the print scale settings before you actually print the worksheet. Because your worksheet might look dramatically different on the screen than it does on paper, you could be disappointed by the printed version of your worksheet after you spent so much time formatting it on the screen.

This doesn't mean you have to abandon the way you like to view the worksheet on the screen. You can print the worksheet larger than it appears on your monitor by increasing the scale at which it is printed. On the File menu, click Page Setup. In the Scaling section of the Page tab, increase the setting in the Adjust To box. The higher the percentage, the larger the worksheet content will appear when the worksheet is printed, without changing the worksheet's actual formatting. ▶

Warning

The one potential drawback to increasing the print scale of the worksheet is that the worksheet will print out on more pages. However, bear in mind that you might end up with those additional pages anyway, if you increase the font size in the worksheet.

The format of my text isn't consistent throughout my worksheet

Source of the problem

Not all worksheets are developed in a single session. For example, you sit down to set up the basic layout, enter your column and row labels, and enter some content. Then at a later time, you finish making your entries, create your formulas, and move things around as you reconsider your layout. Your process might vary, but unless you complete the entire worksheet and apply all the formatting in one session, you're likely to end up with some inconsistencies in your worksheet's appearance. (If other people work on your worksheet, they can introduce even more inconsistencies.) ▶

The larger your worksheet is, the more likely these inconsistencies will occur because you can't see all of it at once. You might forget to make the labels bold in one section of the worksheet, or change the font in one area and not in another. Why are these inconsistencies a problem? Because you don't want your piecemeal development process to be obvious, and because you want your worksheet to look as uniform and well-planned as possible. Further, having consistent formatting throughout makes a worksheet easier to edit later because as you cut and copy text from place to place, the formatting will come with it.

	A	B	C	D	E	F
1			Sales by Division			
2			2000			
3		Qtr. 1	Qtr. 2	Qtr. 3	Qtr. 4	TOTALS
4	Philadelphia	5250678	5786452	6,425,646	7854251	$ 25,317,027
5	New York	4875986	6785428	7,452,987	2578456	$ 21,692,857
6	Chicago	3587452	7458976	5,487,653	5648752	$ 22,182,833
7	Atlanta	4789521	3789451	1,258,795	3567894	$ 13,405,661
8	Phoenix	5784236	6785497	6,456,781	4526781	$ 23,553,295
9	San Francisco	6452179	7425891	5,784,896	6457251	$ 26,120,217
10	TOTAL	$ 30,740,052.00	$ 38,031,695.00	$ 32,866,757.78	$ 30,633,385.00	$ 132,271,890
11						
12			2001 Projections			
13		Qtr. 1	Qtr. 2	Qtr. 3	Qtr. 4	TOTALS
14	Philadelphia	6038280	6654420	7389493	9032389	$ 29,114,581
15	New York	5607384	7803242	8570935	2965224	$ 24,946,786
16	Chicago	4125570	8577822	6310801	6496065	$ 25,510,258
17	Atlanta	5507949	4357869	1447614	4103078	$ 15,416,510
18	Phoenix	6651871	7803322	7425298	5205798	$ 27,086,289
19	San Francisco	7420006	8539775	6652630	7425839	$ 30,038,250
20	TOTAL	$ 35,351,060	$ 43,736,449	$ 37,796,771	$ 35,228,393	$ 152,112,673

To correct the appearance of spotty formatting, you need to apply consistent styles throughout your worksheet. If, for example, you want all of your labels to be in a certain font and size, you need to apply the formatting to all of them at once. If you

Tip

To prevent inconsistencies in the first place, don't do any formatting until most of your content is in place. Even though you'll be adding content on an ongoing basis, wait until all your labels, formulas, and the majority of your content is entered. That way, you can select similar content throughout the worksheet and apply the formatting consistently. If your worksheet is one of two or more that will have the same layout and formatting, group the worksheets first, and then enter and format your labels and common content for maximum consistency throughout the workbook. (See "I don't want to have to build identical worksheets individually" on page 142.)

want totals and other important entries to stand out, choose attention-getting formats and apply them. If that sounds like what you're already doing, yet your worksheet formatting still isn't uniform, you can employ some simple techniques to prevent and also correct inconsistencies.

How to fix it

1. Make a list of all the parts of your worksheet that require special formatting.

2. One by one, go through the worksheet and select all of the content that needs a particular type of formatting—all the labels, for example, or all the totals. To select noncontiguous ranges of the worksheet, hold down the Ctrl key while you make your selections.

3. With the cells selected, apply your formats using the buttons on the Formatting toolbar.

Ya gotta have style

If you've used a word processor such as Microsoft Word, you're probably familiar with the concept of styles. A style is a group of formats that can be applied to selected content with one command (the application of the style) rather than repeatedly applying several formats, step by step. By default, Excel has six different styles: Normal, Comma (with decimal places), Comma [0] (without decimal places), Currency (with decimal places), Currency [0] (without decimal places), and Percent. You can adjust these styles to suit your needs, and also create new styles of your own.

To edit an existing style, click Style on the Format menu to display the Style dialog box. ▶

In the Style Name list, click the style you want to edit. Select the check boxes for the attributes—Number, Alignment, Font, Border, Patterns, and Protection—that you want the style to contain. Click the Modify button to display the Format Cells dialog box, and then apply the formatting you want for all the selected attributes. Click OK to close the Format Cells dialog box, and then click OK again to close the Style dialog box and apply the style changes.

To create a new style, click Style on the Format menu, and in the Style Name box, type a new style name to replace the name that is currently displayed. Click the Modify button, and in the Format Cells dialog box, apply all the formatting that the new style should include when it's applied to your worksheet. Click OK to return to the Style dialog box, click the Add button to add your new style to the list of available styles for your workbook, and then click OK.

Although you can apply the styles you created only in the workbook for which you created them, you can apply the Excel default styles from the Style Name list at any time. Select the cells to which you want to apply a style, and click Style on the Format menu. In the Style Name list, click the style you want to apply, and then click OK.

I'm not sure how to format paragraph text in my worksheet

Source of the problem

Many worksheets consist solely of numbers, with a brief amount of text to identify the numbers. Normally these worksheets track scientific or financial information and rarely, if ever, require any special formatting, other than to display numbers as currency or to make labels or important data bold. There are, however, worksheets that require a lot of text—rows of text-based data, labels between worksheet sections, and sometimes even paragraphs of text.

How can a worksheet, which is really just a grid of tiny cells, contain paragraphs? Easy. Because a worksheet is not designed for paragraph text, the tools to easily accommodate paragraph text aren't right there on the toolbars like the rest of the more commonly used tools. However, you can format any cell or range of cells to let text wrap within it. And by adjusting the width of a column, you can control both the width of the paragraph and the wrapping required to fit paragraph text into a cell. ▶

A16			Projections are based on each department manager's estimates based on communications and published reports from vendors.		
	A				
3	Product Line	Current Rate	Proposed Increase	Projected Rate	
4	Clothing	0.2	0.015	0.203	
5	Accessories	0.35	0.02	0.357	
6	Shoes	0.025	0.01	0.02525	
7	Linens	0.4	0.015	0.406	
8	Window Treatments	0.055	0.022	0.05621	
9	Lighting	0.035	0.0125	0.0354375	
10	Carpeting	0.02	0.005	0.0201	
11	Housewares	0.025	0.012	0.0253	
12	Floral	0.03	0.008	0.03024	
13	Seasonal Items	0.05	0.0035	0.050175	
14	Averages	**0.119**	**0.0123**	**0.12087125**	
15					
16	Projections are based on each department manager's estimates based on communications and published reports from vendors.				
17					
18					

How to fix it

1. Select the cell or cells in which you want to wrap paragraph text.

2. Right-click the selection, and then click Format Cells on the shortcut menu.

Tip

When a single cell contains a paragraph, it normally becomes taller. Its height increases to accommodate the amount of text in it and, in turn, the text wraps to accommodate the column width. Bear in mind that the height of the rest of the cells in that row will increase along with the affected cell, even if the other cells contain little or no content. If you later widen the column, you'll need to adjust the row height manually if all of the height is no longer needed. To adjust the row height, point to the bottom seam of the row's heading, and then drag upward to decrease the row's height.

3. In the Format Cells dialog box, click the Alignment tab, and in the Text Control section, select the Wrap Text check box. ▶

4. Click OK to close the dialog box and apply the format to the selected cell. Existing text or new text you enter will wrap within the column's current width.

5. As needed, widen the column by dragging the column heading's right seam to make the paragraph the width you need it to be.

It's like you're floating

What if you don't want the paragraph to be in a specific cell? When you type a lot of text in a cell and you set the cell to wrap the text, the row the cell is in can get very tall, and the grid structure for that row might look weird with one cell filled with text and the rest of the cells overly tall for their contents. The alternative is to let the cell be yards long as a single string of text, which also looks weird.

How to avoid this phenomenon? Put the text in a text box. The text box will float over the surface of your worksheet, and you can place it wherever you want, even making its background clear so that if it overlaps any portion of the worksheet, the content underneath it isn't obscured. On the Drawing toolbar, click the Text Box button. (If the Drawing toolbar isn't visible, click the Drawing button on the Standard toolbar.)

Tip
To make your text box transparent, select the box, click the arrow next to the Fill Color button on the Drawing toolbar, and then click No Fill.

When the mouse pointer changes to a crosshair, click and drag to draw a rectangle the approximate size you think you'll need for your text. As soon as you release your mouse button, the insertion point is activated in the text box. Type your content, and the text will wrap to the confines of the box. ▶

You can always resize the text box by dragging its size handles—when the mouse pointer becomes a two-headed arrow, drag the corner handles outward to increase, or inward to decrease, the size of the box. You can also move the box by first selecting it and then when the mouse pointer becomes a four-headed arrow, dragging it.

I can't center a title across the top row of my worksheet

Source of the problem

Your worksheet contains several rows and columns of data, and you've typed a title in one of the first cells. Now you want that title to be centered across the span of columns containing data, or at least across the first screen of columns. A title is helpful, even if your worksheet is in a workbook with a file name that expresses the book's content, and even if your worksheet tab has a name on it. People often forget to read the sheet tabs unless they're leafing through looking for a particular sheet, and it's not a good idea to type really long tab names, anyway. What's more, the sheet tab name and the worksheet title may not be the same.

So you've got a title, and now you want to center it. ▶ How? Well, you don't move it to a cell that looks like it's roughly centered on the screen. Even if that were possible, if someone using a different size monitor or display resolution opens the file, the title won't appear centered for that person. If you print the worksheet, the title probably won't fall dead center, either.

	A	B	C	D	E	F	G	H	I
1	Insurance Costs								
2									
3	Carrier Code	Monthly Cost per Person	Medical	Dental	Eye	Prescriptions	TOTAL COST	Cost to Insure Current Staff	
4	A-45	$ 175.00	75	50	25	25	$ 350.00	$ 28,700.00	
5	A-72	$ 200.00	55	45	20	10	$ 330.00	$ 27,060.00	
6	B-36	$ 185.00	80	50	25	50	$ 390.00	$ 31,980.00	
7	B-58	$ 225.00	75	75	50	55	$ 480.00	$ 39,360.00	
8	C-75	$ 500.00	25	25	25	25	$ 600.00	$ 49,200.00	
9	D-63	$ 550.00	0	0	10	0	$ 560.00	$ 45,920.00	
10									
11									
12									

The ideal method for centering a title across a span of columns is to use Excel's Merge And Center button. This way, the title will remain centered no matter how wide the columns are, or might become, due to future formatting.

How to fix it

1. In the row containing your worksheet title, select the cells that span the distance across which you want to center the title. For example, if your worksheet fills columns A through H, and your title is in A1, select cells A1 through H1. ▶

	A	B	C	D	E	F	G	H	I
1	Insurance Costs								
2									
3	Carrier Code	Monthly Cost per Person	Medical	Dental	Eye	Prescriptions	TOTAL COST	Cost to Insure Current Staff	
4	A-45	$ 175.00	75	50	25	25	$ 350.00	$ 28,700.00	
5	A-72	$ 200.00	55	45	20	10	$ 330.00	$ 27,060.00	
6	B-36	$ 185.00	80	50	25	50	$ 390.00	$ 31,980.00	
7	B-58	$ 225.00	75	75	50	55	$ 480.00	$ 39,360.00	
8	C-75	$ 500.00	25	25	25	25	$ 600.00	$ 49,200.00	
9	D-63	$ 550.00	0	0	10	0	$ 560.00	$ 45,920.00	
10									
11									
12									

2. Click the Merge And Center button on the Formatting toolbar.

Once your cells are merged and your title is centered, you can apply any formatting you wish, and any formatting already applied (other than alignment) will remain intact. If you add columns to your worksheet within the range of the merged cell, the cell will expand to center your title over all the columns. If you delete a column within the range, the merged cell will shrink to accommodate the new number of columns.

The cloud surrounding that silver lining

Merge And Center is very useful, and when people find out about it, it elicits a real "ooh, ahhh" reaction. There are, however, some drawbacks to it. The problems can occur not so much in using it, but in applying it too soon. Below is a list of things you can't do to a merged cell or to a column containing one. If you want to do these things, wait until after you've done them to use Merge And Center:

Tip
While you can make your worksheet title as long as you want, it's a good idea to be as succinct as possible when creating a title. For example, "Third Quarter Sales" is preferable to "Our Sales in the Third Quarter." By keeping the amount of text to a minimum, you can increase the size of the text to make it stand out and still not overwhelm the rest of the worksheet.

- Select an entire column and move it. If you try to move a column that includes the merged cell, a prompt appears indicating that you "cannot change part of a merged cell." In other words, by selecting the column, you've selected part of the merged cell, but that part can't be moved along with the rest of the cells in the column.

- Sort the data in a column that includes the merged cell.

  Excel 2000
  If you're using Excel 2000, you can select the entire column that includes the merged cells, but you need to be aware of a small trick. Click Sort on the Data menu, and if the Sort Warning dialog box appears, click either Expand The Selection or Continue With The Current Selection, and then click the Sort button. In the Sort dialog box, click the Header Row option in the My List Has section, and then click OK. Excel will proceed with the sort, but ignore the header row (in this case, the merged cell).

  Excel 97
  If you're using Excel 97, an error message indicates that you can't sort the cells. If you need to sort the data in cells that appear underneath the merged cell title, select only the cells that contain the data you want to sort (but not the merged cell), and then click Sort on the Data menu.

- Apply formats from other areas of the worksheet with Format Painter. If you take formatting from somewhere else in the worksheet and attempt to apply it to a column that includes a merged and centered cell, a prompt tells you that you can't change part of a merged cell. The only way this can be done is if you apply the formats to the entire row that houses the merged and centered cell. Remember that in doing so, the merge and center format is removed and replaced by whatever new formatting you are applying.

People keep changing my text formatting, and I don't want them to

Source of the problem

You've taken the time to format your worksheet content just the way you like it. You've selected fonts, resized some of your text, created styles and applied them to headings and totals, and you've made your worksheet into a thing of beauty. Then what happens? Some joker opens your worksheet to look at it or do some editing, and the next thing you know, your formatting is changed. Maybe the other user copied content from one place to another and it came with formatting that doesn't belong where the content ended up. Or maybe he or she just didn't like your font and went ahead and changed it. The nerve! Well, rather than strangling someone (or wasting your energy imagining such a thing), just prevent it from happening in the first place. Apply protection to your worksheet so that content can still be edited, but no one can ever fiddle with your formats again.

How to fix it

1. Select the entire worksheet by pressing Ctrl+A.

2. Right-click the selection, and then click Format Cells on the shortcut menu.

3. In the Format Cells dialog box, click the Protection tab, and clear the Locked check box. This will allow the cells in your worksheet to be edited after you apply protection, but other people won't be able to reformat your worksheet in any way. ▶

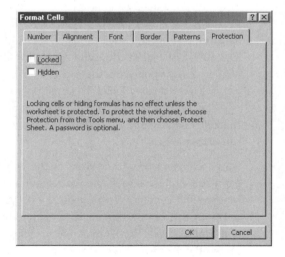

4. To apply worksheet protection, point to Protection on the Tools menu, and then click Protect Sheet. In the Protect Sheet dialog box, type an optional password if you want, and then click OK.

Here an edit, there an edit

If you want to prevent not only formatting changes but edits to your worksheet, you can isolate areas and lock them. This process relies upon the fact that you turned off the locked status for the whole worksheet. Before applying protection, select the range of cells that you don't want anyone to edit, right-click the selection, and then click Format Cells on the shortcut menu. In the Format Cells dialog box, click the Protection tab, select the Locked check box, and click OK. Next point to Protection on the Tools menu, and click Protect Sheet. Although the cells you didn't select can be edited, the locked range is protected from any editing. However, the entire worksheet is completely protected from changes to formatting. The entire Formatting toolbar is useless—the Formatting buttons are dimmed, and clicking them produces no effect. ▶

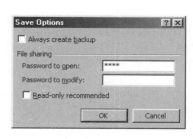

And now for the very cautious

If you want to keep people out of your worksheet entirely, seal the file with password protection. On the File menu, click Save As.

Excel 2000 In the Save As dialog box in Excel 2000, click the Tools button, and then select General Options from the drop-down menu to display the Save Options dialog box.

Excel 97 In the Save As dialog box in Excel 97, click the Options button to display the Save Options dialog box.

In the Save Options dialog box, type a password for opening or modifying the file, or both, and then click OK. ▶

For each password you type, a Confirm Password box will appear, requiring you to reenter the password, just to make sure you didn't make a mistake the first time. (It would be a real pain to have set the password to "aardvark" but have spelled it with only one "a" and not know why your password doesn't work!) Click OK to confirm each password, and then click Save to close the Save As dialog box.

TIP If you want to create a foolproof password but one that you won't forget, use the method Augustus Caesar invented: Take a word you wouldn't forget, such as your child's name or your mother's maiden name. Now, those don't seem too secure, because people who know you might be able to guess them. But wait! Think of a number—3, for example—and move each letter in your word three letters down in the alphabet. "Ann" becomes "DQQ," which no one is likely to guess. All you need to remember is the word and a single digit. You can even write the number somewhere, because no one will suspect that the "3" you wrote in the lower left corner of your calendar has anything to do with your password.

Forn

Are you having trouble getting your gridlines to show when you shade your cells? yes

no

Are you having trouble copying formatted cells? **yes**

Go to...

When I move a cell's content, the formatting comes with it, page 138.

no

Are you having trouble applying AutoFormats? **yes**

no

Are you having trouble applying a background to your worksheet? **yes**

no

Are you having trouble working with more than one worksheet? **yes**   Has Excel rejected your worksheet tab name? **ye**

no

If your solution isn't here
Check these related chapters:
Columns and rows, page, page 14
Formatting numbers, page 114
Formatting text, page 124
Or see the general troubleshooting tips on page xv.

Are you spending too much time creating identical worksheets? **ye**

Quick fix

When you apply shading to cells, the gridlines are hidden by the shading color. To have visible gridlines and shaded cells, you must apply cell borders. Select the cells in question, right-click the selection, and then click Format Cells on the shortcut menu. On the Border tab, click both the Outside and Inside buttons, and then click OK.

Go to...

I can't control how the AutoFormat command is applied, page 140.

Go to...

The Background command is unavailable, page 144.

Quick fix

To name a worksheet, double-click the tab, type the new name, and then press Enter. The new name can have up to 31 characters and can include spaces and punctuation, as well as numbers. However, Excel can't accept the special characters / \ : [ ] or ? and will reject names with these characters in them.

Go to...

I don't want to have to build identical worksheets individually, page 142.

When I move a cell's content, the formatting comes with it

Source of the problem

It's so simple to move cell content around on your worksheet—just click the cell, point to its border, and when your mouse pointer becomes a left-pointing arrow, drag the content to a new cell. Easy, right? Well yes, unless you've already formatted your worksheet. If you've already applied borders, cell shading, text formatting, or a combination of any of these elements, all that formatting will move with the content when you move it. This can be a problem if the new location isn't meant to be formatted the same way the original location was. Further, if you move content as opposed to copying it, you leave a formatting and content hole in your wake after you drag the cell to its new location. ▶

What can you do about this particular problem? You have to change the way you move and copy content, changing from the aforementioned easy dragging method to one of two slightly more complex techniques.

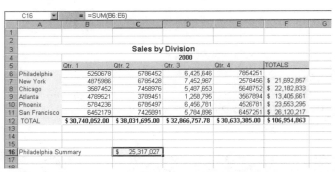

Moving the content of F6 leaves a hole.

Using the Paste Special command or a shortcut menu variant, you can choose what gets moved or copied—the content with the formatting, just the formatting, or just the content.

How to fix it

To use Paste Special, follow these steps:

1. Select the cell or range to be moved or copied.

2. Right-click the selection, and then click Copy on the shortcut menu. Yes, you're going to copy the content even if you want to cut it. If you click Cut instead of Copy, the Paste Special command you'll use in step 4 will be unavailable on the shortcut menu. You can always go back and delete the original content after you've pasted it.

> **Tip**
>
> You can use the Paste Special technique between worksheets and workbooks as well. Select the content to be moved or copied, right-click the selection, click Copy, and then switch to the target cell in another sheet or another open workbook. Right-click the target cell, click Paste Special, click Values in the Paste section, and then click OK.

3. Right-click the cell (or first cell of the target range) where you want to paste the content, and then click Paste Special on the shortcut menu.

4. In the Paste Special dialog box, click the Values option in the Paste section to indicate that you want to paste only the cell content. (Don't worry if your dialog box looks a little different.) ▶

5. Click OK to paste the content to the new location.

Tip

If you want to create a connection between copied content in its original location and the target cell, click the Paste Link button in the Paste Special dialog box. After creating this link, any updates to the original cell will be reflected in the target cell.

6. If you don't want the original content you copied, select the cells containing the content, and then press Delete. If you want to remove the original cell formatting as well as the content, select the original cells, point to Clear on the Edit menu, and then click All.

To drag the content of cells without moving the formatting, follow these steps:

1. Select the cell or cells to be copied.

2. Point to the cell or range border. When the mouse pointer changes to a left-pointing arrow, hold down the right mouse button and drag the cell or range of cells to its new location.

3. Release the right mouse button, and click Copy Here As Values Only on the shortcut menu to copy the content, but not the formatting. ▶

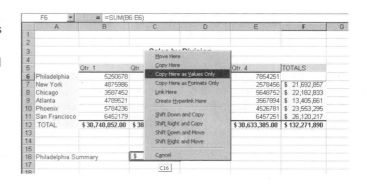

Tip

The "fix" discussed in this section is more of a prevention than a cure. If you've already dragged a cell's content from one place to another, and the formatting came with it, you can use the Format Painter to copy formatting from adjoining cells into the cell in which you pasted the content, and into the cell in which the content originally resided. Select the cells containing the format you want to copy, and then click the Format Painter button on the Standard toolbar. When the pointer changes to a paintbrush, drag through the cells that you want to apply the copied format to.

I can't control how the AutoFormat command is applied

Source of the problem

The AutoFormat command allows you to instantly apply a collection of formats to a range of cells. Using this command can save you a lot of time when compared to applying each format individually. Additionally, the AutoFormats that come with Excel offer professional-looking, highly legible effects that you can apply to any of your worksheets that are constructed with AutoFormat in mind. ▶

So what could possibly go wrong? Lots of things, if you don't know how to control the way Auto-Format changes the appearance of your worksheet. By default, all AutoFormats can change the font, size, cell shading, borders, and column widths of the worksheet content to which you apply them. What if you've already adjusted your column widths and have them where you want them? Applying the AutoFormat can change them. What if you like everything about a particular AutoFormat except the font, and you've already chosen and applied the font you want to use? Your preferred font will lose out to the font included in the AutoFormat unless you customize the way the AutoFormat is applied.

	A	B	C	D	E	F	G	H
		H6		=				
1								
2								
3				Sales by Division				
4				2000				
5			Qtr. 1	Qtr. 2	Qtr. 3	Qtr. 4	TOTALS	
6	Philadelphia		5250678	5786452	6,425,646	7854251	$ 25,317,027	
7	New York		4875986	6785428	7,452,987	2578456	$ 21,692,857	
8	Chicago		3587452	7458976	5,487,653	5648752	$ 22,182,833	
9	Atlanta		4789521	3789451	1,258,795	3587894	$ 13,405,661	
10	Phoenix		5784236	6785497	6,456,781	4526781	$ 23,553,295	
11	San Francisco		6452179	7425891	5,784,896	6457251	$ 26,120,217	
12	TOTAL	$ 30,740,052.00	$ 38,031,695.00	$ 32,866,757.78	$ 30,633,385.00	$ 132,271,890		
13								
14								
15								
16								
17								

How to fix it

1. Select the portion of your worksheet you want to apply the AutoFormat to. To select the entire worksheet, press Ctrl+A.

2. On the Format menu, click AutoFormat.

3. In the AutoFormat dialog box, click once to select an AutoFormat from those displayed in the list box. Don't double-click the AutoFormat, or it will be applied without giving you the chance to customize it.

4. Click the Options button. The dialog box expands to offer a Formats To Apply section, which contains check boxes for AutoFormat features. Leave the check boxes selected for those formats that you want to apply, and clear the check boxes for those formats that you want to remove. For example, if you don't want your column widths or row heights to change, clear the Width/Height check box. (The AutoFormat dialog box for Excel 97 looks different from the one shown here for Excel 2000, but don't worry—they work in the same way.) ▶

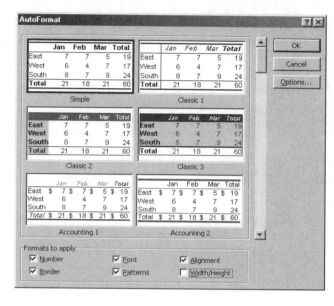

5. When you've made all of the adjustments you need, click OK to apply the customized AutoFormat to the selected range of cells.

Yecch! I don't like this AutoFormat!

If you apply an AutoFormat and hate it, or if your worksheet content or layout changes and the format applied is no longer appropriate, you can remove it. No, you don't need to reformat the worksheet manually by removing shading and borders, or changing fonts—you can use None AutoFormat instead. Simply select the range of cells that have an AutoFormat applied to them, click AutoFormat on the Format menu, and in the AutoFormat dialog box, click once on None in the list of sample AutoFormats. If you want to keep some of the formatting that's in place, such as column widths or borders, click the Options button, and clear the check boxes in the Formats To Apply section for features that you don't want changed. Then click OK to remove the AutoFormat.

Tip

You can also use the None AutoFormat to remove formatting you've applied manually. Suppose you've applied shading, borders, or fonts, and tinkered with column widths, and now you want to return to the default worksheet appearance. Select the cells that are formatted, click AutoFormat on the Format menu, click None, and then click OK to remove the formats you don't want.

I don't want to have to build identical worksheets individually

Source of the problem

Your workbook needs to contain two or more sheets with very similar content and layout, and you're grimacing at the thought of building Sheet1, then repeating yourself in Sheet2. Even if you've been crafty enough to think of copying content from Sheet1 to Sheet2 (to save yourself the typing and formatting), the process still feels like it's too much trouble. Shouldn't there be a way to build several identical worksheets in the same workbook without redoing the work or copying and pasting between sheets? Yep, there should be, and there is!

Creating multiple sheets is simple, requiring only that you group the sheets you want to mass-produce, and then restrict your entries to the content that will be the same on all sheets. Say you want to create a series of department expense reports. You're in charge of three departments, and you want to build the same report form for each department. If you create three sheets (one for each department) and then group them, the column and row labels, formulas, and formats you build on any one of the three grouped sheets will appear on all three sheets.

However, you'll want to ungroup the worksheets before you enter material that is specific to one sheet so that changes you make don't end up on all sheets.

> **Tip**
> When your sheets are grouped, everything you do to one sheet—every thing you type, every command you give, every formula you build—applies to the corresponding cell or cells in every sheet in the group. This includes mistakes! If you find an error on one sheet that was part of a group when you worked on it, the error will appear on all the sheets that were originally grouped. To fix the error on all of the sheets, regroup them, and correct the mistake. Of course this fix will work only if you haven't made erroneous edits separately to one or more of the sheets when they were ungrouped.

How to fix it

1. Click the first sheet tab that you want to include in the group.

2. Hold down the Shift key, and click the last sheet tab in the series to be grouped. All sheets between and including the first and last sheets become grouped. ▶

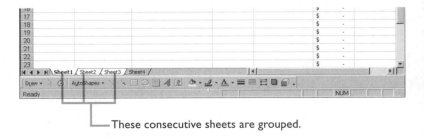

These consecutive sheets are grouped.

If you want to select nonconsecutive sheets, hold down the Ctrl key instead of the Shift key, and then click each sheet tab that you want to make part of the group. ▶

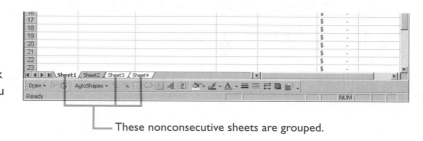

These nonconsecutive sheets are grouped.

Tip

When they're not grouped, you can rearrange your worksheets by clicking the tab of the sheet you want to move and then dragging the sheet icon that appears under the mouse pointer. A small triangle appears, indicating where the sheet will be moved to when you release the mouse button.

Tip

It's a good idea to name your worksheet tabs before grouping them, if only to make it easy for you to tell your sheets apart. This is especially important if you don't want to group all the worksheets in the workbook. If you have sheets that you don't want to be set up the same way as the ones you're building in the group, you might accidentally include them when you group your sheets. If a generically named "Sheet4" shows up in the group, you'll know you've included a sheet you didn't intend to.

Breaking up is hard to do (well, not really)

Once you have entered the common material in all the sheets in a group, you'll want to ungroup the sheets so that you can start entering the content that's specific to the individual sheets. To ungroup sheets, use one of the following techniques:

- Click the tab of any sheet not in the group.

- Right-click any tab in the group, and then click Ungroup Sheets on the shortcut menu. ▶

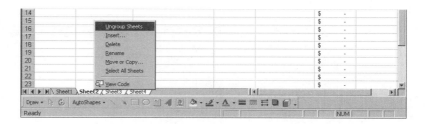

The Background command is unavailable

Source of the problem

There's nothing more annoying than opening a menu only to find that the command you wanted is unavailable. Well, maybe parking tickets or finding out the milk is sour after you've poured it on your cereal are more annoying, but you get the idea. Why is a command unavailable anyway?

When a command is dimmed on the menu (or when a toolbar button is dimmed on the toolbar), the command or button is inappropriate to use under the current circumstances. The "current circumstances" include which cells (if any) are selected, what's on your worksheet, what view you're in, and what other commands you might have used previously. Any or all of these influences can cause a command to be unavailable.

If the Background command is unavailable on the Sheet submenu, two or more worksheets are probably grouped. (Unfortunately, you can't use the Background command on grouped sheets.) ▶

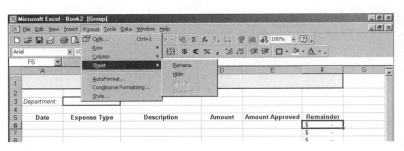

How to fix it

1. To ungroup sheets, right-click any sheet tab in the group, and then click Ungroup Sheets on the shortcut menu.

2. Once the sheets are ungrouped, click the sheet you want to apply a background to, point to Sheet on the Format menu, and then click Background to display the Sheet Background dialog box. ▶

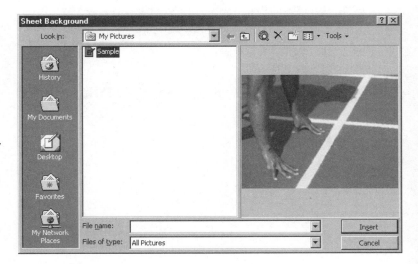

3. In the Sheet Background dialog box, locate the graphic file you want to use as a background, and then double-click its icon to use the file as a background on the sheet.

Background basics

When applying a background, it's a good idea to keep the following issues in mind:

- Legibility. Will the background image make the worksheet content hard to read? Choose an image that isn't too dark, bright, or busy. You might have to change text colors just so you can read text on the background, and even then, the background can still be distracting. ▶

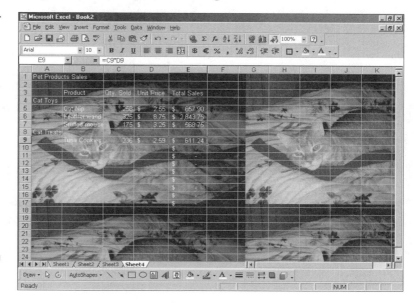

- Usability. Backgrounds aren't printed when you print a worksheet. If you print a worksheet that contains a background, any formatting you did to make content show on top of the background might not look right on plain paper. For example, if you made your text light colored to show on top of a dark background, it might be unreadable on a sheet of white paper.

- Web practicality. If your entire workbook is saved as a web page, the background on the sheet will show online. However, the background you applied will not appear in the .htm file in your browser if you save only a single sheet or section as a web page. The background will appear on the web page only if you save an entire workbook as a web page. For more information on saving a workbook as a web page, see "Saving" on page 244.

Tip
If your workbook is bound for the web, make sure all the graphics used for the background as well as any other graphic images you've inserted are smaller than 50KB, so that they don't take too long to load when someone visits your web site. Also, make sure that the files are in either .GIF, .JPG, or .PNG format. Web browsers can't display other graphic formats.

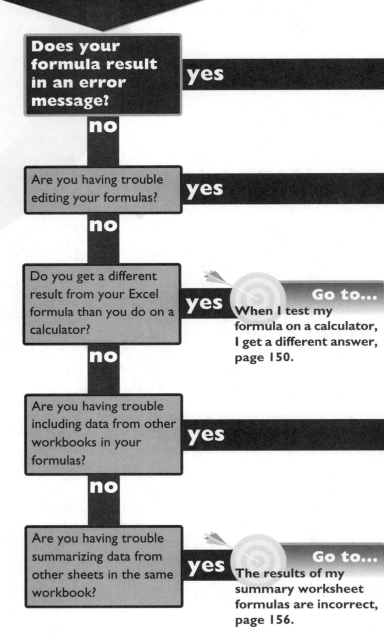

Does your formula result in an error message?　　yes

no

Are you having trouble editing your formulas?　　yes

no

Do you get a different result from your Excel formula than you do on a calculator?　　yes

Go to...
When I test my formula on a calculator, I get a different answer, page 150.

no

Are you having trouble including data from other workbooks in your formulas?　　yes

no

Are you having trouble summarizing data from other sheets in the same workbook?　　yes

Go to...
The results of my summary worksheet formulas are incorrect, page 156.

Formulas

Go to...
My formula causes an error message to appear, page 148.

Are you having trouble determining which cells were used in your formula?

yes

no

Quick fix
To see formulas instead of their results, click Options on the Tool menu. On the View tab, select the Formulas check box under Window Options, and then click OK to close the dialog box and view your formulas. If you want to see the results again, clear the Formulas check box in the Options dialog box.

When you edit cells in your formula, does the result stay the same?

yes

Go to...
When I edit the cells referenced in my formula, the result doesn't change, page152.

Quick fix

1. Open the workbook where you want the formula and the one that has the data you need.

2. Click the cell where you want the formula, and start typing the formula as usual.

3. To cite a cell from the other workbook, switch to that workbook, and click the desired cell.

4. Continue selecting cells in any open workbook (each separated by the appropriate operator, such as the + sign), and then press Enter to complete the formula.

If your solution isn't here
Check these related chapters:
Functions, page 158
Macros, page 180
Templates, page 292
Or see the general troubleshooting tips on page xv.

My formula causes an error message to appear

Source of the problem

Formulas can be both the best part of Excel and the most problematic. Not because they're difficult or they don't work reliably, but because they provide a place for everything that can go wrong to converge. Problems such as not knowing the right formula to use, which cells to include in the formula, or in what order the different parts of the formula should be calculated—or making a simple error when you enter addresses and numbers to build the formula—can make formulas seem more troublesome than they are.

Any combination of these problems can occur and result in an error message when your formula is applied. The error message is helpful in that it gives you some tips on how to investigate the nature or cause of the problem. ▶

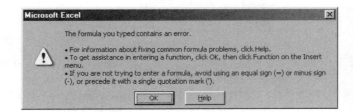

How to fix it

To correct the formula error, you might need to start from scratch, but the solution could be as simple as adding a missing parenthesis to complete the formula's proper structure. The solutions are as varied as the problems themselves. The good news is, the solutions are generally straightforward and easy to implement. The table on the facing page lists the errors that might show up where you expect to see the results of your formulas, and what you can do to fix these errors.

Tip
Sometimes it helps to know how your worksheet material and its formulas relate to each other. Click a cell containing a formula, point to Auditing on the Tools menu, and then click Trace Precedents to highlight the cells that are used in the formula. Likewise, click a cell that might be referenced in a formula, point to Auditing on the Tools menu, and then click Trace Dependents. You'll see the formulas (if any) that reference the cell you're in.

Error	How to fix it
#DIV/0!	This error appears if you try to divide by zero. Change the zero to some other number.
#N/A	This error means "not available." If cells referenced in a formula are unavailable, the error appears in the cell that contains the formula. Possible causes of this error include deleting a worksheet or workbook containing a cell referenced in a formula. To fix this, restore the missing material, or edit the erroneous formula to reference identical material in a new cell or worksheet.
#NAME?	If text that Excel doesn't recognize appears in a formula, this error appears. This can be due to a misspelling or to using text without quotes around it (such as ="the total is"&G22 where G22 contains a total and the text in quotes is inserted with the number). You can also see this error if you forget the colon when referencing a range of cells, as in B12:G15. The solution? Click cells rather than type their names to insert them in a formula, and watch your punctuation.
#NUM!	Most often seen when the result of a formula is a number too large or too small to be displayed in Excel, this error indicates a problem with a number in the formula or in the result of the formula. To make sure you never see this error, your results must be between $-1*10^{307}$ and $1*10^{307}$, where * is the multiplication sign. That shouldn't be tough for most users!
#REF!	If your formula refers to cells that have been edited after you constructed the formula, or if the target cell reference is deleted, this error appears. When editing your worksheet, be careful not to replace referenced cell data with additional formulas. And when deleting content, make sure any formulas you have constructed don't reference what you're deleting.
#VALUE!	If you enter a non-numeric character in a cell referenced in the formula, this error appears. This error might also appear if you enter a range (such as A3:B5) in a formula that requires only a single number or cell.
Circular Reference	When you include in a formula a cell that contains the formula itself, an error message appears notifying you of a circular reference. You need to edit the formula to remove the reference to the formula cell.

Formula do's and don'ts

● Do keep track of parentheses. There must be an even number of them in every formula. Make sure every left (open) parenthesis has a right (close) parenthesis mate.

● Do use colons to indicate a range of cells. A5:B6 means all the cells between and including A5 and B6. A5,B6 means that both A5 and B6 are arguments in a function. A5-B6 means A5 minus B6. Only the colon indicates a range.

● When referencing cells in another worksheet (in the same or a different workbook), do make sure the sheet name (even if it's just Sheet1) is enclosed in single quotation marks, followed by an exclamation point. If the sheet is in another workbook, that workbook's name is enclosed in brackets and appears before the sheet name within the single quotation marks.

When I test my formula on a calculator, I get a different answer

Source of the problem

The big difference between how calculators and Excel formulas work with equations is that on the calculator, the math is done in the order you press the keys. If you press 5 - 2 * 3, the 2 is subtracted from the 5, and the result is multiplied by 3. If, however, you type =5-2*3 in a cell, Excel will multiply the 2 times the 3 first, and then subtract that result from 5. Same formula, different answer. Why? Order of operations.

Excel performs calculations within a formula in this order:

1. Parentheses

2. Exponents

3. Multiplication

4. Division

5. Addition

6. Subtraction

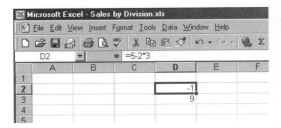

In school, you might have learned to remember this standard mathematical order of operations with the phrase "Please Excuse My Dear Aunt Sally." Lame, maybe, but it worked. I'm remembering it an undisclosed number of years later, aren't I?

So how would you tell Excel to subtract the 2 from the 5, and then multiply by 3? With appropriately placed parentheses! ▶

How to fix it

To edit an existing formula and change the order of operations, follow these steps:

1. Click the cell containing the formula that needs to be edited.

2. On the Formula bar, click to position your insertion point in the formula.

3. Using the left and right arrow keys as needed, reposition your insertion point where you want to insert the missing parentheses, and type the parentheses.

To build a new formula, controlling the order of operations from the start, follow these steps:

1. Click the cell where you want to type the formula, and type an equal sign to begin the formula.

2. Select cells to insert in a formula, or type cell references, numbers, and operators to manually build a formula. Press Enter when you have completed building the formula.

3. As you build the formula, place parentheses around the portion of the formula that should be calculated as a separate entity. If more than one set of items needs to be calculated on its own, place the individual elements of the formula in order—from left to right, and each element in parentheses. For example, =((6*10)-(4*2))/2 will be calculated as 6 times 10, less the result of 4 times 2, and the result of those three calculations will be divided by 2. Placing an extra set of parentheses around the two sets of operations— ((6*10) -(4*2))/2—makes sure that the division by 2 doesn't get calculated before the result of 6 times 10 is reduced by the result of 4 times 2. ▶

Tip
Always make sure there are an even number of parentheses in your formulas. Make sure every left (open) parenthesis has a right (close) parenthesis to go with it. If even one is missing, your formula will display an error message. When the error message appears, click Yes if you want Excel to try to fix the parentheses for you, or No if you want to fix the error yourself. See "My formula causes an error message to appear" on page 148.

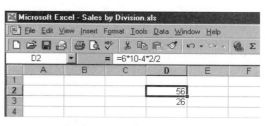

When I edit the cells referenced in my formula, the result doesn't change

Source of the problem

One of the coolest things about an electronic spreadsheet is watching formulas get updated when cells are edited. A grand total in a series of summed columns? No big deal. But change one of the cells in the series and see that grand total change automatically? What a rush! OK, maybe I need to get a life, but if you have

ever performed bookkeeping or data analysis on paper, you know the thrill of using a computer to do things faster, and to not have to erase, recalculate, and rewrite the results when something changes in the data. ▶

But where's the thrill if you edit the cells that are referenced in your formula and nothing happens? This can certainly be a letdown. In addition to being disappointed, you might be concerned as to what's wrong with your formulas. If one is not working, can you rely on

any of the formulas you entered? Of course you can. The problem is most likely a case of not knowing which cells are truly referenced by the formula in question, and it's easy enough to find out which ones are.

Excel calls the cells that are referenced in a formula *precedents*. The formulas that reference a cell are called *dependents*. These terms are based on the concept that the cells precede a formula, and the formula depends on the content of the cells. You can reveal the precedents and dependents for any cell or formula by using Excel's auditing tools to display arrows that point to and from the related content. These auditing tools even have their own toolbar. ▶

How to fix it

To reveal the cells that are referenced in a formula, follow these steps:

1. Click the cell containing the formula you want to examine.

2. On the Tools menu, point to Auditing, and then click Trace Precedents. An arrow points through all precedents to the cell containing the dependent formula. ▶

3. Look at the arrow that points from the precedent cells to the cell containing a formula. If the arrow doesn't point from cells that you want it to, the cells you intended to include in the formula aren't actually included. Edit the formula to refer to the cells you need to use in the formula's calculation.

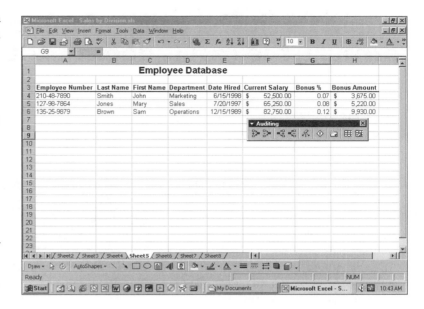

The arrow indicates the precedent of this formula.

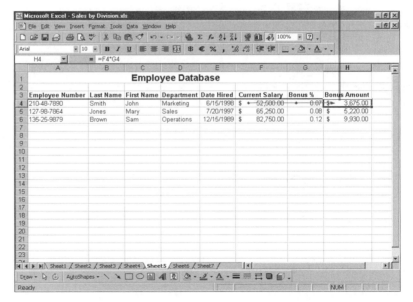

This solution is continued on the next page.

When I edit the cells referenced in my formula, the result doesn't change

(continued from page 153)

To check for formulas that refer to a specific cell, follow these steps:

1. Click a cell that might be used in a formula in your worksheet.

2. On the Tools menu, point to Auditing, and then click Trace Dependents. An arrow points from the cell to all formulas that depend on the cell. ▶

3. View the arrow that points from the cell you selected to its related worksheet formula.

> The arrow indicates the dependent formulas of this cell.

Tip

To display the Auditing toolbar, point to Auditing on the Tools menu, and then click Show Auditing Toolbar. Strangely, this toolbar isn't listed when you point to Toolbars on the View menu to display the Toolbars submenu.

What's that little grid thingy?

If you see a precedents or dependents arrow pointing to or from a small grid icon, that indicates that the formula (dependent) or cell in the formula (precedent) is on another worksheet or workbook. ▶

To reveal the location of the external dependent or precedent, double-click the grid icon. The Go To dialog box appears, showing the address of the cell, including the workbook name and sheet name. (Don't worry if your dialog box looks a bit different from this one.) ▶

Select the address in the Go To box so that the address appears in the Reference box, and then click OK to switch to the sheet containing the dependent or precedent.

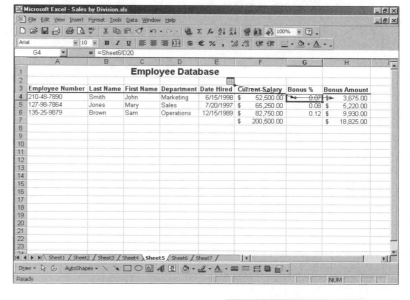

The results of my summary worksheet formulas are incorrect

Source of the problem

Formulas that summarize data from other worksheets can go wrong for a variety of reasons. The two most common are an error in the way the formula was created, and a change in the sheets and data to which the summary formula refers. If your summary formula results in an error message, there's something wrong with the formula itself in a grammatical way—missing parentheses, cells not containing numbers referenced in the formula—and you should check "My formula causes an error message to appear" on page 148.

If, on the other hand, the result is just plain old wrong, the problem is that a cell or range is being referenced in error, or the data that the formula references has moved or changed, and you're unaware of it. Either situation is easily straightened out through the use of Excel's auditing tools and some basic formula-creation tips.

If you're using a worksheet that someone else created or one you don't use that often, it's easy to forget how things relate to each other. You can use Excel's auditing tools to identify the cells referenced in a formula, as well as the formulas that reference a specific cell. So if the results of your summary worksheet are incorrect, you need to check your summary formula for the cells that are referenced in it.

> **Tip**
> To quickly see which cells are referenced in a formula, click a formula cell and check out the Formula bar. Although the cell in the worksheet contains the result, the Formula bar shows the formula that produces the result.

How to fix it

1. Click the cell containing the summary formula.

2. On the Tools menu, point to Auditing, and then click Trace Precedents.

3. Examine the arrow that points to the summary formula. The arrow points from a small grid icon that indicates a cell reference outside of the active worksheet. ▶

	A	B	C	D
	C5	= =B5/Sheet6!$F$12		
1				
2	Region Summaries			
3				
4	**Region**	**Sales**	**Percentage of Total Sales**	
5	Philadelphia	$ 25,317,026.70	19%	
6	New York	$ 21,692,857.00	16%	
7	Chicago	$ 22,182,833.00	17%	
8	Atlanta	$ 13,405,661.00	10%	
9	Phoenix	$ 23,553,295.00	18%	
10	San Francisco	$ 26,120,217.00	20%	
11				
12				
13				

To view the external cell reference indicated by the grid icon, double-click the icon. The Go To dialog box appears, showing the address of the precedent (the cell reference contained in the formula) that's not on the active sheet. The address includes the workbook name, and also the name of the worksheet on which the precedent can be found. (Don't worry if your dialog box looks a bit different from this one.) ▶

If you want to go to the cell that's referenced, select the address in the Go To box so that it also appears in the Reference box, and then click OK. (You can also click Cancel to close the Go To dialog box after making a note of the address, and then go to that workbook or worksheet on your own.) See "When I edit the cells referenced in my formula, the result doesn't change" on page 152.

One cell, many formulas

To check for the formulas (summary and otherwise) that refer to a specific cell, click the cell that you believe is referenced in your summary formula. On the Tools menu, point to Auditing, and then click Trace Dependents. Examine the arrow pointing from the selected cell to the summary formula in question. Edit the formula if necessary so that it refers to the correct cells. ▶

Tip

For quick access to the Trace commands, display the Auditing toolbar. Point to Auditing on the Tools menu, and then click Show Auditing Toolbar. This toolbar is not available when you point to Toolbars on the View menu and display the toolbars submenu.

B10	▾	=	26120217	
	A	B	C	D
1				
2	Region Summaries			
3				
4	**Region**	**Sales**	**Percentage of Total Sales**	
5	Philadelphia	$25,317,026.78	19%	
6	New York	$21,692,857.00	16%	
7	Chicago	$22,182,833.00	17%	
8	Atlanta	$13,405,661.00	10%	
9	Phoenix	$23,553,295.00	18%	
10	San Francisco	$26,120,217.00	20%	
11				
12				
13				

Tip

If you want the cells to display your formulas instead of their results, click Options on the Tools menu. On the View tab of the Options dialog box, select the Formulas check box in the Window Options section, and then click OK. All of the formula results in your current worksheet will appear as formulas until and unless you clear the Formulas check box in the Options dialog box.

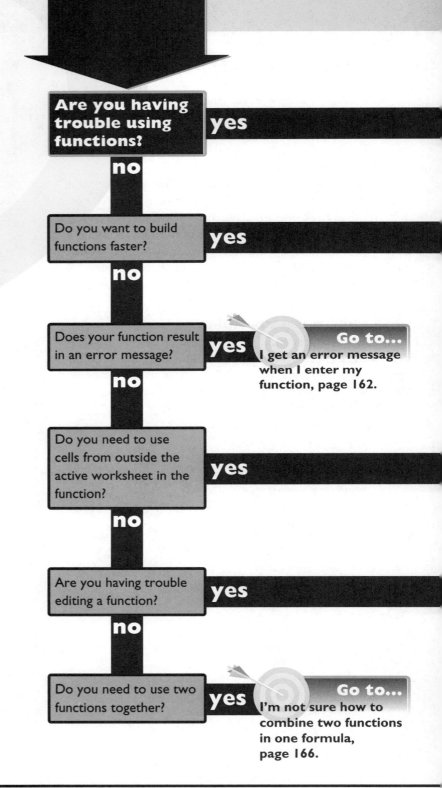

Are you having trouble using functions? yes

no

Do you want to build functions faster? yes

no

Does your function result in an error message? yes

Go to...
I get an error message when I enter my function, page 162.

no

Do you need to use cells from outside the active worksheet in the function? yes

no

Are you having trouble editing a function? yes

no

Do you need to use two functions together? yes

Go to...
I'm not sure how to combine two functions in one formula, page 166.

Functions

Are you unsure how to build a function?

yes Go to... **I don't know how to construct the function I need, page 158.**

no

Are you having trouble understanding how a function works?

yes Go to... **I don't know what to include in this function, page 160.**

Quick fix

Once you understand the structure of a function, you can build it manually. For example, to build the AVERAGE function, type =*average* and then the cell range in parentheses. Insert the range of cells to be averaged either by typing the range, (A5:A20), for example, or by selecting the range using your mouse. Press Enter to implement the function.

Go to... **Cells I need to include in my function aren't in my active worksheet, page 164.**

Quick fix

If a function no longer works properly after you've edited it (or the cells to which it refers), it's often a good idea to simply delete it and repeat the function building process. Use the Paste Function dialog box to guide you. Click Function on the Insert menu to open this dialog box.

> **If your solution isn't here**
> Check these related chapters:
>   Currency, page 46
>   Formatting numbers, page 114
>   Formulas, page 146
> Or see the general troubleshooting tips on page xv.

I don't know how to construct the function I need

Source of the problem

The structure of most formulas can be determined by talking them through: "This cell should equal this other cell here, minus this cell, divided by three." So the formula is simple—subtract one cell from another and divide the result by three. But what if you want to determine how much your car payment will be if you finance it for five years at an interest rate of 7%? What if you want to know how much an investment will be worth in 10 years, assuming a standard rate of return? Or how much an asset will depreciate before next year's taxes are due? Even if you understand the concepts of loan payments and interest rates and depreciation, the structure of the formulas to calculate them might not be so obvious. When you want to create a formula for a mathematical, statistical, scientific, or accounting procedure, you'll find what you need in Excel's functions.

Functions are preset formulas that you can use by inserting information—cell addresses, numbers, even text—into prescribed positions. Excel provides a dialog box through which you can select the right function for the formula you want to create and learn how that formula is constructed. Once you find the function you need, you can proceed to build your formula.

Tip

Don't be put off by some of the functions Excel offers. For example, one of the functions will return the hyperbolic cosine of a number. I admit that I understand only "the," "of," and "a number" in that last sentence, but I feel better knowing that Excel can help me if I ever need to use that function. Stick with the functions you need to use, and ignore the ones that make you scratch your head.

How to fix it

1. Click the cell in which you want to create a formula.

2. Click the Paste Function button on the Standard toolbar.

3. In the Paste Function dialog box, click a function category in the Function Category list, and view its corresponding list of functions in the Function Name list. ▶

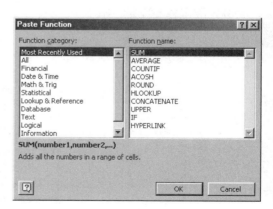

4. Because the function names don't always make it clear what a function is or does, you'll need to click them in the list to read a description of what they do and when they're used. The description appears in the dialog box below the lists of categories and functions.

5. When you find the function you need, double-click it. The Formula palette docks in the upper left corner of your worksheet. ▶

6. Enter a number or cell address in the Formula palette's first argument box. (You can also select the information requested by clicking cells in your worksheet.)

7. To move to the next box, press Tab or click the box. The description of the argument changes to match the number for each box. As you fill in the requested information, a calculation result appears in the Formula Result section at the bottom of the Formula palette. ▶

8. When you've filled in all the information the Formula palette asks for, click OK. ▶

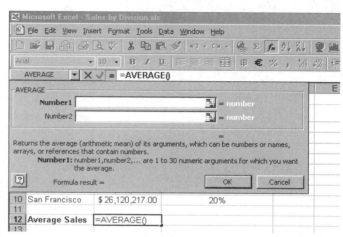

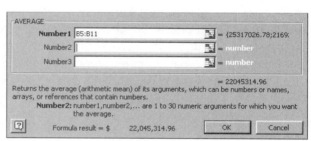

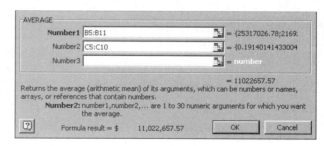

> **Tip**
>
> You don't have to fill in all of the information requested in the Formula palette argument boxes. If a box label is **bold**, an entry is required in that argument box. If the box label is plain text, you can skip entering a value in the box.

I don't know what to include in this function

Source of the problem

Your worksheet requires a rather complex formula, you've found the function that creates it, and you're ready to start building the formula using the Formula palette. Despite the step-by-step process involved in selecting and building a function, you might have some trouble deciphering the descriptions in the Formula palette. Each number, cell reference, or value that the function requires is explained, but sometimes the descriptions aren't terribly clear or they assume too high a level of familiarity with the accounting, statistical, or scientific concept on which the function is based. You might find out that you don't understand the function as you're building it, or when the function result turns out to be wrong.

In either case, all is not lost. You can use Excel's Help feature when you're really stuck. You can use Help proactively (before you attempt to create the formula), or reactively (when you're in the middle of building the function and smacking your forehead in frustration). You can also print Help pages for future reference.

Tip

A quick way to test a function is to build it with easy, round numbers so you'll know right off the bat if the result is wrong. If you're building a PMT (payment) function to determine a payment on a loan, test the function with simple numbers—10,000 for the loan amount, 10 months to pay it back, and 10% interest. Even the most mathematically challenged should be able to spot an error if the numbers are ones that you can calculate in your head.

How to fix it

1. On the Help menu, click Microsoft Excel Help.

2. Type the name of a function in the Office Assistant's text box. ▶

Tip

If you're not using the Office Assistant, you can click the Index tab of the Microsoft Excel Help window—or the Help Topics: Microsoft Excel window if you're using Excel 97—and type the name of the function in the box provided. Then click the topic you want in the list of the closest matches.

3. Click Search to see a list of Help articles that cover the function for which you're seeking information. The first option in the list should pertain directly to the function name you typed.

4. Click the option that matches the function you typed. The Help window opens, displaying the Help page for the option you clicked. The Help page repeats the function's description and includes a detailed breakdown of the arguments the function needs to do its work. The Help page might also include links to related Help pages. (Don't worry if your Help window looks a little different from this one.) ▶

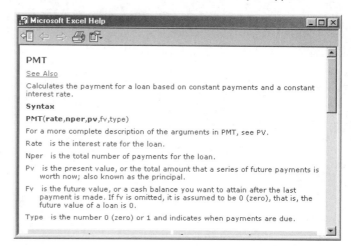

Boy, do I hate that stupid paper clip!

You're not alone. Many users grimace the minute he shows up. But don't despair. You can use a different Office Assistant character, or tell Excel you don't want to use the Office Assistant at all.

To change to a different character (like Links, the little orange cat), click the Microsoft Excel Help button, and right-click the Office Assistant that appears. On the shortcut menu, click Choose Assistant. ▶

On the Gallery tab of the Office Assistant dialog box, scroll through the available characters by clicking the Next and Back buttons. When you find a character you like, click OK. (You might have to insert the Office CD if all of the characters weren't loaded when you installed Excel or any other components in the Office suite.)

If you don't want to use an Office Assistant, you can turn it off and go directly to the Microsoft Excel Help window when you use Help. To turn the Office Assistant off, right-click it, and click Options on the shortcut menu to display the Office Assistant dialog box. On the Options tab, clear the Use The Office Assistant check box, and then click OK.

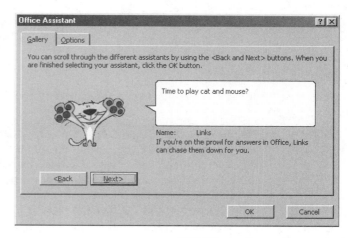

Tip
If you're building a function, you can click the Help button (which looks like a dialog bubble with a question mark in it) in the Formula palette to open the Help page about the function at hand.

I get an error message when I enter my function

Source of the problem

There's a difference between a wrong answer (15 when you were expecting 150) and an error. An error comes in the form of an on-screen message, advising you that the formula you've attempted to use is structured incorrectly, or in the form of an error in the cell itself.

In the case of structural problems, the error message appears as a prompt and usually offers help—some indication of what went wrong.

It also tells you how to access a Help page to get more information about the problem at hand. ▶

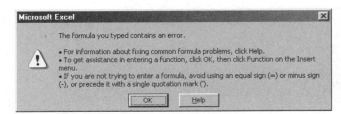

Errors in the cell come in seven varieties, and the solutions vary depending on the error. The solutions normally require editing the cell's formula by changing a cell reference or reducing the number of arguments you've included. If the editing seems to be too complex, just delete the cell contents, and start over!

How to fix it

Here's a table describing the most common function errors in Excel:

Error	How to fix it
#DIV/0!	This error appears if you include the number zero in the function and other numbers within the function will be divided by that zero. References to a cell containing zero (if that cell is in a divisor position within the function) will also result in this error. Change the cell reference to a cell containing a number other than zero, or edit the zero out of the function directly.
#N/A	If cells referenced in a function are unavailable, this error appears in the cell that contains the function. Possible causes include deleting a worksheet or workbook containing a cell that is referenced in a formula, or deleting the formula that the cell containing the error is trying to locate. To fix this, restore the missing material in the referenced worksheet or workbook, or edit the erroneous function to reference identical material in a new cell or worksheet.

Error	How to fix it
#NAME?	If text that Excel doesn't recognize appears in a function, this error appears. This can be due to a misspelling or to using text without quotes around it (in a Criteria argument, for example). You can also see this error if you forget the colon when you reference a range of cells, as in =AVERAGE(B12:G15). Be sure to always use a colon when referring to a range of cells in a function, or any formula for that matter.
#NUM!	With regard to functions, this error normally indicates that the function was expecting a number, and the cell referenced contains text. Check the cells your function references, and either edit them or redirect the function to a cell containing a number.
#NULL!	If your function refers to two ranges that should intersect but don't, this error will appear. For example, if a SUM function refers to ranges B1:B10 and D1:D10, the lack of an intersecting cell will cause the #NULL! error to appear because Excel will try to find a cell that's in both ranges. Add a comma between the two ranges to tell Excel to add the two ranges separately and not to look for an intersecting cell.
#REF!	This is a "reference" error. If your function refers to cells that have been edited after you constructed the formula, or if the target cell has been deleted, this error appears. When editing your worksheet, be careful not to replace referenced cell data with formulas or additional functions, and when deleting content, make sure any formulas you have constructed with the function or functions don't reference what you're deleting.
#VALUE!	If you enter any nonnumeric characters in a cell referenced in the function, and the function requires numeric content, this error appears. It might also appear if you enter a range in a function (such as A3:B5) when the formula requires only a single number or cell. The solution? Be sure not to use ranges when you need a single number (or a cell containing a single number), and check the content of all cells referenced in a function to make sure they contain what the function requires.

Put the "fun" back into functions

All this talk about errors can make functions seem unpleasant and difficult to use. However, if you understand a function's purpose in your worksheet, and you know what information the function needs to give you the result you want, you won't have any trouble. You might even enjoy the process, because Excel functions make creating complex formulas much easier than creating them "from scratch." Additionally, the process is relatively foolproof. (You can run into snags, however, if you work carelessly or don't pay attention to the "grammar" of a function.)

Remember that you must provide a series of arguments in the right order, containing the right stuff, and in precisely the way the function was designed to work. Always use a colon between cell addresses in a range (A1:B15), use a comma to indicate two separate ranges with no intersecting cell (A1:B6,B10:G25), and put quotes around criteria—as in =COUNTIF(A6:A16,"Atlanta").

Cells I need to include in my function aren't in my active worksheet

Source of the problem

Creating a function can be confusing enough without trying to reference cells from outside the active worksheet, right? Well, it's actually really simple to include cells from other worksheets in the current workbook, or from another workbook entirely. You can reference these cells and ranges manually by typing the workbook or worksheet name (or both) and cell addresses in the formula.

Or you can use the Formula palette (which appears when you choose a function in the Paste Function dialog box) and select the cell ranges you need with your mouse pointer.

The keys to successfully referencing external cells are knowing which cells you want from which worksheets and workbooks before you get started, and making sure that the cells you're referencing contain the sort of data the function requires. For example, be sure to use numbers, not text, if the cell is part of a calculation. Use single cells or numbers if a range won't work in the function you want (or, conversely, use ranges if single numbers or cells won't work), or use text or some other value in quotes if the function is looking for a comparison value. Excel will alert you with an error message if you violate any of these rules (see "I get an error message when I enter my function" on page 164), so you'll know right away that you need to do something differently. You can always start over with a list of where to find the information you need—be it in the current worksheet, another worksheet or workbook, or obtained from someone or somewhere else (such as an interest rate or tax percentage that's not stored in a worksheet).

Tip
Another good reason to keep workbook file and sheet tab names short and simple is so that you can type them in formulas without serious risk of creating typos. If your file and tab names are complex, it might be difficult for you to refer to them manually as you build formulas and functions.

How to fix it

1. Click the cell that will house the formula, and then click the Paste Function button.

2. In the Paste Function dialog box, select a function category in the Function Category list, and then double-click the function you need in the Function Name list. ▶

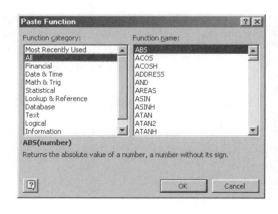

3. As soon as the Formula palette appears and is docked in the upper left corner of the worksheet, you can begin building the formula. Click the first box to type the cell reference or value. ▶

4. To include a reference to a cell outside the active worksheet, you have two options: To reference a cell within the active workbook but on a different sheet, click that sheet's tab. To reference a cell in another workbook, make sure the second workbook is open and click the workbook's name on the Window menu. When the workbook appears, click the tab of the worksheet containing the cell you want to reference.

5. In the worksheet that contains the cell or range you want to reference, click the cell or drag through the range to select it. The Formula palette is on-screen, so you can see the formula with the workbook, sheet, and cell references included. ▶

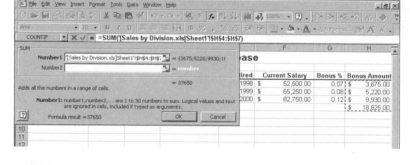

6. Continue building your function in the Formula palette, and click OK when you're done.

Don't forget the @!?*!! punctuation

If you decide to enter the external cell or range references

Tip

When you've finished selecting a cell or range in a worksheet in another workbook, don't return to the original active worksheet until you've moved on to the next argument box in the Formula palette. If the external reference is the last thing you need for the formula, click OK in the Formula palette, or press Enter. If you go back to any cell in the original active worksheet, you'll accidentally add that cell's address to the function.

manually, be sure to add the appropriate punctuation to the workbook and worksheet names. Workbook file names are enclosed in square brackets, and worksheet names are followed by an exclamation point. As you can see in the graphic above, the entire external location (workbook name and sheet name) is enclosed in single quotation marks.

I'm not sure how to combine two functions in one formula

Source of the problem

So one function isn't good enough for you, eh? You want two, three, maybe four functions all rolled up into one formula, and you don't know how to do it. Or maybe you've tried, and it didn't work. In either case, there are some key things to remember when building nested functions:

Tip
Want to find the Help file on nesting functions? If you're using the Office Assistant, type *nesting functions* in the Office Assistant box, and click Search. If you're using the Index tab, type *function*, and scroll through the related topics to find "About nesting functions within functions." (In Excel 97, the topic is titled "About multiple functions within functions, or nesting.")

- Set some limits. The bottom line: You can't nest more than seven functions. If you are trying to nest more than that, there's your problem. The solution? Get rid of one of the functions by incorporating an already-calculated part of the formula in another cell, and reference that cell in the function instead.

- If you've tried to combine or nest functions and an incorrect result or an error message appeared, the problem is most likely the function's structure. Where you insert the second-level function (say, a SUM function within an AVERAGE function) is important.

- Be completely familiar with the proper way to build each of the individual functions you want to nest. Often, it's not the nesting that's gone wrong, but the way one of the functions is set up.

With these considerations in mind, it's fairly straightforward to build a function that contains a second function within it, for example, a SUM function within an AVERAGE function.

How to fix it

1. Click the cell that will contain the formula.

2. Click the Paste Function button to display the Paste Function dialog box.

3. Select a category in the Function Category list, and then double-click the function you want in the Function Name list. (If you're not sure which function to pick, try clicking All in the Function Category list, and then scrolling through the alphabetical Function Name list to find one.)

4. When the Function palette appears, the Name box to the left of the Formula bar becomes the Function box. To supply the first argument (for example, the sum of a series of numbers), click the arrow to the left of the Function box, and in the drop-down list, click the name of the function you want to nest inside the first function.

5. On the worksheet, drag through the range of cells to be added. (You might have to click the Collapse button to temporarily hide the Formula palette; click the Expand button after you finish selecting the range you want.) When you release the mouse button, both the nested function and range appear in bold on the Formula bar. ▶

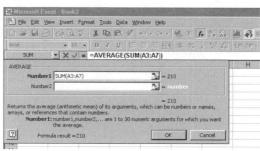

6. Click the second argument box, and then click the Function box to insert the displayed function.

7. Drag through the second range of cells. Again, a nested function and range appear on the Formula bar. ▶

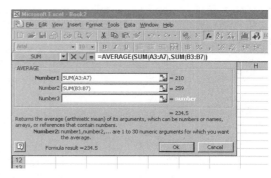

8. Click OK, and view the results in your worksheet. For example, if you used the SUM function inside the AVERAGE function, you've averaged two sums. ▶

The correct formula appears in the Formula bar and should look similar to the following (your cell ranges might vary):

=AVERAGE(SUM(A3:A7),SUM(B3:B7))

This combination of functions adds cells A3 through A7, and averages that result with the sum of B3 through B7.

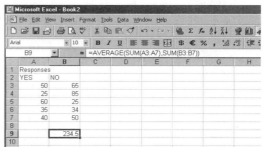

Parenthetically speaking

The placement of parentheses is essential in forming nested functions, especially if you're entering the functions manually. There should be one set of parentheses around the nested function or functions, and parentheses within each nested function if any ranges are referenced. If you type the function in the Formula bar and include the wrong number of parentheses, you'll see the pairs appear in color and the odd one (if you have a single parenthesis that's missing its mate) appear in bold. Get rid of the extra or give it a mate (whichever is appropriate), and the formula should work without an error message appearing.

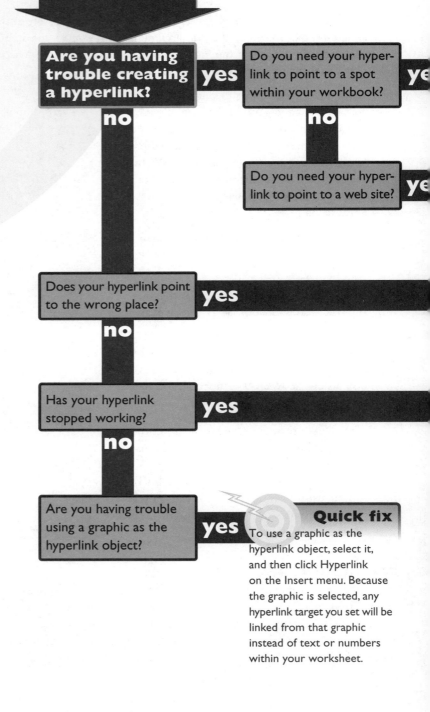

Are you having trouble creating a hyperlink?

yes → Do you need your hyperlink to point to a spot within your workbook?

no

Do you need your hyperlink to point to a web site?

no

Does your hyperlink point to the wrong place?

yes

no

Has your hyperlink stopped working?

yes

no

Are you having trouble using a graphic as the hyperlink object?

yes

Quick fix

To use a graphic as the hyperlink object, select it, and then click Hyperlink on the Insert menu. Because the graphic is selected, any hyperlink target you set will be linked from that graphic instead of text or numbers within your worksheet.

Hyperlinks

Go to...

I'm not sure how to link to a spot in my current workbook, page 172.

Go to...

I don't know the exact web address that my hyperlink should point to, page 174.

Quick fix

If the target of your hyperlink has been moved, renamed, or deleted, the link won't work anymore. To make the hyperlink work again, you need to relocate the target and edit the hyperlink so that it points to its new location. Right-click the hyperlink, then click Edit Hyperlink on the shortcut menu. In the Edit Hyperlink dialog box, type the new target location.

Does your hyperlink do nothing when clicked?

yes

Go to...

I click a hyperlink in my worksheet, and nothing happens, page 176.

no

Do you get a new worksheet when you click a hyperlink?

yes

Go to...

When I click my hyperlink, it creates a new, blank workbook, page 178.

If your solution isn't here

Check these related chapters:

Drawing shapes and lines, page 66

Macros, page 180

Saving, page 244

Or see the general troubleshooting tips on page xv.

I'm not sure how to link to a spot in my current workbook

Source of the problem

When most people think of hyperlinks, they think of text or graphics on a web page that take you to other web pages when you click them. Few people are aware that you can create hyperlinks that open new and existing documents, or that move you to other locations that are within your current file.

Given the size of an Excel workbook, and the fact that data can be spread out over more than 16 million cells per sheet, it would be rather handy to be able to click one cell or a graphic image and be instantly taken to another cell on the same worksheet or on a different worksheet in the same workbook. Because people aren't aware of this capability within Excel, they usually have no idea how to make it happen.

Tip

When you're planning your inter-worksheet hyperlinks, remember that the target within your worksheet can be a cell, a range of cells, or a chart. You can also create hyperlinks that point to other workbook files, and to specific sheets within them.

Creating hyperlinks is simple, and it involves a very short series of steps, beginning with choosing the item that will serve as the link. In Excel, your choices are a cell, a chart, or a graphic object—an AutoShape, a WordArt object, or anything else you've drawn using the Drawing toolbar. It's a good idea to have planned your hyperlinks before you sit down to create them. Jotting down a list of what links to what, or at least planning it in your head, will save you a lot of time making changes and corrections.

How to fix it

1. Select the worksheet entry (a cell or range of cells) or object (graphic or chart) that will serve as the hyperlink object.

2. On the Insert menu, click Hyperlink.

3. Click Place In This Document in the Link To section of the Insert Hyperlink dialog box. (If you're working in Excel 97, click the Browse button next to the Named Location In File (Optional) box.)

4. In the Type The Cell Reference box, type the cell or range that the hyperlink should point to. (If you're working in Excel 97, make sure the Sheet Name option is selected in the Browse Excel Workbook dialog box, and then in the Reference box, type the cell or range the hyperlink should

point to. The dialog box in Excel 97 looks a bit different than this one.) ▶

5. In the list of sheets provided in either the Insert Hyperlink dialog box (if you're working in Excel 2000) or the Browse Excel Workbook dialog box (if you're working in Excel 97), select the sheet within your current workbook that the hyperlink should point to.

6. Click OK once if you're working in Excel 2000, or twice if you're working in Excel 97. When you point to the hyperlink object, the pointer becomes a pointing finger, indicating that clicking the link will access the target cell or range. ▶

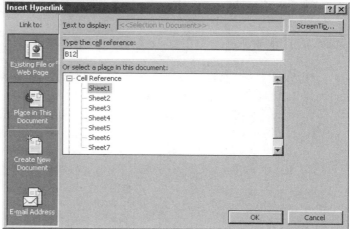

Psssst! It's a ScreenTip

Excel 2000 If you want some descriptive or instructional text to appear when people move their mouse pointer over a hyperlink, you can create a ScreenTip. Just like the little boxes that pop up when you point to a toolbar button, this ScreenTip will appear whenever anyone hovers a mouse pointer over the hyperlink for more than a second. Your ScreenTip might say "Click here to view last year's data for this same time period" or something like that—something that tells the person what to expect at the other end of the hyperlink. To create a ScreenTip for an existing hyperlink, right-click the hyperlink object, point to Hyperlink on the shortcut menu, and then click Edit Hyperlink. In the Edit Hyperlink dialog box, click the ScreenTip button to display the Set Hyperlink ScreenTip dialog box. ▶

In the ScreenTip Text box, type the text you want to appear in the ScreenTip. You can use as many as 90 characters, but it's better to use 50 or fewer characters to keep it concise and easy to read. Click OK to return to the Edit Hyperlink dialog box, and click OK again to implement the ScreenTip.

Tip
It's a good idea to test your hyperlink and its ScreenTip—make sure the hyperlink points to the location you want it to, and that the ScreenTip is spelled and worded correctly—before making your workbook available to others. Better for you to spot the mistake than to have someone else tell you about it!

I don't know the exact web address that my hyperlink should point to

Source of the problem

A hyperlink that points to a web page can give your lowly worksheet a global reach. Whether the hyperlink points to your company web page or to supporting or related information on someone else's site, it's important that the hyperlink work properly, taking users to the exact spot on the exact web page you intended.

What if you don't know the exact web address? It's a good idea to know this information before you start the hyperlink creation process, but if you're like me and don't read directions or plan ahead before setting out on a trip, you might find yourself sitting in front of the computer saying, "Wait a minute, I don't know where this hyperlink is supposed to point!" For the preparation-challenged, the Insert Hyperlink dialog box gives you the chance to browse the web in search of the page your hyperlink should point to.

Tip

A web address is also called a URL, which stands for Uniform Resource Locator. Some geeks pronounce it "Earl," but being a non-geek myself, I say the letters U-R-L. The choice is up to you, but if you choose the geek way, people might snicker at you behind your back.

How to fix it

1. Select the cell, range, graphic, or chart that will act as your hyperlink object.

2. On the Insert menu, click Hyperlink.

3. Click Existing File Or Web Page in the Link To section of the Insert Hyperlink dialog box. (If you're working in Excel 97, go to step 4.) ▶

4. Click Inserted Links in the Or Select From List section, and look through the corresponding list of sites to see if you

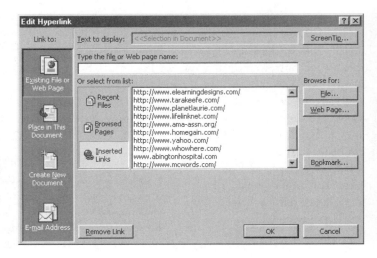

can find the page you want. (If you're working in Excel 97, look through the most recently visited sites in the Link To File Or URL drop-down list.)

5. Assuming you don't find the web site you need in the list, open your default web browser by clicking the Web Page button in the Browse For section. (If you're working in Excel 97, click the Browse button next to the Link To File Or URL box. When the Link To File dialog box appears, click the Search The Web button—the button with the globe at the top of the dialog box—to open your default browser.)

6. In the browser window, you can take two approaches to finding the site you're looking for: If you have no idea what the web address for the site you need is, go to a search site such as *www.yahoo.com*, *www.hotbot.com*, or *www.google.com*, and in the Search box, type keywords such as the name of the company or organization that owns the site you're seeking. If you know the web

site address but not the specific page you want your hyperlink to point to, type the address in the browser's Address or Location bar, and press Enter. When you get to the main site, use the site's links to locate the specific page you need to complete the entire hyperlink web address. ▶

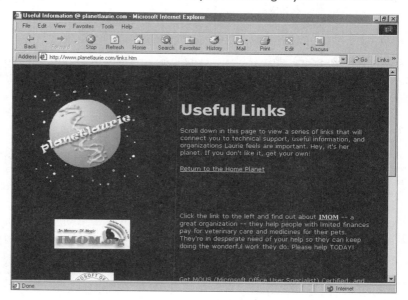

7. Once you find the page and it's displayed in your browser window, switch back to Excel (press Alt+Tab, or use the taskbar buttons). You'll see that the address you were just visiting has been automatically inserted in the Insert Hyperlink dialog box.

8. Click OK to insert the hyperlink.

Tip
Hyperlinks can also point to web pages on your company's intranet. Some companies don't want to post the kind of data your worksheet might refer to on an Internet-based web server, preferring to keep what could be confidential info in-house.

Tip
It's a good idea to test your hyperlinks immediately after setting them up and to continue to test them. Web sites close or get reorganized (which can change the address of a specific page within the site), and content moves from one page to another, potentially leaving your hyperlink connected to inaccurate or nonexistent content.

I click a hyperlink in my worksheet, and nothing happens

Source of the problem

You click a hyperlink, and you expect to be taken to a web site or to a specific location in a worksheet. But it doesn't work. Isn't that aggravating? I hate it when that happens. The problem is easy enough to fix, but you'll want to know what happened so it doesn't happen again, right?

Before you get started though, here are some questions for you to consider:

● Are you sure what you're clicking is a hyperlink? If the hyperlink is the content of a cell, it should be in color (blue or purple, if you're using default settings for hyperlinks) and be underlined. Also, your mouse pointer should turn into a pointing finger when you point to it.

● When you point to the hyperlink (whether it's a cell's content or a graphic object), does a ScreenTip appear with the location of the hyperlink's target?

● Did the hyperlink work before? If so, could anything have changed?

Your answers can shed light on the nature and source of the problem. If the text in the cell isn't underlined, or if your mouse pointer doesn't change when you point to a cell or graphic, the cell or graphic probably isn't a hyperlink. If everything looks as it should, perhaps the hyperlink points to itself. It's possible to link to the cell that's serving as the hyperlink object—not on purpose, but accidents happen!

If the hyperlink used to work, something has to have changed. Perhaps the target file or web site has moved. Whatever the cause, the solution is to edit the hyperlink.

How to fix it

1. Right-click the cell or graphic, point to Hyperlink on the shortcut menu, and then click Edit Hyperlink. (Don't worry if your dialog box doesn't look exactly like this one.) ▶

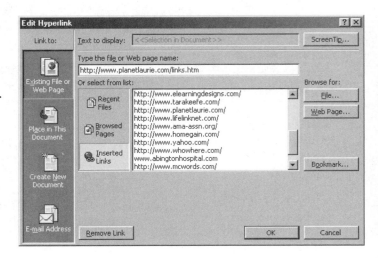

2. If the hyperlink is linked to a place within the worksheet (or to a cell or range within another worksheet or workbook), the address appears in the Type The Cell Reference box. If your link points to a web site or another file (other than a different workbook), the address will appear in the Type The File Or Web Page Name box. (If you're working in Excel 97, the address will appear in the Named Location In File (Optional) box if the link points to a place in the same worksheet or to a cell or range in another worksheet. If the link points to a web site or a different file including a different workbook, the address will appear in the Link To File Or URL box.)

3. Examine the address in the box, and then edit the hyperlink by either reestablishing a target for the hyperlink within the worksheet, or reentering the name of the file or web page to which the hyperlink should point.

4. When you've reset the hyperlink information, click OK.

No thanks, just browsing

If your hyperlink points to a web site and you think the existing address is the correct one (despite the link not working), click the Web Page button in the Browse For section of the Edit Hyperlink dialog box to open your default browser. (If you're working in Excel 97, click the Browse button next to the Link To File Or URL box. When the Link To File dialog box appears, click the Search The Web button, the button with the globe at the top of the dialog box.)

When your browser opens, use a search site such as *www.yahoo.com* or *www.google.com* to search for the site, or try entering the web address you think is right, using the browser's Address or Location bar. ▶

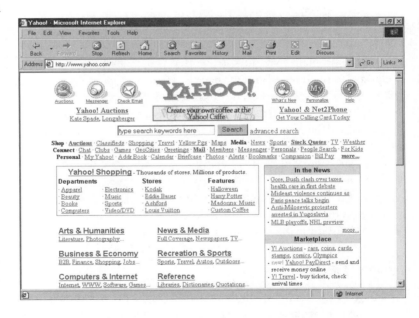

Once you locate the working web site, switch back to Excel (where you left the Edit Hyperlink dialog box open) and you'll see that the address has been inserted in the Type The File Or Web Page Name box. (In Excel 97, the Link To File dialog box closes when you switch back to Excel and you'll see the address in the Link to File Or URL box.)

When I click my hyperlink, it creates a new, blank workbook

Source of the problem

This problem comes up only in Excel 2000, and it isn't really a problem, in that a certain type of hyperlink is meant to open a new, blank workbook. But if opening a new workbook isn't what you want your hyperlink to do, or if you don't expect this result from a hyperlink someone else created, it can be an unpleasant surprise. Regardless, if you don't know how to fix it, it's a problem.

In addition to linking to files and web sites, Excel hyperlinks can be set up to link to any of the following:

- a place in your existing worksheet (a cell or range thereof)

- a new, blank workbook created at the time the hyperlink is clicked (available only in Excel 2000)

- an e-mail address in a new message window (available only in Excel 2000)

If the problem hyperlink is one that you created, it's relatively easy to see how you might have created this type of hyperlink by mistake—the version of the Insert Hyperlink dialog box that appears when the Create New Document button is clicked does ask for a file name and path to that file, so you might have thought you were setting up a link to an existing file.

If you're working with a hyperlink created by someone else, let's just assume they were sleepy or just not thinking straight at the time they created it, and let it go. Take a deep breath, and move on—you'll just fix the problem and have the satisfaction of knowing that you did a good deed!

> **Tip**
>
> Before clicking a hyperlink, check its ScreenTip by moving your mouse pointer over the link. Even if the person who set up the hyperlink didn't create a custom ScreenTip, there should be a default one—probably the name of the file or web site the link points to. If the ScreenTip doesn't list a web site, workbook file name that you recognize, or say "mailto: name@domain.com" (for an e-mail link), chances are that clicking the link will create a new, blank workbook.

How to fix it

1. Right-click the hyperlink that's generating a new workbook whenever it's clicked, and on the shortcut menu, point to Hyperlink, and then click Edit Hyperlink.

2. In the Edit Hyperlink dialog box, observe the panel of buttons in the Link To section. Most probably, the Existing File Or Web Page button is selected. To change the hyperlink to a different type—one that links to a web page or a location in an existing worksheet or workbook, or one that generates an e-mail message—click the appropriate button in the Link To section.

3. Type a file name and location or a web address in the Type The File Or Web Page Name box, or click an address in the Or Select From List section. Click Remove Link if you'd rather not link the selected cell or object at all. ▶

4. Click OK to return to your worksheet.

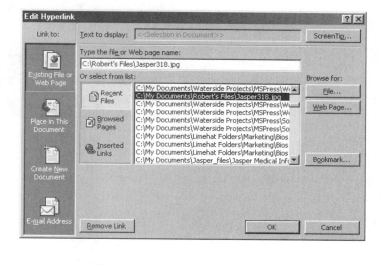

Now I want a new, blank workbook!

You didn't want one before, but now you see the merits. If your worksheet contains data that people test and play with, you can create a link that gives them a blank workbook into which they can copy the data. They can then play without risk of mangling the original data. Click the cell, range, or object that will be the hyperlink object, and on the Insert menu, click Hyperlink. In the Insert Hyperlink dialog box, click Create New Document in the Link To section. (The dialog box displays different settings if you selected another type of hyperlink when you last inserted or edited a hyperlink.) In the Name Of New Document box, type the name and extension of the file you want the link to create ("playdata.xls" for example, for a workbook that is a testing location for data). ▶

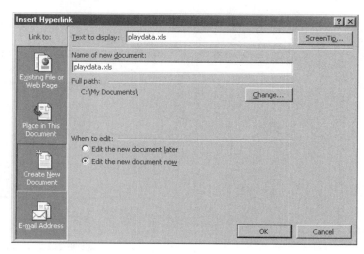

Click the Change button if you don't want the file to be stored in the My Documents folder, which is the default location. When the Create New Document dialog box appears, find where you want to store the new file, type the new file's name (including its extension) in the File Name box, and click OK. If you want to keep working in the current worksheet, click the Edit The New Document Later option. (Otherwise, the new file will open when you click OK.) Click OK to create the hyperlink and the new file that the hyperlink targets. If you clicked the Edit The New Document Later option, the new file won't open right away—it will be created and stored in the directory that you set in the Full Path section so that you can edit it at your leisure.

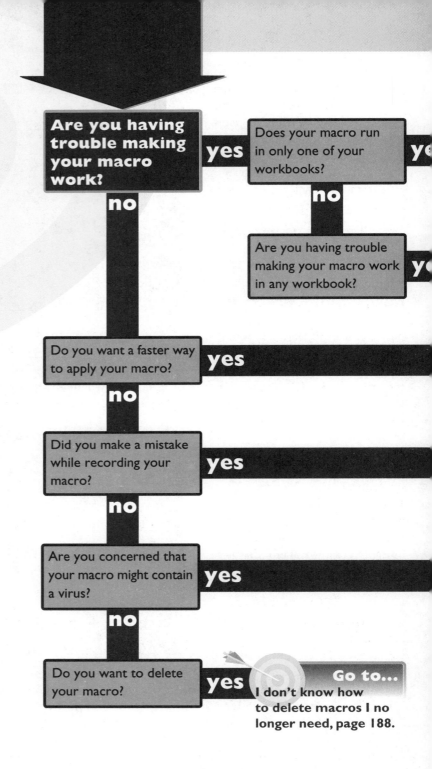

Are you having trouble making your macro work?

yes → Does your macro run in only one of your workbooks? **ye**

no ↓

Does your macro run in only one of your workbooks?

no ↓

Are you having trouble making your macro work in any workbook? **y**

Do you want a faster way to apply your macro? **yes**

no ↓

Did you make a mistake while recording your macro? **yes**

no ↓

Are you concerned that your macro might contain a virus? **yes**

no ↓

Do you want to delete your macro? **yes**

Go to...
I don't know how to delete macros I no longer need, page 188.

Macros

Go to...
My macro won't run in the active workbook, page 182.

Go to...
My macro doesn't work at all, page 184.

Quick fix

1. To create a keyboard shortcut for your macro, point to Macro on the Tools menu, click Macros, and then click the Options button.

2. In the Options dialog box, type a letter (that you will press in conjunction with the Ctrl key) to run your macro.

3. Click OK to close the dialog box.

Go to...
I made an error while recording my macro, page 186.

Quick fix

Computer viruses can be stored in macros, and if you enable a macro in a worksheet that someone sent you via e-mail or on a disk, you risk infecting your computer. Run your virus scan software on any downloaded files, and if they are not infected, go ahead and enable macros when you open the workbook.

If your solution isn't here
Check these related chapters:
   Printing, page 234
   Workspace customization, page 304
Or see the general troubleshooting tips on page xv.

My macro won't run in the active workbook

Source of the problem

You recorded a macro but when you try to invoke it in your current workbook, nothing happens. If you assigned a keyboard shortcut to your macro, pressing the key sequence doesn't work. If you go to the Tools menu and click Macros, the macro isn't listed, so you can't even try to run it that way. What's going on?

The cause of your dilemma is most likely that you are not working in the workbook in which you created the macro. When you create a macro, you specify a storage location for it—and the default location is This Workbook, which means the one you're working in when you create the macro. Personal Macro Workbook is the location that you want to use if the macro you're recording should be available to all workbooks. The simplest method of fixing the problem requires rerecording the macro and opting to save the new version to the Personal Macro Workbook. Yes, that sounds like a lot of work, especially if your macro is a long one, encompassing a lot of steps. Think of it this way, though—you'll know where to store your macros in the future, and you'll only have to rerecord a macro for this purpose once!

How to fix it

1. In any open workbook (it doesn't matter which one, because you'll be storing the macro in the Personal Macro Workbook), point to Macro on the Tools menu, and then click Record New Macro.

2. In the Macro Name box of the Record Macro dialog box, type a name for your macro, replacing the default generic name (such as Macro1).

3. Type a keyboard letter in the Shortcut Key box if you want to be able to invoke your macro by pressing a key combination. (Keep in mind that you must type a letter, not another character such as a ? or ~, in the Shortcut Key box.)

Tip

So what's this Personal Macro Workbook? It's a workbook that opens as soon as you elect to store a macro in it during the current Excel session. It isn't available from the Window menu, so is essentially invisible unless you click Unhide on the Window menu and then click OK to unhide the workbook file (called Personal.xls by default). If you close this workbook before closing Excel, make sure you save any changes to it; otherwise the macros you recorded in the current Excel session will be lost! If you click Unhide and don't see Personal.xls listed (or if the Unhide command is unavailable on the Window menu), no macros were saved to the Personal Macro Workbook in your current Excel session.

4. Click Personal Macro Workbook in the Store Macro In drop-down list. ▶

5. Type a description to elaborate on the macro's purpose.

6. Click OK, and begin recording your macro.

7. When you have finished recording your macro, click the floating Stop Recording button. Be sure to save changes to the Personal Macro Workbook if you either close the Personal.xls workbook or exit Excel.

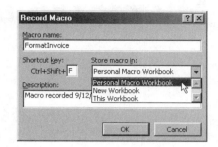

If you really don't want to rerecord...

Feeling adventurous? You can copy your existing macro—you know, the one you stored in a specific workbook and not in the Personal Macro workbook. Open the Microsoft Visual Basic editor and copy the macro from the open workbook into the Personal Macro Workbook. The macro will now be available in both the current workbook and in all other workbooks because it's stored in the Personal Macro Workbook.

In the workbook containing the macro you want to copy, point to Macro on the Tools menu, and then click Macros. (Make sure Personal.xls is open, even if it's hidden.) Click the macro in the Macro Name list, and then click the Edit button to display the Microsoft Visual Basic editor window. ▶

On the View menu, click Project Explorer to make sure that the Project panel is visible. With your

Tip

Many Ctrl+[letter] combinations are used by application commands. To expand the possibilities when you create a keyboard shortcut for a macro, add the Shift key to the key combination, giving yourself 26 new keyboard shortcuts to choose from.

The macro will be copied to the Personal Macro Workbook.

This macro is to be copied.

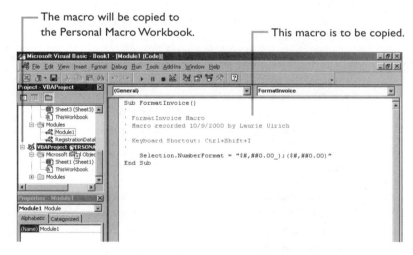

macro's program code visible, look in the Project panel for the module that represents the macro you want to copy. If necessary, select the module, and drag it to VBAProject Personal.xls. Close the Microsoft Visual Basic editor window by clicking the Close button in the upper right corner. Back in your open workbook, point to Macro on the Tools menu, and click Macros. In the Macro Name list of the Macro dialog box, verify that your macro now appears listed with PERSONAL.XLS! in front of it, indicating that a copy of your macro is stored in that workbook. From now on, your macro will run in any workbook.

My macro doesn't work at all

Source of the problem

Unlike a macro that works in only one worksheet (see "My macro won't run in the active workbook" on page 182), a macro that won't run at all probably needs to be edited or rerecorded. When you run a macro that doesn't work, either nothing happens or you get an error message.

The causes of this problem with your macro include the following:

- The macro contains procedures that are in conflict with the current circumstances when you go to run it. For example, a macro that involves printing won't work if your computer can no longer access a printer, and a macro that hides a column will stop if the column is already hidden. Such a conflict results in an error message that alerts you to the problem the macro has encountered.

- The macro doesn't really exist. Perhaps you created and stored it in one workbook, and now that workbook is gone (or was never saved at all). If this is the problem, the macro won't be in the Macros dialog box list, and if you try to invoke it using a keyboard shortcut, nothing happens.

- The macro has been deleted by you (and you forgot) or by another user.

- The macro is stored in a workbook that you haven't opened, so you can't find it. If you want the macro to be available to all workbooks, you should store the macro in the Personal Macro Workbook. You can store an existing macro in this workbook by opening the workbook where the macro is currently located, and then copying the macro to the Personal Macro Workbook. (See "My macro won't run in the active workbook" on page 182.)

If you aren't sure of the cause, the quickest way to be able to perform whatever tasks the macro automated is to rerecord the macro. If the macro is gone, you can reuse the macro name and shortcut with no problem. If it still exists but has some error in it, you can replace the malfunctioning macro with the new one, and in doing so, make it possible to reuse the keyboard shortcut.

Before you go to the trouble, however, find out if the macro exists anywhere—in the Personal Macro Workbook or in any of your other saved workbooks.

Tip

Some macros work only partially—they do some of the things intended and then stop. In this case, rerecording the macro is your best bet. Unless you're a Microsoft Visual Basic programmer (or at least have some knowledge of Visual Basic), you'll spend more time editing the macro's programming code than you would recording it again.

Tip

When you exit Excel after you copy or store a macro in the Personal Macro Workbook, you'll be asked if you want to save changes to the Personal Macro Workbook. Click Yes. If you click No, the macros you just copied to or stored in the Personal Macro Workbook will be lost.

How to fix it

To determine if the macro is still on your computer, follow these steps:

1. Open all the workbooks in which you might have created (and also stored) the macro you're looking for.

2. In any one of them, point to Macro on the Tools menu, and then click Macros.

3. If necessary, click All Open Workbooks in the Macros In drop-down list. ▶

4. Select the macro in the Macro Name list, and click the Run button. The macro will likely run fine.

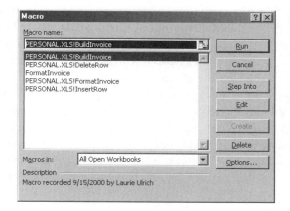

Tip

If you have an idea of when you recorded the macro, view the list of your workbooks by the date they were created. In Details view in Windows Explorer or My Computer, open the folder in which you save your workbooks, and in the right pane, click the Modified heading at the top of the Modified column. (Click Details on the View menu if you can't see a Modified column.) Find workbooks with dates around the time you think you created the macro. Open these workbooks when you begin your search for the missing macro.

If your macro does exist, and you need to copy it to the Personal Macro Workbook so you can run it from any worksheet, see "My macro won't run in the active workbook," on page 182.

If your macro exists, and you can't make it work in the worksheet it was stored in, you can edit the macro if you know Visual Basic. Assuming you just said "Yeah, right," simply rerecord your macro by following these steps:

1. In any workbook, point to Macros on the Tools menu, and then click Record New Macro.

2. In the Macro Name box, type the name of the macro you want to replace. If you want, type a letter in the Shortcut Key box. (Press Shift while typing the letter to expand your keyboard shortcut options.) You can then simultaneously press this letter key and Ctrl (and Shift, if you used that too) to run the macro.

3. In the Store Macro In drop list, select Personal Macro Workbook so that the macro can be run from any worksheet.

4. If you want, type a description in the Description box, and then click OK. Click Yes when the prompt appears asking if you want to replace the existing macro with the same name.

5. Record your macro, and then click the floating Stop Recording button when you are finished.

I made an error while recording my macro

Source of the problem

If you made an error while recording your macro, the problem will make its presence known either as you're recording the macro or the first time you try to run the macro (and something undesirable happens). With the former, after you smack yourself in the forehead, you're faced with the decision—do I continue recording and then edit the macro later, or do I click Stop Recording now and start over? Well, that depends on the nature of the error. If the error is fundamental—you opened the wrong file, or you set up the worksheet with an entirely inappropriate layout—it's probably best to rerecord the macro, reusing the name and keyboard shortcut. (See "My macro doesn't work at all" on page 184.) But perhaps the error is relatively minor. Did you misspell something when you inserted text? Did you enter the wrong number in a cell? Did you apply formatting and choose the wrong font or font size? These errors are all easy to edit, even if you're not a Visual Basic programmer, so you can probably fix the mistakes yourself by editing your macro.

If you've discovered the error after completing the macro-creation process, simple errors are still easy to fix.

How to fix it

1. Open the workbook in which your macro is stored. (If it's stored in the Personal Macro Workbook, open any workbook.)

2. If you stored the macro in the Personal Macro Workbook, click Unhide on the Window menu, and then click Personal.xls in the Unhide dialog box. Click OK to unhide the workbook. (You can't edit a macro that's stored in a hidden workbook.)

3. On the Tools menu, point to Macro, and then click Macros.

4. In the Macro dialog box, click the macro you want to edit, and then click the Edit button to display the Microsoft Visual Basic editor window.

> **Tip**
> Visual Basic might not seem so basic if you're not familiar with it. It's a simple programming language that uses standard instructions to complete a series of tasks. You can learn more about it by reading *Microsoft Visual Basic Professional 6.0 Step by Step*, from Microsoft Press.

5. In the Microsoft Visual Basic editor window, read the code in the Module window. ▶

6. The text or numbers you've typed appear in quotes. Edit them by positioning your insertion point in the text and typing a correction using the Backspace and Delete keys as needed. To correct formatting, find the format setting, and change the font, size, alignment, color, or other format. Type the new format (such as Bold) after the equal sign; if the original setting was in quotes, keep the quotes intact.

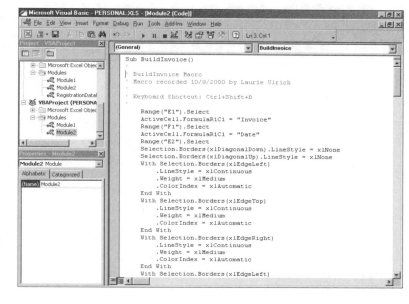

7. When you've completed your edits, press Ctrl+S to save the open macro.

8. Click the Close button at the right side of the title bar to return to Excel.

You'll want to test your macro right away to make sure your edits worked. If they didn't, go back and re-edit, repeating steps 3 through 8. If you're unable to solve the problem, you'll want to rerecord the macro from scratch. If the problem isn't resolved after two attempts at editing, it will take less time to start over than to keep editing, especially if you're unfamiliar with Visual Basic.

An ounce of prevention is worth a pound of rerecording

To avoid macro errors in the future, keep the following in mind as you record your macros:

- Planning is key. Write down the macro's tasks in the order they should be recorded. The order in which they're recorded is the order in which they'll be done when you run the macro.

- The macro recorder is recording *everything* you're doing, including making erroneous selections from menus, inserting typos that you backspace through and type again, creating formulas that don't work and have to be redone, moving content from cell to cell, and selecting elements with your mouse. Do a test run before you start recording so that you keep the mistakes (even those that you fix and that don't mess up the macro's performance) to a minimum.

- The Description box in the Record Macro dialog box is very handy, especially if others will be using your macros. The contents of that box will appear in the Visual Basic editing window and can help to clarify what your macro is supposed to do, long after you might have forgotten.

I don't know how to delete macros I no longer need

Source of the problem

There's no harm in keeping macros around after they're no longer useful, unless you want to reuse the keyboard short-cut assigned to one, or you are recording a similar macro and want to reuse the name or use one like it, or you're just very tidy and like to throw things away when you no longer need them. What makes a macro obsolete? Maybe it was used for a particular set of circumstances, and those circumstances no longer exist. Perhaps you found a better way to do something, and the macro that automated the old way is no longer useful. Whatever the reason, macros are simple to delete.

How to fix it

1. If the macro you want to delete is stored in one of your workbooks, open that workbook. If the macro is stored in the Personal Macro Workbook, click Unhide on the Window menu, make sure Personal.xls is selected in the Unhide dialog box, and then click OK.

2. On the Tools menu, point to Macro, and then click Macros.

3. In the Macro dialog box, click All Open Work-books in the Macros In drop-down list. ▶

4. Click the macro you want to delete in the Macro Name list.

5. Click the Delete button. A prompt appears, asking you to confirm your intention to delete the macro. This is your chance to change your mind. If you really want to delete the macro, click Yes; if you decide you don't want to delete it, click No. ▶

> **Tip**
> Deleting macros might be *too* simple. Although the deletion process results in a prompt that you must respond to be-fore the deletion occurs, many users quickly click OK to con-firm prompts, without reading their messages. Be sure you're deleting the right macro, not the one above or below it in the Macro Name list!

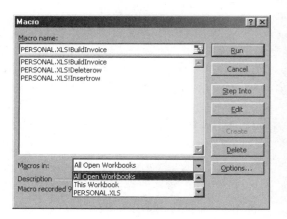

When you don't know where it's been

Sometimes you might want to delete macros that other people have created, just to make the workbook where the macros were stored safe to view and use. Why? Macros can contain viruses, which is why Excel might prompt you before it opens a worksheet containing macros, asking if you want to enable those macros when the file is opened. Choosing to disable them will prevent any infected macro from giving your computer a virus; choosing to enable them puts your computer at risk if you don't have virus protection software installed.

If someone has sent you a workbook, always scan it before you open it, using your virus protection software. This is a good rule of thumb even if you don't know if the workbook contains macros in the first place. If you don't have virus protection software, get some. Having the software, however, doesn't make you immune to viruses—new ones are being developed daily, so your virus protection software might not have the "cure" for the latest virus you might have caught.

Of course, you can open the file, choose to disable the macros, and then delete the macros from the file. This might result in limiting the workbook's functionality, especially if the macros are important to the way the author intended you to use the worksheets and their data. Deleting the macros won't limit your ability to view, edit, and work with the data, however.

Tip

If someone you don't know sends you a workbook and you didn't ask for it, don't even open it. Regardless of the sender, always scan any attachments to e-mail messages, and always scan any files you download from the Internet.

Tip

Once a macro is gone, it's really gone. You can't undo the deletion of a macro, so be very sure you want to delete it before you click Yes to confirm the deletion. If the macro was in the Personal Macro Workbook, you can't get the macro back, even by saying No to saving changes to the Personal Macro Workbook when you exit Excel—the deletion is permanent.

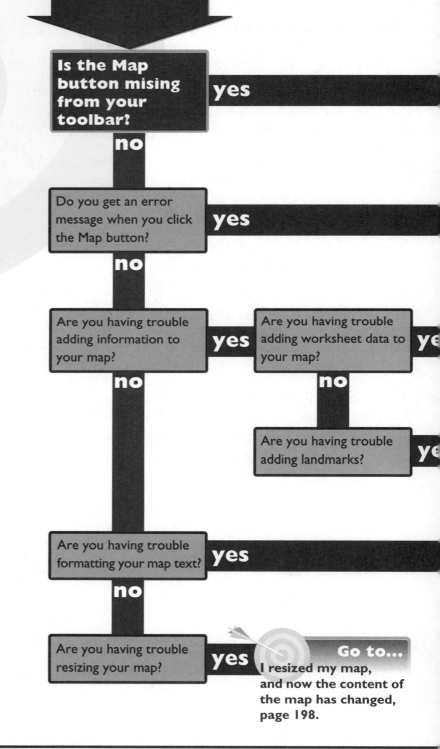

Is the Map button mising from your toolbar?

yes

no

Do you get an error message when you click the Map button?

yes

no

Are you having trouble adding information to your map?

yes

Are you having trouble adding worksheet data to your map?

ye

no

no

Are you having trouble adding landmarks?

ye

Are you having trouble formatting your map text?

yes

no

Are you having trouble resizing your map?

yes

Go to...
I resized my map, and now the content of the map has changed, page 198.

Maps

Quick fix

1. On the Tools menu, click Customize.

2. On the Commands tab, click Insert in the Categories list.

3. In the Commands list, select Map, and drag the command to the toolbar you want, depositing the command wherever you want the button to be.

4. Click Close when you are finished.

Quick fix

Even if you have the Map button on your toolbar, it is possible that Microsoft Map is not installed on your computer. If this is the case, you will receive an error message accompanied by a prompt telling you to insert the Microsoft Office CD-ROM. Follow the installation instructions that appear on your screen.

Go to...

I'm not sure how to get data from my worksheet to appear on a map, page 192.

Go to...

I don't know how to add roads and cities to my map, page 194.

Go to...

My map labels are hard to read, page 196.

If your solution isn't here

Check these related chapters:

Drawing shapes and lines, page 66

Formatting text, page 124

Or see the general troubleshooting tips on page xv.

I'm not sure how to get data from my worksheet to appear on a map

Source of the problem

The mapping capabilities of Excel come from a program called Microsoft Map that runs within the Excel application. Microsoft Map allows you to select geographic names within your worksheet and plot them on a map. (Note they must be appropriate abbreviations, such as two-character states, or correctly spelled city, state, or country names.) These maps can accompany your data to provide additional information or a geographi-

cal subtext for the information that is in your worksheet. ▶

If you can't get your information to appear in the map, the problem is most probably due to misspellings, incorrect abbreviations, or the inclusion of non-geographic information in the selected range of cells. The solution to the problem, therefore, is to make sure that your cell content is correct, and that you are selecting a range of cells

that contains geographic information that Microsoft Map can digest and turn into plotted locations on a map.

How to fix it

If you're having trouble creating a map based on data in your worksheet, follow these steps:

1. Select a range of cells that contain city names, state names, or country names. (If the cells contain abbreviations, make sure they're the correct ones, or Microsoft Map won't be able to plot them.)

Tip

Microsoft Map is being phased out of the Office suite and will not be included in versions later than Office 2000. In the meantime, some of the features in the versions of Microsoft Map that come with Office 97 and 2000 might not run properly. The features documented in this chapter, however, work as they are described.

2. Click the Map button on the Standard toolbar, and notice that your mouse pointer becomes a crosshair.

3. Drag to draw a rectangle, estimating the size of your map. When you release the mouse button, a map appears, containing the cities, states, or countries you selected in your worksheet. A dialog box might precede the appearance of the map, asking you to confirm which map you want to use, especially if the geographic locations in your worksheet can appear on more than one of the Map program's stored maps. ▶

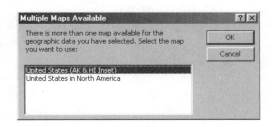

If you've already created a map and want to add your data to it, follow these steps:

1. Double-click the map in your worksheet to make the map the active object on-screen and to display the Microsoft Map program toolbar.

2. On the Insert menu, click Data. When the Microsoft Map dialog box appears, select the range of cells that contains your geographic information.

3. With the range displayed in the dialog box, click OK to plot the geographic locations listed in the selected cells on your map.

A legend in your own map

As soon as your map forms, or as soon as you plot data from your worksheet in it, a legend appears, indicating what data is plotted. If the legend doesn't offer any important information, you can delete it by selecting it and pressing Delete. You can also edit it. Right-click the legend, and click Edit on the shortcut menu. You can change the legend title and subtitle, and on the Value Shading Options tab, you can change the color of the plotted regions (cities, states, or countries) on your map.

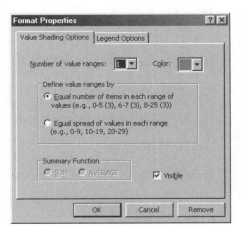

Click OK to apply the changes to your legend, your map, or both. ▶

I don't know how to add roads and cities to my map

Source of the problem

A map with colored regions on it, indicating cities, states, or countries, isn't very compelling if it doesn't contain other information to make the map relevant to the data in the worksheet. For example, if your worksheet shows sales data for a series of U.S. states, having major roads and cities on that map makes the map more meaningful to people viewing it. Also, because more populated areas tend to have more roads and more cities (and in fact, only fairly large cities make it into the Map program's geographic database), including them in the map also shows which areas are more active than others. ▶

In addition to plotting the locations included on your worksheet, it's easy to add streets, roads, and other cities to your map as well. You can add them to the entire map, or to specific regions.

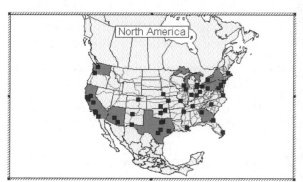

How to fix it

1. Double-click your map to activate the Microsoft Map program tools.

2. On the Map menu, click Features.

3. In the Map Features dialog box, scroll through the list of locations and features (such as highways or lakes). In the list, select the check box for each feature you want to add. ▶

4. If you want to apply a custom color or symbol to the features you add, click the Custom option, and then choose a color or symbol, depending on the corresponding map feature. (Colors apply to roads and regions; symbols apply to cities.)

5. Click OK to plot the features you selected on the map.

Able to label

You can label the roads, states, and cities on your map to add more information and relevance to the map. In your active map, click the Map Labels button on the toolbar. In the Map Labels dialog box, click the Map Feature To Label arrow to display a drop-down list of the features (such as a country's major lakes, highways, or cities) that you can label. After selecting the feature you want to label, click OK, and then move your mouse pointer (which appears as a crosshair) over the map. As you hover over a feature on your map, the label for that feature appears. Click once to add the label to the map. Keep moving the mouse pointer over the surface of the map. As you move over other objects of the type you have selected for labeling, those labels will appear. Click once more to add the corresponding label for each new object. ▶

Repeat these steps to add labels to additional features. (If you want to add a label for a feature that isn't included in the Microsoft Map program, add a pushpin to your map and enter your own label. See "My map labels are hard to read" on page 196.)

Tip

If you want to make more features available, click the Add button in the Map Features dialog box. You can add such features as small cities (in addition to the major cities listed by default) and airports to the list of plotted objects on your map.

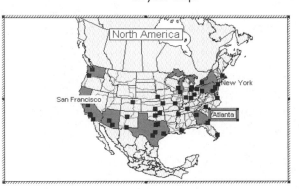

Tip

In congested areas of most countries, there will be several cities you could label, with roads leading between them. Don't try to label all of them, or your labels will overlap and visually cancel each other out because your map will become too "busy." Stick to labeling major places that are directly relevant to your worksheet, and label only those roads and airports that people who view the map will use or recognize.

My map labels are hard to read

Source of the problem

By default, map labels appear in small, black text. Major geographic divisions are labeled with all capital letters; smaller items, such as cities and lakes, are labeled with the first letter of each word capitalized. This is fine unless you've fancied up the map by applying a different background color to your plotted regions, or you have labeled areas or geographic features that are physically close to each other. ▶

If some of your labels are hard to read, you can format them by changing the font, size, and color so that they stand out against the other map labels and objects.

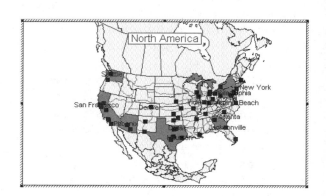

How to fix it

1. Right-click the label you want to reformat. On the shortcut menu, click Format Font.

2. In the Font dialog box, reset any of the font properties you want to change, such as the font style, size, or color.

3. Click OK to apply the formats. ▶

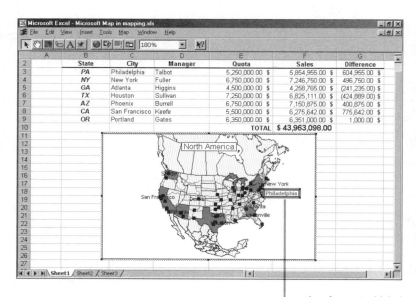

A reformatted label stands out better.

4. Repeat steps 1 through 3 for any other labels that need reformatting. When all of the illegible labels are reformatted, the map should look better, with important items standing out.

An uncharted desert isle

What if you want to plot and label places that Microsoft Map doesn't recognize? You can add pushpins to your map and type whatever label you want for each of them. This makes it easy to plot towns, cities, office locations, and points of interest (parks, landmarks, historically significant places), making your map truly relevant to your worksheet data and interesting to look at.

To add a pushpin to your map, double-click the map, and then click the Custom Pin Map button on the toolbar. When the Custom Pin Map dialog box appears, type a name for the label in the Type A Name For The New Custom Pin Map You Want To Create box, and then click OK. When your mouse pointer turns into a pushpin symbol, point to the spot on the map where you want to insert the pushpin and label, and click to insert the pin. Next to the pushpin, type a label for the pushpin directly on your map, and then press Enter. ▶

Continue clicking places on your map to add other pushpins, and type a label for each pin after you have added it. When you've finished placing pushpins in your map, click the Select Objects arrow on the toolbar to return the pointer to its regular shape.

Tip
No amount of formatting can make a map legible if it has too many labels. Before you increase the font size or make your labels a more dynamic color, consider thinning your labels so that only key items are labeled, and so that you aren't labeling things that are too close together. There is no formatting that will make overlapping labels legible!

┌ Add a pushpin to your map to
  mark relevant points of interest.

Tip
You can move the pushpin labels you created with the Add Text button so that the labels don't overlap each other or other map features, such as roads and regional labels. Click the pushpin label you want to move. A box forms around the label. Point to the box, and when the mouse pointer turns into a four-headed arrow, drag the label to a new position near the pushpin.

I resized my map, and now the content of the map has changed

Source of the problem

Whether you create a map by selecting one of Microsoft Map's large regional maps, or the program selects one for you based on selected geographical names in your worksheet, one country or group of countries is the focal point of the map. If you attempt to resize the map to make it larger, however, the focal point changes. The entire map becomes larger, and other regions that were on the periphery of the map are now included. What was the center of the map is no longer in the middle of the map object, and you can't tell which country or region is the map's focus. For example, in a map of North America that focuses mainly on the United States, resizing the map will bring in northern parts of Canada and most of Mexico, and the U.S. portion of the map looks less significant than it did when the map was its original size. ▶

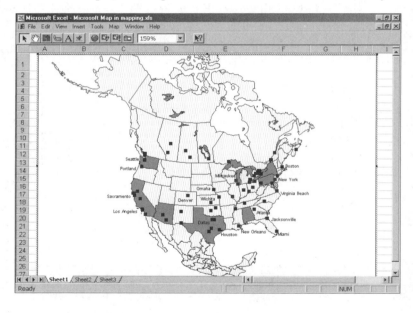

If the reason you are resizing the map is to enlarge the area that is the focus of the map—the parts you've added features and labels to, the areas that are plotted based on data from your worksheet—you need to resize it when you're not in the Microsoft Map program. Resizing the map as an object in the Excel worksheet will increase the size of the area in the center of the map without resizing the whole map so that it displays items from its outer reaches.

How to fix it

1. Make sure the map is not active by clicking any cell in the worksheet. If the Microsoft Map toolbars were displayed, they are now replaced by Excel's toolbars.

2. Click the map once to select it. Be sure not to double-click it, as that will reactivate both the map and the Map program tools.

3. Point to a corner handle, and when your mouse pointer turns to a two-headed arrow, drag outward to increase the size of the map. (Use the corner handle to simultaneously resize the map both horizontally and vertically, retaining the map's current proportions.) ▶

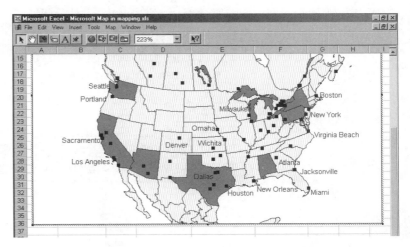

But can you refold the map?

Big paper maps fold in about fifty different directions, causing most people to wad them up and throw them in the back seat of their car. Luckily, the map in your Excel worksheet can be tucked nicely alongside your data or placed on a worksheet all by itself. It can be grouped with surrounding related graphic content. You can also add callouts that point to places on the map (a handy alternative to using map labels), and add other AutoShapes, text boxes, lines, and arrows on top of and alongside the map. ▶

Once you've positioned and formatted these elements, you can group them with the map so that they can't be separated. To group your map with other graphic objects, click the map once, and Hold down the Shift key as you click the other graphic objects that you want to group with the map. When they're all selected (handles appear around each item), click the Draw button on the Drawing toolbar, and then click Group on the menu that appears.

Tip
Once you resize the map, you might need to move it so that it isn't covering up any part of your worksheet data. To move it, point to the map, and when your mouse pointer becomes a four-headed arrow, drag the map to a new position.

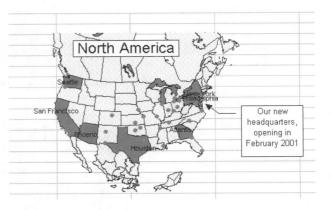

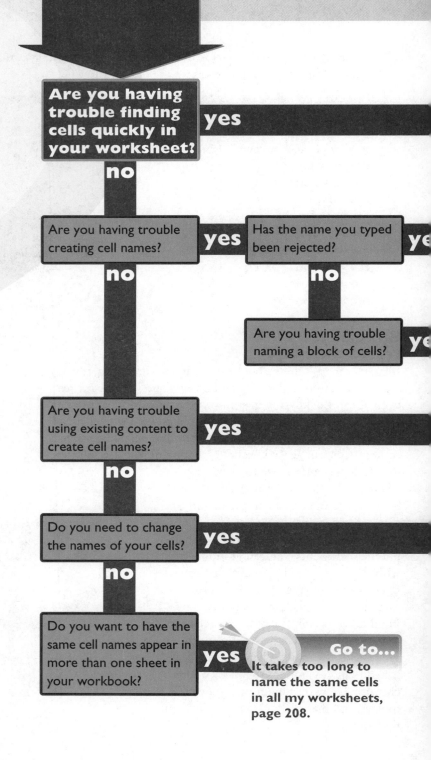

Are you having trouble finding cells quickly in your worksheet?

yes

no

Are you having trouble creating cell names?

yes

Has the name you typed been rejected?

ye

no

Are you having trouble naming a block of cells?

ye

Are you having trouble using existing content to create cell names?

yes

no

Do you need to change the names of your cells?

yes

no

Do you want to have the same cell names appear in more than one sheet in your workbook?

yes

Go to...

It takes too long to name the same cells in all my worksheets, page 208.

Naming cells

Go to...
It's taking too long to find cells in my worksheet, page 202.

Quick fix
Excel won't accept numbers, punctuation, or spaces in cell names. For example, the name Total Sales would be rejected, but Total_Sales would be accepted.

Go to...
I'm not sure how to apply a name to a range of cells, page 204.

Go to...
I don't know how to turn column and row headings into names, page 206.

Quick fix
To change the name of a cell, click the cell, and then click the name in the Name box. Type a new name and press Enter. To remove a name and go back to a simple cell address, select the cell or cells containing the name, point to Name on the Insert menu, click Define, select the name in the Define Name dialog box, click Delete, and then click OK.

If your solution isn't here
Check these related chapters:
Outlining, page 210
PivotTables, page 220
Searching for data, page 256
Or see the general troubleshooting tips on page xv.

It's taking too long to find cells in my worksheet

Source of the problem

You've been searching for a particular worksheet entry, be it a number or text, by searching manually—looking through the worksheet for the missing content—or by clicking Find on the Edit menu and entering search criteria. Both methods, especially the first one, are time consuming, and with the latter approach, if you set up the Find criteria incorrectly, you might not find what you're looking for after all. There has to be a faster, more efficient way of finding worksheet content, right? Right, there is.

In Excel, you can name cells in your worksheet, giving them logical names that you can use to look for them and to refer to them in formulas. If, for example, you have a number in the worksheet that's the total sales for all of your company's divisions, you can call it DivSalesTotal or something similar, and no longer will you have to remember that the total is in cell G10. You can name the totals for each division as well, giving them names such as PhilaSales or AtlantaTotal. These names are what you call these cells in your mind, being much more representative of the actual content of the cell than referring to them by cell address or by having to remember which part of the worksheet they're stored in.

So you can name cells. How does that help you find them? As long as you've appropriately named cells, you can use the Name box to find the named cells you need to locate. All you have to do is click a cell name in the Name box drop-down list. ▶

Excel finds and selects the cell that matches the name you clicked.

> **Tip**
> Cell names must start with a letter and cannot contain spaces or any punctuation, including dashes, slashes, or apostrophes.

Use the Name box to find cells in your worksheet.

To use the Name box feature to find cells, you must go through your worksheet and name important cells—cells you have looked for or think you'll need to look for in the future. This can be helpful not only for you, but also for others who use your worksheet and might not be as familiar with its layout as you are.

How to fix it

1. Click the cell that you want to name.

2. In the Name box, click the cell address once. The address becomes highlighted and moves to the left side of the box.

3. Type the name you want to give the cell.

4. Press Enter to confirm the name. If you click the named cell again, you'll see the name you typed in the Name box.

A cell by any other name...

You're not stuck with the names you give to cells. If you spell something wrong, or later think of a better name or more appropriate abbreviation for a cell name, you can edit the names. You can also delete cell names if you've named the wrong cell or simply don't want a particular cell to be named anymore. To rename a cell, click the cell, and then click the current name for that cell in the Name box once. When the name becomes highlighted, type the new name over it. Press Enter to confirm the new name.

Oddly, the old name remains in place, but if you click the Name box drop-down arrow, you'll see the new name in the list. So now you have to delete the old name so that only the new name points to the cell. On the Insert menu, point to Name, and then click Define. In the Names In Workbook list in the Define Name dialog box, scroll as needed to find the name you want to get rid of, and click it to select it. ▶

Click the Delete button, and then click OK to close the Define Name dialog box.

Tip

If you need to create the illusion of a space within your cell name, use an underscore. TotalSales looks more polished to some people as Total_Sales, and is more legible in the Name box list.

Tip

You can always keep both names for the cell rather than deleting the old one in favor of the new. In fact, it can be helpful to give certain cells more than one name to account for all the ways different users might want to refer to them.

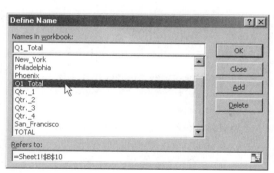

I'm not sure how to apply a name to a range of cells

Source of the problem

Some individual cells in your worksheet are happily named, feeling all puffed up because they have real names, not just cell addresses.

Other cells are jealous. Now you want to name cell ranges, creating groups of cells, both contiguous and noncontiguous, with names like Regional_Totals and List_of_Departments. There's no stopping you now!

So how do you name a range? You can use the same technique you would employ to name a single cell (by using the Name box—see "It's taking too long to find cells in my worksheet" on page 202), and you can also use the Define command and the Define Name dialog box. You need to know both techniques because there are benefits to each, and you might find situations that make one preferable to the other. One requires you to select the range before you start the naming process, the other allows you to specify the range after you've created the name.

see "It's taking too long to find cells in my worksheet" on page 202

> **Tip**
> Naming ranges is a great way to turn your worksheet into a searchable database. Do you currently store a list of employees and keep that list in order by department? You can apply a name to the range of cells that lists all the employees in a given department, and name the range using the department name. Do you need to see all the people in the Sales department? Choose Sales_Dept_Staff from the Name box list, and the information about people in that department is selected and ready to be viewed, copied to a worksheet, or printed out.

How to fix it

To name a range of cells using the Name box, follow these steps:

1. Select the range of cells that you want to name. You can select noncontiguous cells by holding down the Ctrl key as you drag through or click cells anywhere in your worksheet.

2. Click the Name box once. Don't worry that only one cell address—the first cell in the selected range—appears. It doesn't mean that you're naming only that cell. ▶

Replace this address by typing a new name for the selected range.

3. Type the name you want to apply to the selected range.

4. Press Enter to confirm the name.

5. Click the Name box drop-down list, and then select the name you just created—the range of cells is instantly highlighted.

To name a range of cells using the Define command, follow these steps:

1. In the worksheet containing the range you want to name, point to Name on the Insert menu, and then click Define.

2. In the Names In Workbook text box of the Define Name dialog box, type the name you want to give to the range of cells.

3. Click the Collapse button at the end of the Refers To box to collapse the dialog box so that you can see the range that you want to name.

4. Drag through the range of cells you want to name. ▶

5. Click the Expand button to return the dialog box to full size. The range of cells you selected appears in the Refers To box and includes the sheet name.

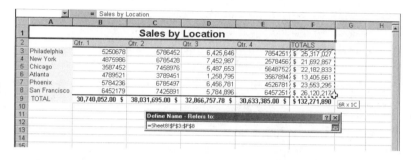

6. Click OK to define the name and close the dialog box.

Tip

You don't have to be creating a cell or range name in order to use the Define Name dialog box. You can use it to edit existing names, review the cells and ranges to which the names apply, and delete obsolete names or names you don't want to give to cells or ranges anymore.

I don't know how to turn column and row labels into names

Source of the problem

You've taken the time to build your worksheet with column and row labels that clearly identify your worksheet content, and you wish you could somehow use those labels to create names for cells in your worksheet. It would be a big pain and a waste of time to go in and select each of the important cells or ranges in a worksheet and apply names to them individually. What's more, it would make it so much easier to use the worksheet names if they were the same as the labels that already exist. Using labels for names would help you and others who use the worksheet to find data and to use the names in formulas.

Instead of creating names for individual cells, let Excel's Create Names feature build a series of names for the cells in your worksheet based on the column and row labels you already have.

Tip

Did I say "use the names in formulas"? You bet I did. Rather than referring to cells by their cell addresses when using them in a formula, type the cell name, as in =SUM(Regional_Totals), where Regional_Totals is a column of numbers in a named range. If you plan to use names in formulas, keep them simple so that you can type them without risk of typos. Using names in formulas also helps other users of the worksheet decipher your formulas, instantly knowing what the calculation does by reading the formula itself.

How to fix it

1. Select the section of your worksheet that contains the column and row labels you want to use, plus the data to which they refer.

2. On the Insert menu, point to Name, and then click Create.

3. In the Create Names dialog box, select the column and row check boxes that match the location of your labels. For example, if your labels appear in the worksheet both across the top and down the left side, select the Top Row and Left Column check boxes. ▶

A range with labels is selected.

	A	B	C	D	E	F
1			Sales by Location			
2		Qtr. 1	Qtr. 2	Qtr. 3	Qtr. 4	TOTALS
3	Philadelphia	5250678	5786452	6,425,646	7854251	$ 25,317,027
4	New York	4875986	6785428	7,452,987	2578456	$ 21,692,857
5	Chicago	3587452	7458976	5,487,653	5648752	$ 22,182,833
6	Atlanta	4789521		,795	3567894	$ 13,405,661
7	Phoenix	5784236		,781	4526781	$ 23,553,295
8	San Francisco	6452179		,896	6457251	$ 26,120,217
9	TOTAL	30,740,052.00 $	38		30,633,385.00 $	$ 132,271,890

Create Names

Create names in
- ☑ Top row
- ☑ Left column
- ☐ Bottom row
- ☐ Right column

[OK] [Cancel]

4. Click OK. When you open the Name box drop-down list, you'll see your column and row labels listed.

To use the label-based names in formulas or to quickly access and select a range of cells, select the name from the list. When you select, for example, the name based on the fourth label in the left column, the cell adjacent to that label will be selected. ▶

Atlanta ▾	=	4789521				
	A	B	C	D	E	F	G
1			**Sales by Location**				
2		Qtr. 1	Qtr. 2	Qtr. 3	Qtr. 4	TOTALS	
3	Philadelphia	5250678	5786452	6,425,646	7854251	$ 25,317,027	
4	New York	4875986	6785428	7,452,987	2578456	$ 21,692,857	
5	Chicago	3587452	7458976	5,487,653	5648752	$ 22,182,833	
6	Atlanta	4789521	3789451	1,258,795	3567894	$ 13,405,661	
7	Phoenix	5784236	6785497	6,456,781	4526781	$ 23,553,295	
8	San Francisco	6452179	7425891	5,784,896	6457251	$ 26,120,217	
9	TOTAL	30,740,052.00 $	38,031,695.00 $	32,866,757.78 $	30,633,385.00 $	$ 132,271,890	
10							
11							

Tip

The rules for acceptable cell and range names still apply, even when you use existing column and row labels to create them. Your names can't start with a number, you can't use spaces, and you can't use punctuation such as dashes and slashes. If, however, your labels contain any of these verboten elements, Excel will adjust the names accordingly by adding underscores in front of names that start with a number and in between words separated by spaces.

Tip

When you move a named cell or range from one place to another on a worksheet, or to another worksheet within the same workbook, the address changes to point to the cell or range in its new location. If, however, you cut or copy a named cell to a new workbook, or if you copy a named cell or range within the same workbook, the name for the pasted cell or range will have to be recreated in the cell's or range's new home.

Give us their names

If you open someone else's worksheet and click the Name box drop-down list to see if there are any named cells or ranges, you won't be able to tell which cells or ranges the names refer to without selecting them, one by one.

Instead of going on such a wild goose chase, why not create a list of the workbook's names and the cells and ranges to which they apply? It'll save you opening the Define Name dialog box (in case you were thinking that was a convenient alternative), because there you have to click the names and view the Refers To information, plus shrink or move the dialog box aside to see the worksheet. No, it's much better to have a list of all the names and their cells in one place. You can squirrel the list away on a sheet that will never be printed, or hide the column it's in if you don't want it to be visible until you need to refer to it.

Sold? Well, OK then. Click the cell at the beginning of the blank range where you want to stash the name list. Keep in mind that the list will occupy two cells per name: one for the name itself, and one for the cell or range to which it refers. On the Insert menu, point to Name, and then click Paste. In the Paste Name dialog box, click the Paste List button. Voilà—the list appears in your worksheet.

Tip

If you move your named cells or ranges, the list you pasted with the Paste List feature won't change automatically. You'll have to delete the list and paste it again to reflect the named cells' or ranges' new locations.

It takes too long to name the same cells in all my worksheets

Source of the problem

Some workbooks contain two or more worksheets that have the same exact layout. While the data might vary from sheet to sheet, the column and row labels are the same, and the worksheet is set up in the same cells on all of the sheets. You might have even created the worksheets at the same time by grouping them before entering the common content.

If you're naming cells in these sheets, it can seem like a waste of time to go into each sheet and create names for the cells. In fact, you might have already spent a great deal of time doing just that, leading you to this very page in this book. Your belief that there has to be a better way is justified. There should be, and there is.

In Excel, you can create 3-D cell references, which means that names are created for cells in multiple worksheets at the same time. You need to create the names only once, but all the names will be created simultaneously in all the worksheets.

How to fix it

To create names that will apply to multiple worksheets, follow these steps:

1. On the Insert menu, point to Name, and then click Define to display the Define Name dialog box.

2. In the Names In Workbook text box, type the name you want to apply to the cell or cells in multiple sheets.

3. Click in the Refers To box, and delete any current content by selecting any and all existing sheet and cell references and then pressing the Delete key.

> **Tip**
> If you want to group a series of contiguous sheets, use the Shift key instead of the Ctrl key. Also, you need to click only the first and last tabs in the series.

4. Type = (an equal sign) in the Refers To Box.

5. Click the tab for the first worksheet to be used in the multiple-sheet reference. The sheet name appears in the Refers To box.

6. Hold down the Shift key, and click the tab for the last worksheet to be included in the multiple-sheet reference. Any tabs between the first and last tabs you clicked are also included in the multiple-sheet reference. (The name of the last tab you clicked now appears in the Refers To box, with a colon separating it from the name of the first sheet tab you clicked.)

7. Click the individual cell or drag through the range of cells that you want to be referenced by the name you typed. The cell or range appears in the Refers To box, after the sheet tabs' reference.

8. Click the Add button. The name is now stored, and is associated with the cell or range you specified. (Note, however, that you'll be able to access the multiple-sheet name only through the Define Name dialog box; the name won't appear in the Name box or its drop-down list.)

9. Repeat steps 2 through 8 for any additional names you want to create.

10. Click OK to close the dialog box and return to your worksheet.

To create names from column and row labels in all the identical worksheets in your workbook, follow these steps:

1. Group the sheets (if they're not currently grouped) by clicking the tab of the first sheet you want to include in the group, holding down the Shift key, and then clicking the tab of the last sheet you want to include in the group. (To select nonconsecutive sheets in a group, hold down the Ctrl key as you click sheet tabs.)

2. In any worksheet in the grouped sheets, select the range of cells that contains both the column or row labels and the data they identify. Excel assumes that the labels are the same in all of the grouped sheets, and that the labels and data are in the same cells on all of the sheets.

3. On the Insert menu, point to Name, and then click Create.

4. In the Create Names dialog box, select the Create Names In check boxes that match the location of your labels. In many worksheets, the column labels are in the top row of the selected range and the row labels are down the left side— therefore, you'd select Top Row and Left Column from the list of options. ▶

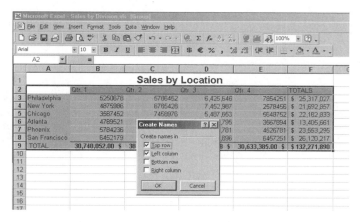

5. Click OK.

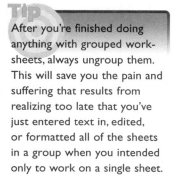

After you're finished doing anything with grouped work-sheets, always ungroup them. This will save you the pain and suffering that results from realizing too late that you've just entered text in, edited, or formatted all of the sheets in a group when you intended only to work on a single sheet.

Testing, 1, 2, 3...

Before you release your worksheet to the rest of the world— making it available to others on your company's network or sending it to someone as an e-mail attachment—test the names on each sheet. Make sure there are no misspellings or misdi-rected names. If you find errors, delete the names by pointing to Name on the Insert menu, clicking Define, selecting the name you want to delete in the Names In Workbook section, clicking Delete, and then clicking OK. Recreate the name, taking care not to misspell anything this time.

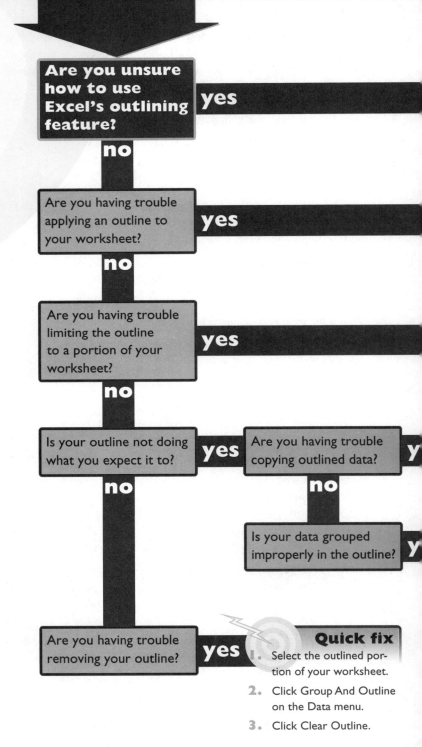

Are you unsure how to use Excel's outlining feature?

yes

no

Are you having trouble applying an outline to your worksheet?

yes

no

Are you having trouble limiting the outline to a portion of your worksheet?

yes

no

Is your outline not doing what you expect it to?

yes

Are you having trouble copying outlined data?

y

no

Is your data grouped improperly in the outline?

y

Are you having trouble removing your outline?

yes

Quick fix

1. Select the outlined portion of your worksheet.
2. Click Group And Outline on the Data menu.
3. Click Clear Outline.

Outlining

Go to...
I'm not sure if my worksheet can be turned into an outline, page 212.

Go to...
When I use the Auto Outline command, I get an error message, page 214.

Quick fix
1. Select the part of the worksheet you want to outline.
2. Point to Group And Outline on the Data menu, and then click Auto Outline.

Go to...
When I copy summary data to another worksheet, the details are copied too, page 216.

Go to...
My worksheet content doesn't fall into appropriate outline groups, page 218.

If your solution isn't here
Check these related chapters:
Sorting data, page 266
Subtotal reports, page 284
Or see the general troubleshooting tips on page xv.

I'm not sure if my worksheet can be turned into an outline

Source of the problem

Obviously, not all worksheets can be broken down into levels of hierarchical or topical content in an outline, and you're wondering if your worksheet falls into the "Yep" or "Nope" category.

What makes a worksheet outline-worthy? The way it's structured, and the data it contains. If it's a highly segmented worksheet that's not stored in regular rows and contains no totals or subtotals, nope, it can't be turned into an outline. If your worksheet is a list of records stored in rows, and the rows are in a specific order and are subtotaled within that sort order, yep, it can be turned into an outline. Worksheets that contain lists that are sorted by a column with many duplicate entries are the best outlining candidates. ▶

Tip

For a really dynamic outlined worksheet, you can subtotal the items in the sorted groups. Click Subtotal on the Data menu. In the Subtotal dialog box, click Sum, Average, or Count in the Use Function list, and click OK. This process creates collapsible and expandable horizontal levels. If you want, you can then create vertical outline levels by grouping your columns.

	A1		=	Course Enrollments				
	A	B	C	D	E	F	G	H
1			Course Enrollments					
2								
3	Application	Course #	Course Name	Course Date	Cost per Student	Number Enrolled	Total Class Revenue	Trainer Assigned
4	Access	MSAD1	Access Application Development	11/10/00	$ 400.00	4	$ 1,600.00	Moore
5	Access	MSA1	Access level 1	10/12/00	$ 300.00	6	$ 1,800.00	Cook
6	Access	MSA2	Access level 2	10/25/00	$ 325.00	8	$ 2,600.00	Cook
7	Access	MSA3	Access level 3	10/30/00	$ 350.00	8	$ 2,800.00	Cook
8	Excel	MSE3	Excel level 3	11/5/00	$ 350.00	9	$ 3,150.00	Corson
9	Excel	MSE2	Excel level 2	10/20/00	$ 325.00	7	$ 2,275.00	Elmaleh
10	Excel	MSE1	Excel level 1	10/8/00	$ 300.00	10	$ 3,000.00	Fuller
11	FrontPage	FPWD1	Web Design w/FrontPage, level 1	11/5/00	$ 400.00	12	$ 4,800.00	Fuller
12	FrontPage	FPWD2	Web Design w/FrontPage, level 2	11/15/00	$ 500.00	12	$ 6,000.00	Fuller
13	PowerPoint	MSP1	PowerPoint level 1	10/15/00	$ 300.00	6	$ 1,800.00	Talbot
14	PowerPoint	MSP2	PowerPoint level 2	10/30/00	$ 350.00	8	$ 2,800.00	Talbot
15	Publisher	MSPUB	Publisher Basics	11/13/00	$ 350.00	8	$ 2,800.00	Kline
16	Windows	MSWU	Windows 98 User	11/2/00	$ 300.00	10	$ 3,000.00	Corson
17	Windows	MSNTA	Windows NT Administration	11/6/00	$ 500.00	5	$ 2,500.00	Elmaleh
18	Word	MSW2	Word level 2	10/15/00	$ 325.00	8	$ 2,600.00	Fuller
19	Word	MSW3	Word level 3	11/1/00	$ 350.00	12	$ 4,200.00	Kline
20	Word	MSW1	Word level 1	10/5/00	$ 300.00	9	$ 2,700.00	Talbot
21					Total	142	$ 50,425.00	
22								
23								

This worksheet is sorted by the first column, creating groups by alphabetized application names.

Once you've determined, based on the considerations just mentioned, that your worksheet is indeed outline-worthy, you can go ahead and create the outline.

How to fix it

1. Sort your list by at least one column in your worksheet, preferably a column containing a lot of duplicates, which will break your list into groups of similar content.

2. Click any cell in the worksheet except the title. Point to Group And Outline on the Data menu, and then click Auto Outline. Two outline level buttons appear to the left of the row numbers,

above the column letters, or both, depending on the type of information and how it is arranged in your worksheet. ▶

Break it down

Perhaps you were hoping to be able to collapse the outline at two or more points across the rows or columns, but there's only one outline level. What to do? Group your rows or columns in the outline with the Group command on the Group And Outline submenu, turning one or all of the groups into additional outline levels. Looking at your data, think which columns or rows you'd like to hide, and select the headings of the rows or columns in a group that you'd like to isolate in the outline. ▶

Having selected the rows you want to group, point to Group And Outline on the Data menu, and then click Group. A level indicator appears. To add another group, select the first group and then drag through the second group's row headings. On the Data menu, point to Group And Outline, and then click Group again, and another level indicator appears. You can expand a collapsed level by clicking the plus sign near the last row in the level. Conversely, you can collapse an expanded level by clicking the minus sign.

And break it down again

Having broken your sorted rows into groups, you can also break your columns into collapsible levels. Select the column headings, point to Group And Outline on the Data menu, and then click Group. You'll end up with horizontal and vertical outline levels that can be expanded and collapsed.

When I use the Auto Outline command, I get an error message

Source of the problem

"Can't create an outline?" Well, why the heck not? You thought you did everything right—you made sure your database had all the elements that are needed to turn a worksheet into an outline (see "I'm not sure if my worksheet can be turned into an outline" on page 212), and you pointed to Group And Outline on the Data menu and then clicked Auto Outline. But instead of seeing outline levels appear on your worksheet, you see an error message. Possible reasons for this message include:

- There is no real database. If Excel doesn't detect a worksheet that is laid out as a database (if it has inconsistent layout, blank columns or rows, or missing column and row labels), it won't create an outline.

- You didn't select the whole database. When you tried to select the entire database, you missed some of the cells, so Excel is confused as to what you want to outline and displays the error message. ▶

- You selected a cell that doesn't contain data or a label. If you select your worksheet title (usually in cell A1 or A2) rather than a data or label cell, the error message appears because Excel doesn't see any contiguous data that can be turned into an outline.

This is sort of a case of "Doctor, it hurts when I go like this." The doctor replies, "Well, then don't go like that!" The way to prevent this error message from appearing is to not do any of the things just listed—don't select the worksheet title or a range of cells within the database before issuing the Auto Outline command, and make sure your worksheet contains data in a layout that's conducive to outlining.

How to fix it

1. Check your data for content or layout that will prevent the Auto Outline command from working. Make sure all of your labels are there, and that there are no blank rows or columns within the database.

2. Click a cell within the data—not the cell containing the worksheet title, but a cell containing a label or data.

3. On the Data menu, point to Group And Outline, and then click Auto Outline to make two outline levels appear down the left side of your worksheet.

Just asking...

Another message that you might see when attempting to use the Auto Outline feature is one that asks, "Modify the current outline?" You'll see this when you've already used the Auto Outline command on the active worksheet, or when you've used the Subtotals command on the Data menu to create a subtotal report using your data. Because the subtotal report breaks your data into levels (based on sorted rows), it is considered to be an existing outline. ▶

If you were unaware that an outline already existed (perhaps someone else applied it) and you want to remove this outline before applying a new one, click any cell in your data (other than the title cell), point to Group And Outline on the Data menu, and then click Clear Outline. However, if your data has been subtotaled, click Subtotals on the Data menu, and in the Subtotal dialog box, click the Remove All button to remove both the subtotals and the outline that resulted from subtotaling. In either case, any existing outline will be removed, and you can go ahead and use the Auto Outline command without fear of unexpected results.

	A1		=	Course Enrollments					
1 2 3		A	B	C	D	E	F	G	H
	1			Course Enrollments					
	2								
	3	Application	Course #	Course Name	Course Date	Cost per Student	Number Enrolled	Total Class Revenue	Trainer Assigned
	4	Access	MSAD1	Access Application Development	11/10/00	$ 400.00	4	$ 1,600.00	Moore
	5	Access	MSA1	Access level 1	10/12/00	$ 300.00	6	$ 1,800.00	Cook
	6	Access	MSA2	Access level 2	10/25/00	$ 325.00	8	$ 2,600.00	Cook
	7	Access	MSA3	Access level 3	10/30/00	$ 350.00	8	$ 2,800.00	Cook
	8	**Access Total**						$ 8,800.00	
	9	Excel	MSE3	Excel level 3	11/5/00	$ 350.00	9	$ 3,150.00	Corson
	10	Excel	MSE2	Excel level 2	10/20/00	$ 325.00	7	$ 2,275.00	Elmaleh
	11	Excel	MSE1	Excel level 1	10/8/00	$ 300.00	10	$ 3,000.00	Fuller
	12	**Excel Total**						$ 8,425.00	
	13	FrontPage	FPWD1	Web Design w/FrontPage, level 1	11/5/00	$ 400.00	12	$ 4,800.00	Fuller
	14	FrontPage	FPWD2	Web Design w/FrontPage, level 2	11/15/00	$ 500.00	12	$ 6,000.00	Fuller
	15	**FrontPage Total**						$ 10,800.00	
	16	PowerPoint	MSP1	PowerPoint level 1	10/15/00	$ 300.00	6	$ 1,800.00	Talbot
	17	PowerPoint	MSP2	PowerPoint level 2	10/30/00	$ 350.00	8	$ 2,800.00	Talbot
	18	**PowerPoint Total**						$ 4,600.00	
	19	Publisher	MSPUB	Publisher Basics	11/13/00	$ 350.00	8	$ 2,800.00	Kline
	20	**Publisher Total**						$ 2,800.00	
	21	Windows	MSWU	Windows 98 User	11/2/00	$ 300.00	10	$ 3,000.00	Corson
	22	Windows	MSNTA	Windows NT Administration	11/8/00	$ 500.00	5	$ 2,500.00	Elmaleh
	23	**Windows Total**						$ 5,500.00	
	24	Word	MSW2	Word level 2	10/15/00	$ 325.00	8	$ 2,600.00	Fuller
	25	Word	MSW3	Word level 3	11/1/00	$ 350.00	12	$ 4,200.00	Kline

Sheet1 / Sheet2 / Sheet3 /

Ready — NUM

Tip
For more information on using the Subtotals command to subtotal your database, see "Subtotal reports" on page 284.

When I copy summary data to another worksheet, the details are copied too

Source of the problem

You've collapsed a level in your worksheet by clicking the outline button, successfully hiding some of your columns or rows. With this detail hidden, you want to copy the displayed data to another worksheet—perhaps to be e-mailed to someone who needs to see only the summary data, or to be accessed via a network drive to which other users have access. When you select the displayed cells and copy them to another worksheet, you get more than you bargained for, however. The outlined data comes complete with the hidden data, which is now displayed in your worksheet, and you didn't want that detail to come along for the ride. What can you do? Excel gives you some special selection tools through the Go To dialog box with which you can select just the cells that are visible on-screen. By using this feature, you can copy only the cells that are showing, preserving the appearance of the data that you've achieved by collapsing your outline. ▶

Using the Go To dialog box rather than a simple Copy command, you can avoid copying hidden cells.

How to fix it

1. Collapse the levels of your outline so that only the portions of your worksheet that you want to copy are visible.

2. On the Edit menu, click Go To.

3. In the Go To dialog box, click the Special button to open the Go To Special dialog box.

4. In the Go To Special dialog box, click Visible Cells Only. (Don't worry if your dialog box looks a little different from this one.) ▶

5. Click OK. The dialog box closes, and though it appears that your entire worksheet is selected, only those cells that are displayed are actually selected—the hidden rows and columns are not included.

6. Press Ctrl+C to place the visible cells on the Clipboard.

7. Move to the target worksheet, and click the first cell. Be sure that the worksheet contains no material that you want to save, because it will be overwritten by the visible cells that you copied, which include all the blank cells as well as the displayed entries in the source worksheet.

8. Press Enter to paste the visible cells in the target worksheet, unaccompanied by the hidden cells.

Error messages that make you want to slap your computer

Some situations will prevent you from using the Visible Cells Only option in the Go To Special dialog box. Among them:

● If a merged cell in the target worksheet is a different size than in the source worksheet, or if the target worksheet has a merged cell containing a title, a message appears telling you that you can't "change part of a merged cell."

● If you've already selected cells using the Go To Special dialog box, a message appears telling you that a selection has already been made.

● If you select a range of cells that includes no hidden cells and then issue the Go To command, when you try to select Visible Cells Only, a message tells you that there is no hidden content.

Obviously, if you split up any merged cells in the target worksheet, click a cell to deselect a previous selection, and make sure you select a range of cells containing hidden columns and rows, these messages won't appear. Equally obvious is the fact that despite your diligent efforts to avoid them, you will at one time or another see these messages and want to slap your computer.

Tip

If your worksheet is small, or if your computer's memory seems overly taxed by copying and pasting an entire worksheet, you can select the range of cells that you want to copy before issuing the Go To command. When you select Visible Cells Only, Go To will select those cells in the range you've highlighted, leaving the rest of the worksheet untouched.

Tip

If you have applied an Auto-Filter to your worksheet (point to Filter on the Data menu, and then click Auto-Filter) and only the rows containing data meeting your filter criteria are displayed, you can copy those rows and not the hidden records. Select the cells you want to copy, press Ctrl+G, click the Special button, click the Visible Cells Only option in the Go To Special dialog box, and click OK.

My worksheet content doesn't fall into appropriate outline groups

Source of the problem

You point to Group And Outline on the Data menu, and then click Auto Outline, and voilà! The worksheet is turned into an outline, with handy collapsible levels that allow you to hide portions of your worksheet at will. Outlining is really a great feature. Or so you thought until you issued the Auto Outline command and ended up with outline levels that make no sense—sure, you could collapse your outline at various points, hiding columns or rows, but why these levels were placed where they were is a mystery. You ended up clearing the outline and starting over, probably with the same result. Now you're really confused.

To put an end to the confusion, it's important to understand how Excel chooses where to place those automatic outline levels. Excel looks for columns and rows containing totals or the results of formulas that use other columns or rows in the worksheet. If you have a column that totals the columns before or after it, that column will become a point at which the outline can be collapsed so that only the totals, not the columns that were totaled, are displayed. Same with a total in a row at the foot of several rows of data—that row will become an outline level, which you can collapse to see just the total of the rows in the list, not the rows that make up that list. ▶

Fixing an outline that doesn't make sense has two solutions—one proactive, the other reactive. To proactively solve this problem, make sure your totaled columns and the column containing the totals are

> **Tip**
> If your column or row containing totals gets those totals from noncontiguous rows or columns in your worksheet, no level will be created. For example, if the numbers in column F are the result of adding columns D and E, column F becomes an outline level. If B and E are summed (or averaged, or used in a formula), and the results appear in column F, column F is not turned into a level. Think about this when planning the order of columns in a worksheet that will be turned into an outline.

contiguous. To reactively solve this problem, you can create your own groups, eliminating the need for Excel's Auto Outline rules to be satisfied by the order and relationship of your worksheet's columns and rows. You can manually group columns and rows that don't result in or have any connection to totals in your worksheet, but that simply contain details that you want to collapse—say, to simplify a worksheet visually or to hide confidential details.

How to fix it

1. If you'll be grouping rows, first sort your worksheet by a field that contains similar content. For example, in a list of classes, you can sort by topic, instructor, or price—anything that will put your list in ordered groups. ▶

	A	B	C	D	E	F	G	H	I
		A3	=	Application					
3	Application	Course #	Course Name	Course Date	Cost per Student	Number Enrolled	Total Class Revenue	Trainer Assigned	
4	Access	MSAD1	Access Application Development	11/10/00	$ 400.00	4	$ 1,600.00	Moore	
5	Access	MSA1	Access level 1	10/12/00	$ 300.00	6	$ 1,800.00	Cook	
6	Access	MSA2	Access level 2	10/25/00	$ 325.00	8	$ 2,600.00	Cook	
7	Access	MSA3	Access level 3	10/30/00	$ 350.00	8	$ 2,800.00	Cook	
8	Excel	MSE3	Excel level 3	11/5/00	$ 350.00	9	$ 3,150.00	Corson	
9	Excel	MSE2	Excel level 2	10/20/00	$ 325.00	7	$ 2,275.00	Elmaleh	
10	Excel	MSE1	Excel level 1	10/8/00	$ 300.00	10	$ 3,000.00	Fuller	
11	FrontPage	FPWD1	Web Design w/FrontPage, level 1	11/5/00	$ 400.00	12	$ 4,800.00	Fuller	
12	FrontPage	FPWD2	Web Design w/FrontPage, level 2	11/15/00	$ 500.00	12	$ 6,000.00	Fuller	
13	PowerPoint	MSP1	PowerPoint level 1	10/15/00	$ 300.00	6	$ 1,800.00	Talbot	
14	PowerPoint	MSP2	PowerPoint level 2	10/30/00	$ 350.00	8	$ 2,800.00	Talbot	
15	Publisher	MSPUB	Publisher Basics	11/13/00	$ 350.00	8	$ 2,800.00	Kline	
16	Windows	MSWU	Windows 98 User	11/2/00	$ 300.00	10	$ 3,000.00	Corson	
17	Windows	MSNTA	Windows NT Administration	11/8/00	$ 500.00	5	$ 2,500.00	Elmaleh	
18	Word	MSW2	Word level 2	10/15/00	$ 325.00	8	$ 2,600.00	Fuller	
19	Word	MSW3	Word level 3	11/1/00	$ 350.00	12	$ 4,200.00	Kline	
20	Word	MSW1	Word level 1	10/5/00	$ 300.00	9	$ 2,700.00	Talbot	
21					Total	142	$ 50,425.00		
22									

When these records are sorted by Application name, they can become outline groups.

2. Select a series of columns or rows on your worksheet by dragging through their column or row headings.

3. On the Data menu, point to Group And Outline, and then click Group. If you're grouping columns, the group will encompass the selected columns, and the column to the right of them will represent the outline level. If you're grouping rows, the group will encompass the selected rows, and the row just below them will represent the outline level. ▶

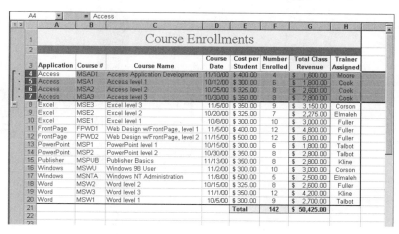

4. Continue selecting groups by repeating steps 2 and 3. Be sure to select the rows or columns in the previous group or groups to get successive groups that don't overlap.

Tip

If you realize that you included too few or too many rows or columns in a group, and the resulting level is in the wrong place, point to Group And Outline on the Data menu, and then click Ungroup. In the Ungroup dialog box, click either Rows or Columns, and then click OK to remove the group.

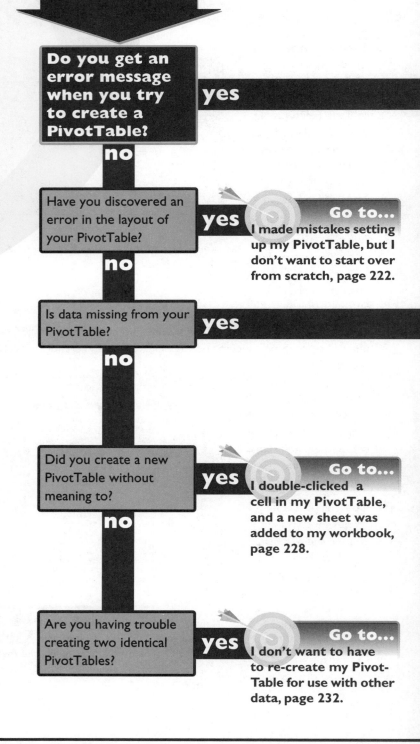

Do you get an error message when you try to create a PivotTable?

yes

no

Have you discovered an error in the layout of your PivotTable?

yes

Go to...
I made mistakes setting up my PivotTable, but I don't want to start over from scratch, page 222.

no

Is data missing from your PivotTable?

yes

no

Did you create a new PivotTable without meaning to?

yes

Go to...
I double-clicked a cell in my PivotTable, and a new sheet was added to my workbook, page 228.

no

Are you having trouble creating two identical PivotTables?

yes

Go to...
I don't want to have to re-create my Pivot-Table for use with other data, page 232.

Quick fix

If your computer tells you there isn't enough memory to create a PivotTable, close any other programs, and then try again. If the problem persists, restart your computer, and then check how much memory it has available. Right-click the My Computer icon, and then click Properties. On the Performance tab in the System Properties dialog box, check the percentage of free memory you have left. It should be at or above 80%.

Is the missing data related to records containing blank fields?

yes

Go to...

My data includes blank fields, but they're not showing up in my Pivot-Table, page 226.

no

Have you refreshed your PivotTable?

yes

Go to...

I refreshed my PivotTable, but the data still doesn't reflect my changes, page 230.

no

Quick fix

To include new or edited data in your PivotTable, click any cell in the table, and then on the Data menu, click Refresh Data. Excel will take a new look at the range of cells used to build your PivotTable, and include the new and changed data in the table.

If your solution isn't here
Check these related chapters:
    Filtering records, page 104
    Subtotal reports, page 284
Or see the general troubleshooting tips on page xv.

I made mistakes setting up my PivotTable, but I don't want to start over from scratch

Source of the problem

Unlike Excel's other relatively automatic report-creation features (Subtotals and Outlines), PivotTable reports requires some setup decisions before Excel can create the report you need. In making those decisions, mistakes and oversights can occur, resulting in a PivotTable report that doesn't include all the information you wanted or that displays the information less effectively than you might like. Starting from scratch is an option when the PivotTable is so out of whack that you can't use it at all, but if you have only a few changes to make—switching some of your fields from columns to rows, changing the calculation performed on the data—it can be easier to edit the PivotTable in place.

With the PivotTable Wizard, you can easily make the following changes to your PivotTable:

- Change the range of cells from which the PivotTable draws data.

- Change the layout of the PivotTable.

- Change the function applied to the Data portion of the PivotTable.

To make these changes, you can use the PivotTable Wizard, or you use the PivotTable toolbar, which appears on the screen as soon as a new PivotTable is created.

How to fix it

To change the layout of your PivotTable using the PivotTable Wizard, follow these steps:

1. Click any cell in the PivotTable.

2. On the Data menu, click PivotTable And PivotChart Report (or PivotTable Report if you're working in Excel 97). Excel displays step 3 of the PivotTable Wizard. (Don't worry if your dialog box looks different from this one.) ▶

3. Edit the layout according to the procedures for your version of Excel, keeping in mind the pointers that follow these steps.

Excel 2000 When the wizard's third step appears, click the Layout button to display a separate Layout dialog box, and then make your edits. Click OK, and then click Finish.

Excel 97 If you're working in Excel 97, your wizard contains four steps instead of three. Because the third step of the PivotTable Wizard is virtually identical to the Excel 2000 Layout dialog box, you just have to click Finish when you have completed editing the layout.

Tip

If you correct the layout of your PivotTable using the steps provided, you'll want to make sure to click a cell directly in the PivotTable to make your changes most quickly. You could click any cell outside the PivotTable (provided the cell is on the same sheet as the PivotTable), but then you'd have to start the PivotTable And PivotChart Wizard from the beginning, as if you were creating a PivotTable from scratch. When the wizard's first step appears, all you have to do is click Next; but when prompted in the second step to select the data you want to use, you'll have to reselect the cells you used when originally building your PivotTable. That's why the PivotTable Wizard skips to the third step when you click a cell directly in the PivotTable—Excel acknowledges that you're just making changes to a PivotTable and saves you the hassle of going through the wizard's first two steps all over. Smart, isn't it?

When editing the layout of your PivotTable, keep these pointers in mind:

- To change which fields are in which parts of the PivotTable, drag the field boxes to the desired locations within the layout diagram. ▶

Tip

In the PivotTable Field dialog box, click the Number button to choose a number format for your data. You can select from the same number format options you'd have available if you clicked Cells on the Format menu. This feature is helpful when the data on which the PivotTable report is based was not formatted before the report was created.

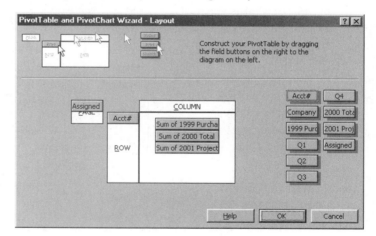

This solution is continued on the next page.

I made mistakes setting up my PivotTable, but I don't want to start over from scratch

(continued from page 223)

● To change the calculation performed on a field in the Data section of the PivotTable diagram, double-click the field name in the Data section. In the resulting PivotTable Field dialog box, choose a different function from the Summarize By list. ▶

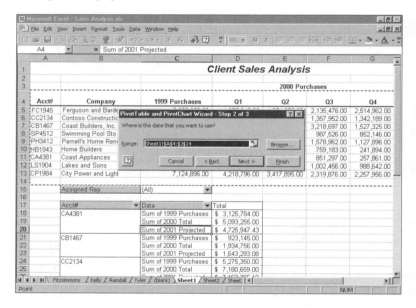

To use the PivotTable Wizard to change the range of cells from which the PivotTable report draws data, follow these steps:

1. If the PivotTable Wizard is not displayed, click any cell in the PivotTable, and click PivotTable And PivotChart Report (or PivotTable Report if you're working in Excel 97) on the Data menu. The wizard opens with its third dialog box displayed.

2. In the wizard's third step, click the Back button. This takes you back to the second step in the wizard, and shows the current range of cells used to build your PivotTable. (Don't worry if your dialog box looks a little bit different from ours.) ▶

3. To select a different range, go to the work-sheet that contains the range you want, and drag through the cells that should be used to build the table.

4. Click Finish to exit the wizard and re-display the PivotTable with the different or additional data included.

> **Tip**
> If you're adding to the existing range, hold down the Shift key and click at the end of the row or column you wish to add. This will add the cells between the original selection and the cell you just clicked to the range used to create the PivotTable.

Using the PivotTable Toolbar

If the problem with your PivotTable isn't so much that it contains a mistake as it is that you want to change your PivotTable's layout, you don't need to go to all the trouble of rerunning the PivotTable Wizard. Instead, you can make use of the Pivot-Table toolbar, which gives you the ability to re-arrange your table, add fields, and make formatting adjustments. ▶

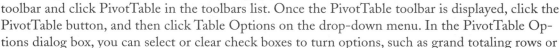

The PivotTable toolbar should appear as soon you click any cell in your PivotTable; however, if it doesn't, right-click the menu bar or any displayed toolbar and click PivotTable in the toolbars list. Once the PivotTable toolbar is displayed, click the PivotTable button, and then click Table Options on the drop-down menu. In the PivotTable Options dialog box, you can select or clear check boxes to turn options, such as grand totaling rows or columns and applying AutoFormats, on or off. From this dialog box, you can also designate a special character to appear in empty cells in the PivotTable. ▶

To add fields to the table, drag the field names on the PivotTable toolbar to the Page, Column, Row, or Data sections of the PivotTable. The mouse pointer changes into a table symbol when it's at a spot that's appropriate to drop the field. If the mouse pointer doesn't change into a table symbol, you won't be able to drop the field icon onto the PivotTable.

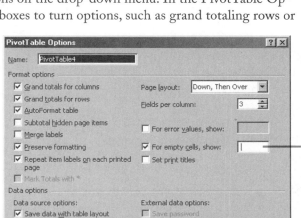

Type the character or word you want to appear in empty cells.

Tip
The PivotTable toolbar needn't be displayed for you to rearrange your table's fields. Simply drag the fields (the gray boxes with names) you want to move from one section of the table to another. In this way, you can add another field to the Page section, for example, or move a field from the Row section to the Column section and vice versa.

My data includes blank fields, but they're not showing up in my PivotTable

Source of the problem

Depending on the nature of the data you're using as a basis for your PivotTable, the database might contain blank fields. For example, if you're listing the purchases of a series of products by a group of your customers, and not all of the customers have purchased all of the different products, there will be blank fields in the database whenever a particular customer didn't buy a particular product. These blanks don't affect the accuracy of your database. ▶

If you want to see those blanks represented in your PivotTable, it can be frustrating—by default, Excel's PivotTable feature does not include empty cells. You can include the blanks, however, by selecting an option in the PivotTable Field dialog box. When you choose to include blanks, your PivotTable becomes more accurate, because intentionally blank cells are part of the information your worksheet stores.

	Acct#	Company	Total Products Purchased	Lumber	Tools	Safety Equipment	Clothing	Plumbing	Electrical	Painting & Coatings
5	FB1945	Ferguson and Bardell	261	53	25	16	12	11	19	125
6	CC2134	Contoso Construction	290	62	45	18	22	10	25	108
7	CB1467	Coast Builders, Inc.	164	36	42	12	10	9	3	52
8	SP4512	Swimming Pool Store	468	86	65	24	13	28	17	235
9	PH3412	Parnell's Home Renovations	144	28	12	5	3	18	22	56
10	HB1943	Home Builders	38	13	5	2				18
11	CA4381	Coast Appliances	313	58	21		16	42	53	123
12	LS1904	Lakes and Sons	1258	122	173	85		236	275	367
13	CP1984	City Power and Light	1053	78	125	46	85	132	127	460
14		TOTALS	3989	536	513	208	161	486	541	1544

This database has blank cells.

How to fix it

1. In the PivotTable, locate the box for the field that contains blank data (the 3-D-looking box with the field name on it).

2. Double-click the box to open the PivotTable Field dialog box.

3. In the dialog box, select the Show Items With No Data check box. ▶

4. Click OK to close the dialog box.

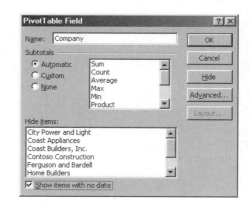

When in doubt, count

If the fields you drag into the Data section of the PivotTable layout diagram contain any blanks, Excel will apply the COUNT function by default. (To access the layout diagram, click a cell within the Pivot Table, click PivotTable And PivotChart Report on the Data menu, click PivotTable, and then click the Layout button in the PivotTable Wizard's third step.) For fields with no blanks, the default is SUM. You can easily change the function to SUM (or to COUNT, AVERAGE, or any other PivotTable function). In the PivotTable, right-click the cell that represents the field for which you want to change the function. Click Field Settings (or Field, if you're working in Excel 97) on the shortcut menu. In the PivotTable Field dialog box, click the desired function in the Summarize By or Subtotals list (depending on which cell you clicked before opening the dialog box). ▶

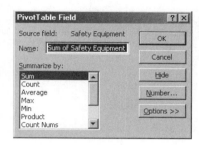

Click OK to close the dialog box. Back in the PivotTable, the numbers in that field will have changed to reflect the new function, and the heading for the numbers will also reflect the new function name.

Tip

If you're changing from a COUNT to a SUM function and the numbers your new function will display represent money, you might want to change the formatting of the results to Currency. In the PivotTable Field dialog box, click the Number button to open another dialog box, through which you can click Currency in the Category list. This dialog box has all the features found on the Number tab in the Format Cells dialog box, so you can also choose the number of decimals to display and the way negative numbers appear in your worksheet.

If you're still in doubt, insert an X

Another option available to you for dealing with blank entries is found in the PivotTable Options dialog box. Right-click any non-blank cell in your PivotTable, and click Table Options (or Options if you're working in Excel 97) on the shortcut menu. In the PivotTable Options dialog box, make sure the For Empty Cells, Show check box is selected, and then enter a character—an X, a zero, a dash, an asterisk, or anything other than a number which would be confusing when viewing the table—and click OK. Any empty cells in your PivotTable will then contain the character you entered.

Tip

You can customize the entry for blank cells based on the table's content. For example, if your PivotTable pertains to sales in various geographic regions, you can type No Sales Here or words to that effect. Your entry in the For Empty Cells, Show box can have up to 255 characters.

I double-clicked a cell in my PivotTable, and a new sheet was added to my workbook

Source of the problem

This isn't so much of a problem as a surprise. You double-click a cell in the calculated portion of your PivotTable (the numbers created by the fields you placed in the Data section of the table's layout), and a new sheet is added to your workbook, containing data from the original database. Each time you double-click a cell in the Data portion of the PivotTable, the same thing happens—a new worksheet, containing data pertaining to the cell you double-clicked, is added to the workbook. You might want to re-arrange the sheets after the new one is added, which you can easily do by dragging the sheet tabs to the left or right to place them in a more preferable order. ▶

Although you can't stop this from happening (except by not double-clicking the cells), you can use it to your advantage. You can create worksheets for important records in your Pivot-Table data to easily isolate data you want to print or use as the beginning of a worksheet that can be edited to contain additional information related or relevant to the PivotTable data.

A new worksheet containing pertinent data is added.

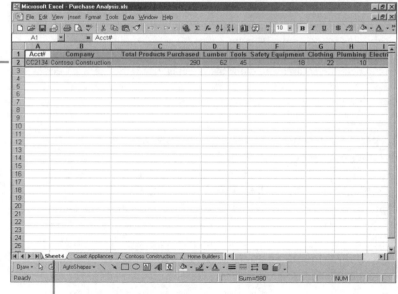

You can drag sheet tabs to rearrange them.

If you accidentally double-clicked a cell and don't want the resulting new sheet, simply remove the sheet from the workbook or delete the content and use the now blank sheet for something else.

How to fix it

1. Double-click the cell in your PivotTable that you want to use to create a new worksheet.

2. In the new worksheet, format the content as desired.

3. Name the worksheet by double-clicking the sheet tab and typing something that will identify and differentiate the worksheet from the others in the workbook.

Tip

If you double-click a cell accidentally and don't want the resulting new worksheet, simply delete it. Make sure the sheet you want to delete is active, then right-click the sheet's tab, and click Delete on the shortcut menu. When you are prompted to verify the deletion, click OK.

Other stuff that happens automatically

If you want to create new PivotTable worksheets from a cell in the current one, right-click the cell. Click Show Pages on the shortcut menu, and then click OK in the Show Pages dialog box. If you have more than one field in the Page section of the PivotTable, you can select which field the detail worksheets will be created for before clicking OK. A worksheet is created for each item in the Pages list, showing the detailed data, with the sheet tabs automatically named for the items. For example, if you have a PivotTable listing products purchased by a series of companies, and the companies are the items you can select from the Show All Pages Of list, a worksheet will be created for each company. ▶

This field was placed in the Page section of the PivotTable layout diagram.

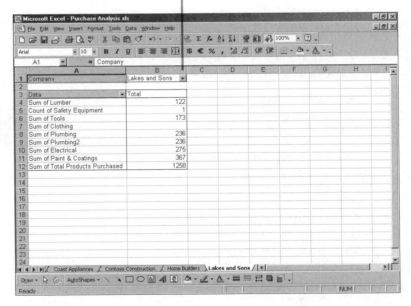

Tip

You can use the Show Pages feature to build several Pivot-Tables and then delete the original PivotTable. This is a quick way to create several duplicate tables and name the worksheets that contain them.

I refreshed my PivotTable, but the data still doesn't reflect my changes

Source of the problem

The process of refreshing a PivotTable involves checking the PivotTable's source cells and changing the content of the PivotTable based on any changes to that range of source cells. If you've clicked the Refresh Data command on the Data menu and your PivotTable wasn't updated, the problem lies in the range of cells specified as the source of your table. If you've expanded the range of cells in your database—by typing new rows of records or by adding columns, for example—those new entries won't fall in the range that Excel is looking at when refreshing your table, so the content of the new cells won't be reflected in the table's cells.

What to do? Establish an expanded range for your PivotTable by rerunning the PivotTable setup process and inserting the new range of cells in the second step of the PivotTable Wizard.

How to fix it

1. Right-click any cell in the PivotTable, and click Wizard on the shortcut menu. The third step of the PivotTable And PivotChart Wizard appears, regardless of what version of Excel you're using.

2. Click the Back button once to access the second step of the wizard. (Don't worry if your wizard looks a little different than ours.) ▶

3. As needed, move the wizard out of the way or click the Collapse button at the end of the Range box.

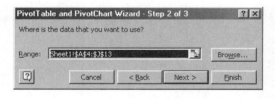

4. Drag through the cells that you want to include as the source range for your PivotTable. (If the range of cells is too large to drag through easily, select the first row with your mouse, and then hold down the Shift key (if you're adding consecutive rows) or the Ctrl key (if you're adding non-consecutive rows). Then click the row headings for rows you want to add until the entire range of cells is selected. You can also hold down the Shift key and select contiguous rows with the Up or Down Arrow keys, if you want. If the range is really huge, you can scroll to the end of the data range, hold down the Shift key, and click the last cell of the desired range. Everything from the

first selected row to the last cell clicked will be selected as the source range for your PivotTable.) The range you select appears in the Range box.

5. If you collapsed the wizard in step 3, click the Expand button to restore its size.

6. Click Finish to redraw the PivotTable, which will now be based on the range of cells you just specified.

What a refreshing idea

If you want your PivotTable to be refreshed each time you open the worksheet that contains the table, right-click any cell in your PivotTable, and click Table Options (or just Options, if you're working in Excel 97) on the shortcut menu. In the Data Options section of the PivotTable Options dialog box, select the Refresh On Open check box, and then click OK. ▶

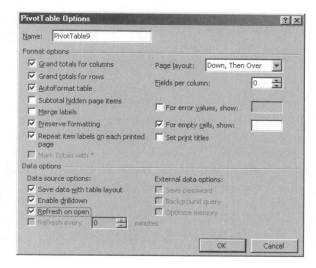

Once this option is turned on, each time you open the worksheet, Excel will check the source range for the PivotTable and update the table to reflect any new data in that range of cells.

Tip One potential problem with using the Refresh On Open option is that if others have been editing your worksheet and have made changes to the source cells for your PivotTable, your table could change in an undesirable way. If, for example, someone has deleted a column or altered a label, or added erroneous data, your table might change in a way that you don't want. If you really need to use the Refresh On Open option, and others have access to your worksheet, consider protecting the source range of cells. (For more information on protecting cell ranges from changes, see "When I put Excel content into an Access database, I have trouble with cells formatted as dates" on page 64.)

I don't want to have to re-create my PivotTable for use with other data

Source of the problem

Suppose you've got the perfect PivotTable, and you have another worksheet that could use the very same PivotTable setup. Or, suppose you want to have two, or more than two, PivotTables side by side, each showing a different aspect of the same target data. In either case, the prospect of starting from scratch to build a new PivotTable doesn't sound terribly appealing. I'm with you!

If you need to use an existing table with different data on a different worksheet, or in another spot on the same worksheet, the solution requires that you copy the table to a new spot and edit its setup to reflect a different range of source cells. If you want to duplicate a table using the same data as the original so that you can display a different portion, all you have to do is copy and paste the original, and then make a few minor adjustments to the duplicate. ▶

How to fix it

To copy a PivotTable, follow these steps:

1. Right-click the PivotTable you want to copy, point to Select on the short-cut menu, and then click Entire Table.

Tip When you copy a PivotTable, clicking Entire Table is much easier than dragging through the table's cells, no matter how small the table is. If you try to drag through the table's cells, you can't start from the first cell, because that's typically a button—clicking it might drop down a list instead of simply selecting the cell. You'd have to start the selection from the last cell in the last column.

2. With the PivotTable selected, press Ctrl+C to copy the PivotTable to the clipboard.

3. Move to the target location for the duplicate PivotTable, and press Enter. The table appears in the new location. (You might have to adjust the layout, formatting, and column widths of the pasted copy to match the original.)

A table so nice, they used it twice

Placing PivotTables side by side on a worksheet is a good way to look at the same data from different perspectives. For example, if your data shows sales for a series of customers over three years, you can have the first table display the first year, the second table display the second year, and the third table display the third year. A fourth table can display the total of all three years. Why not just use the drop-down list and choose a different year? Because with only one PivotTable, you can see the table from only one perspective at a time, and you can't make easy visual comparisons.

Making an attractive PivotTable

Useful for many Pivot-Tables and especially helpful for closely placed duplicates, the Format Report command in Excel 2000 allows you to choose from a series of preset table formats—cell shading, fonts, table layouts—that can help you quickly create a professional look for your PivotTable. In the case of side-by-side duplicates, having each version of the table in a different color helps you tell them apart. (In Excel 97, you can use AutoFormats to dress up your PivotTables.)

Excel 2000 To use this feature, right-click any cell in the PivotTable, and click Format Report on the shortcut menu. In the AutoFormat dialog box, select one of the available table formats, such as Report 3. ▶

Click OK to apply the AutoFormat to your PivotTable.

Excel 97 If you're using Excel 97, click any cell in the PivotTable you want to format, and then click AutoFormat on the Format menu. When the AutoFormat dialog box appears, click one of the available formats in the Table Format list, and then click OK.

> **TIP**
> If you want to use a different range of cells as the source data for a duplicate table, right-click the table, and click Wizard on the shortcut menu. In the PivotTable And PivotChart Wizard, click the Back button to access the wizard's second step, and then establish a different range for the PivotTable. Complete instructions for this process are found in "I refreshed my PivotTable, but the data still doesn't reflect my changes" on page 230.

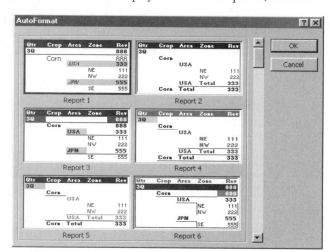

> **TIP**
> One potential drawback to applying preset table formats is that applying these formats can change the layout of your PivotTable and alter the way the PivotTable content is displayed. Be prepared to click Undo to get rid of the formatting if any undesirable change occurs. If you can't undo a change (because you made the change too many actions ago, or you just opened the file), click None in the AutoFormat dialog box, and then click OK to return the table to its original state.

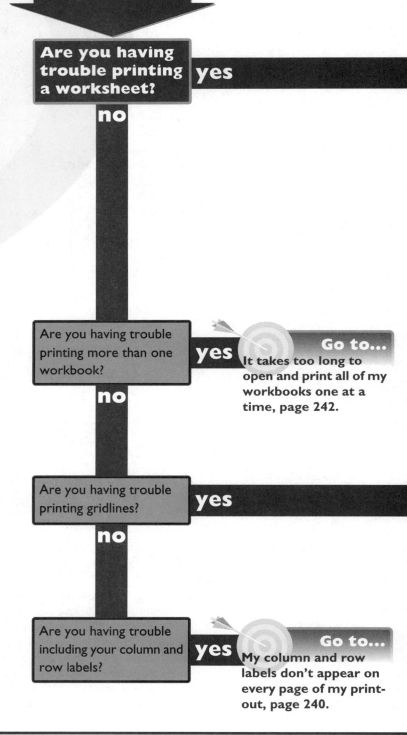

Are you having trouble printing a worksheet?

yes

no

Are you having trouble printing more than one workbook?

yes

Go to...
It takes too long to open and print all of my workbooks one at a time, page 242.

no

Are you having trouble printing gridlines?

yes

no

Are you having trouble including your column and row labels?

yes

Go to...
My column and row labels don't appear on every page of my print-out, page 240.

Printing

Are you having trouble printing your entire worksheet?

yes

Go to...
I can print only part of my worksheet, but I want to print all of it, page 238.

no

Are you having trouble printing your entire worksheet on one page?

yes

Go to...
I can't print my whole worksheet on a single page, page 236.

no

Are you having trouble printing portions of your worksheet?

yes

Quick fix
If you need to print a small section of your worksheet, select the cells you want to print, and click Print on the File menu. In the Print dialog box, click the Selection option in the Print What section. Click OK to print.

Quick fix

1. Click Page Setup on the File menu.
2. In the Page Setup dialog box, click the Sheet tab, and then select the Gridlines check box in the Print section.
3. Click OK, and then click the Print button.

If your solution isn't here
Check these related chapters:
Formatting worksheets, page 136
Workspace customization, page 304
Or see the general troubleshooting tips on page xv.

I can't print my whole worksheet on a single page

Source of the problem

By default, Excel will print your entire worksheet (all the cells containing text and numbers, and any empty rows and columns between those cells) at 100% of its size, on as many sheets of paper as it takes to print everything. This can be frustrating, especially if the working part of the worksheet fits nicely on your computer screen. It should fit as nicely on a single sheet of paper, right?

Regrettably, this assumption can be wrong much of the time. Depending on your monitor's resolution, you might be able to see many more columns across and rows down than could possibly fit on a single sheet of paper. Even a worksheet that uses only six or seven columns might require two sheets of paper, with a stray column or row printing on the second sheet.

The solution requires telling Excel that you want your worksheet to fit on one sheet. This is easy to do using the Page Setup dialog box. (There are a few negative consequences, however, depending on how much of your worksheet doesn't fit on one sheet naturally—namely, by reducing the worksheet size to fit on one sheet, you can end up with tiny, illegible content.)

> **Tip**
>
> Before wasting paper, always check Print Preview. (Click Print Preview on the File menu, or click the Print Preview button on the toolbar.) This will show you how many pages the printout currently requires, and you can then use the Page Setup dialog box to adjust the printed output.

How to fix it

1. If you're in Normal view (as opposed to Print Preview), click Page Setup on the File menu.

2. In the Page Setup dialog box, make sure the Page tab is visible.

3. Click the Fit To option in the Scaling section of the dialog box, and check the number that appears in both the Pages Wide By and Tall boxes. The default setting is 1; if another number appears, overwrite it by selecting it and typing 1. ▶

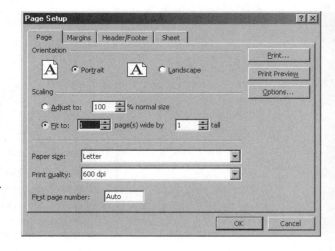

4. Click OK to apply any changes and close the dialog box.

5. Click Print Preview on the File menu to verify that your worksheet will fit on one page, and then print it.

Feeling disoriented?

If your worksheet is printed on two pages because it's too wide, and only one or two columns end up on that second page, try turning the paper on its side so that the worksheet is printed in landscape orientation. This could eliminate the need to reduce the scaling of your worksheet, or require less reduction of your worksheet content because the worksheet has a wider area on which to be printed. If your worksheet is too long for a regular sheet of paper in portrait orientation (the default), changing to landscape orientation won't help. But you can change your paper's orientation and then check to see if the change does the trick. On the File menu, click Page Setup to open the Page Setup dialog box, and make sure the Page tab is visible. In the Orientation section of the dialog box, click the Landscape option, and then click OK. You can't see what your printed worksheet will look like while it is in Normal view, so click Print Preview on the File menu to see how it will look when you print it. If the Next and Previous buttons in the Print Preview window are unavailable, your worksheet will be printed on one sheet of paper. If either or both of the buttons are available, click them (one at a time, of course) to see which parts of the worksheet still stray onto extra pages. ▶

If your worksheet still won't fit on one page, you can reduce the scaling percentage or change the Fit To settings in the Page Setup dialog box as needed.

Tip

When you are in Print Preview, you can click the Setup button to display the Page Setup dialog box. After you make your selections in the dialog box, clicking OK returns you to Print Preview.

Click the Next and Previous buttons to see additional pages.

Preview: Page 3 of 4

Tip

As a general rule, reducing the scaling percentage below 75% can result in a worksheet that is difficult to read. If your worksheet doesn't fit on one page without reducing it to Lilliputian proportions, you might have to stick with printing it on more than one page.

I can print only part of my worksheet, but I want to print all of it

Source of the problem

The Print dialog box offers the All option in its Print Range section, and one would assume that the entire worksheet will be printed if that option is selected. A generally reliable assumption, but if you're reading this part of the book, something tells me you feel as though the Print dialog box duped you—you saw the All option selected (it's the default, after all), and you clicked the OK button. You waited for your worksheet printout to emerge from the printer, and sadly, parts of it weren't included in the print job. What gives?

Allow me to introduce you to a very convenient feature that once used, can be a real nuisance. The feature gives you the ability to select a section of the worksheet and set it as the print area. It's convenient in that it allows you to select an area as small as a single cell and print just that—nothing confidential, nothing that's still being worked on, nothing you don't want to be printed. No need to hide columns or rows, no need to copy sections of the worksheet to another worksheet just to print them on their own. So where's the downside, and how does this have anything to do with the All option not working?

If you've set a print area in your worksheet, it remains set as the print area until and unless you clear it. That means that if you set a print area at 10 a.m., when you go back at 3 p.m. and click Print on the File menu, the only part of your worksheet that will be printed is the content within that print area. This is true even if All is selected in the Print dialog box's Print Range section. Even if you really, really wanted to print the whole worksheet.

The solution? Clear your print area before attempting to print a worksheet. Even if you didn't set one, someone else might have. There's no harm in clearing it before printing your worksheet—you'll save yourself the aggravation and paper for an unusable partial printout.

How to fix it

1. On the File menu, point to Print Area, and then click Clear Print Area. Any print area that was set is removed.

2. On the File menu, click Print. In the Print dialog box, make sure that All is selected in the Print Range section.

3. Click OK to print the entire worksheet.

> **Tip**
>
> To print a small portion of your worksheet without creating a print area, select that portion, and click Print on the File menu. In the Print What section of the Print dialog box, click Selection, and click OK. Only the content of the selected cells will be printed.

What print area??

How can you tell if a print area has been set? By the appearance of a dashed border around the print area itself. This should not be confused with the flashing dashed border that appears when you select a range of cells and copy or cut them to the clipboard. This is a static, thin dashed border around the cells you selected before pointing to Print Area on the File menu and clicking Set Print Area. ▶

If you're thinking that you have to do a preemptive clearing of the print area before you print anything, that's not necessarily the case. If the entire working area of the worksheet can be seen without a lot of scrolling up and down, you can easily see if a print area has been set. If your data is voluminous and spread all over the worksheet, then clearing the print area before any print job is probably a good step to take,

The print area is indicated by dashed lines.

	A	B	C	D	E	F	G	H
1			✧ Course Enrollments					
2								
3	Application	Course #	Course Name	Course Date	Cost per Student	Number Enrolled	Total Class Revenue	Trainer Assigned
4	Access	MSAD1	Access Application Development	11/10/2000	$ 400.00	4	$ 1,600.00	Moore
5	Access	MSA1	Access level 1	10/12/2000	$ 300.00	6	$ 1,800.00	Cook
6	Access	MSA2	Access level 2	10/25/2000	$ 325.00	8	$ 2,600.00	Cook
7	Access	MSA3	Access level 3	10/30/2000	$ 350.00	8	$ 2,800.00	Cook
8	Excel	MSE3	Excel level 3	11/5/2000	$ 350.00	9	$ 3,150.00	Corson
9	Excel	MSE2	Excel level 2	10/20/2000	$ 325.00	7	$ 2,275.00	Elmaleh
10	Excel	MSE1	Excel level 1	10/8/2000	$ 300.00	10	$ 3,000.00	Fuller
11	FrontPage	FPWD1	Web Design w/FrontPage, level 1	11/5/2000	$ 400.00	12	$ 4,800.00	Fuller
12	FrontPage	FPWD2	Web Design w/FrontPage, level 2	11/15/2000	$ 500.00	12	$ 6,000.00	Fuller
13	PowerPoint	MSP1	PowerPoint level 1	10/15/2000	$ 300.00	6	$ 1,800.00	Talbot
14	PowerPoint	MSP2	PowerPoint level 2	10/30/2000	$ 350.00	8	$ 2,800.00	Talbot
15	Publisher	MSPUB	Publisher Basics	11/13/2000	$ 350.00	8	$ 2,800.00	Kline
16	Windows	MSWU	Windows 98 User	11/2/2000	$ 300.00	10	$ 3,000.00	Corson
17	Windows	MSNTA	Windows NT Administration	11/8/2000	$ 500.00	5	$ 2,500.00	Elmaleh
18	Word	MSW2	Word level 2	10/15/2000	$ 325.00	8	$ 2,600.00	Fuller
19	Word	MSW3	Word level 3	11/1/2000	$ 350.00	12	$ 4,200.00	Kline
20	Word	MSW1	Word level 1	10/5/2000	$ 300.00	9	$ 2,700.00	Talbot
21					Total	142	$ 50,425.00	

Tip

Another way to tell if there's a print area set anywhere in your worksheet is to view the sheet in Page Break Preview mode. On the View menu, click Page Break Preview, and you'll see the print area mapped out with a thick blue border around it, on a gray field. To expand or reduce the print area, drag the border out to increase the print area's size, or drag it in to reduce it. Switch back to Normal view, and you'll see the print area has changed to match the dimensions you designated.

just to avoid having to scroll around looking for a previously set print area or wasting paper on a partial printout when you wanted the whole thing.

Maybe you don't need to have it all

When you get to know Excel's Print Area command, you'll find that it's useful for printing what appears to be "all" of your worksheet, when it's actually only the sections that contain information you want to print—you can skip blank sections or cells that contain repetitive or uninteresting data. Using your Ctrl key, select all the areas of your worksheet that you want to print. (They needn't be contiguous, and single cells all around the worksheet can be included in the mass selection.) When the areas are selected, point to Print Area on the File menu, and then click Set Print Area. Any previously set area will be removed, and when you choose to print all of the worksheet, you'll really be printing all of the worksheet that you're interested in, leaving out the cells and ranges that aren't important. Note, however, that if your selected areas are not contiguous, each of them will be printed on a separate page.

My column and row labels don't appear on every page of my printout

Source of the problem

When your worksheet is printed on more than one page, it can be hard to follow the content if the column labels and row labels don't repeat on each page. For the same reason, it's very convenient to freeze the label row at the top of a long database, and have those labels stay on the screen no matter how far down into the database you might scroll. Having those labels remain on each page of the printout can be very helpful as well. No, you don't have to figure out where your page breaks will occur and retype the labels at that point in your worksheet—in fact if you do that, you can render your database useless, making it impossible to sort and use AutoFilter properly.

The solution, you'll be happy to hear, is much simpler. You merely need to tell Excel that you want your column and row labels to repeat on each page, and make sure Excel knows in which cells those labels are currently found. It's important to note, however, that Excel will repeat your column and row labels only on pages that print the content from the sections of your worksheet that the labels apply to. (This sounds like a limitation, but it's not. If your worksheet contains information that doesn't pertain to or fall under the labels, you don't want the labels to appear on those pages, and confuse someone reading the printout.) For example, if your column labels are in cells A3 through H3, only pages containing cells from columns A through H will have the labels printed on them. If your row labels are in cells A4 through A20, only pages with cells between row 4 and row 20 will contain the labels. ▶

The application names are the row labels.

These are the column labels.

	A	B	C	D	E	F	G	H
1			Course Enrollments					
2								
3	Application	Course #	Course Name	Course Date	Cost per Student	Number Enrolled	Total Class Revenue	Trainer Assigned
4	Access	MSAD1	Access Application Development	11/10/2000	$ 400.00	4	$ 1,600.00	Moore
5	Access	MSA1	Access level 1	10/12/2000	$ 300.00	6	$ 1,800.00	Cook
6	Access	MSA2	Access level 2	10/25/2000	$ 325.00	8	$ 2,600.00	Cook
7	Access	MSA3	Access level 3	10/30/2000	$ 350.00	8	$ 2,800.00	Cook
8	Excel	MSE3	Excel level 3	11/5/2000	$ 350.00	9	$ 3,150.00	Corson
9	Excel	MSE2	Excel level 2	10/20/2000	$ 325.00	7	$ 2,275.00	Elmaleh
10	Excel	MSE1	Excel level 1	10/8/2000	$ 300.00	10	$ 3,000.00	Fuller
11	FrontPage	FPWD1	Web Design w/FrontPage, level 1	11/5/2000	$ 400.00	12	$ 4,800.00	Fuller
12	FrontPage	FPWD2	Web Design w/FrontPage, level 2	11/15/2000	$ 500.00	12	$ 6,000.00	Fuller
13	PowerPoint	MSP1	PowerPoint level 1	10/15/2000	$ 300.00	6	$ 1,800.00	Talbot
14	PowerPoint	MSP2	PowerPoint level 2	10/30/2000	$ 350.00	8	$ 2,800.00	Talbot
15	Publisher	MSPUB	Publisher Basics	11/13/2000	$ 350.00	8	$ 2,800.00	Kline
16	Windows	MSWU	Windows 98 User	11/2/2000	$ 300.00	10	$ 3,000.00	Corson
17	Windows	MSNTA	Windows NT Administration	11/8/2000	$ 500.00	5	$ 2,500.00	Elmaleh
18	Word	MSW2	Word level 2	10/15/2000	$ 325.00	8	$ 2,600.00	Fuller
19	Word	MSW3	Word level 3	11/1/2000	$ 350.00	12	$ 4,200.00	Kline
20	Word	MSW1	Word level 1	10/5/2000	$ 300.00	9	$ 2,700.00	Talbot
21					Total	142	$ 50,425.00	
22								
23								

Only pages containing this range of cells will include the repeated column and row labels.

How to fix it

1. On the worksheet you intend to print, click Page Setup on the File menu.

2. Click the Sheet tab.

3. In the Print Titles section of the dialog box, click in the Rows To Repeat At Top box to place your insertion point there.

4. Outside of the dialog box (move it aside as needed), drag through the row or rows that contain your column labels. Note the range of cells that appears in the Rows To Repeat At Top box.

5. Click in the Columns To Repeat At Left box to place your insertion point there.

6. Again, outside of the dialog box, drag through the column or columns containing your row labels. Note the range that appears in the Columns To Repeat At Left box. (You might have to adjust the column settings Excel selects by retyping the letter of the column that "finishes off" your row labels.) ▶

7. Click OK.

8. Although you don't need this last step to make this feature work, you might still want to take it as a wise final preprinting step. On the File menu, click Print Preview to see how your worksheet will look when you print it, and make sure your labels are where you want them, on the pages you need them. If all's well, go ahead and print your worksheet whenever you're ready.

Tip

If your column and row labels appear on more than one of your worksheets, it becomes more important than ever that they be spelled correctly, that they use well-known abbreviation forms, and that they're formatted attractively—bold to make them stand out, for example, or in a different color so that you can distinguish them from the rows and columns containing data.

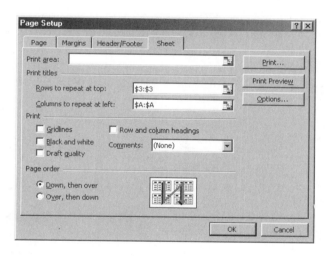

It takes too long to open and print all of my workbooks one at a time

Source of the problem

For people who work with several different workbooks on a consistent basis, it can be a pain to open each of them, one at a time, whenever you need them all open. If you also need to print them, that's another step that has to be repeated for each open workbook. There has to be a better way, right? Yep!

Excel's Open dialog box allows you to select multiple workbooks from within the same folder and open them all at the same time. Moreover, you can choose to open and print all of them at the same time, saving a lot of redundant effort.

Tip

The quick procedure described in this section works only for workbooks that are stored in the same folder. If you want to open all of your workbooks at once, move or copy them to the same folder, and then follow the steps in this section. If the workbooks must remain in separate folders, you'll have to open and print groups of workbooks in each of the separate folders.

How to fix it

1. Make sure your printer is on and ready, with enough paper for the entire print job. On the File menu, click Open.

2. As needed, navigate to the folder containing the workbooks you want to open and print.

3. When the desired workbooks are displayed in the dialog box, click the first one you want to open.

4. Hold down the Ctrl key, and click each of the other workbooks you want to open and print once. (Don't worry if your dialog box looks different from ours.) ▶

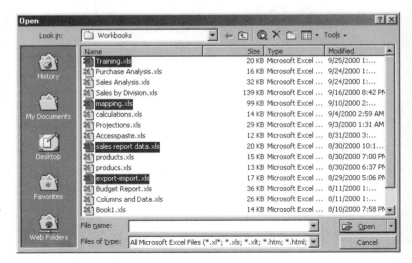

5. Click the Tools button (or the Commands And Settings button, if you're working in Excel 97), and then click Print on the drop-down menu that appears. Without the Print dialog box opening, each of the selected workbooks will be opened, all the contents of all worksheets will be sent to the default printer, and the workbooks will be closed when the print operation is complete.

Open (and close) sesame

You can use a variation of this procedure to open a series of workbooks without printing them. To open several workbooks at once, click Open on the File menu, and in the Open dialog box, move to the folder containing the workbooks you want to open. (Again, they must all be in the same folder.) Use the Ctrl key to select multiple files, and then click the Open button. All of the workbooks will open, and each will be listed on the Window menu.

After the workbooks are open and you've done whatever reviewing and editing they require, you will probably want to save and close them. If you don't want to exit Excel at the same time, there's a trick that allows you to close all open workbooks. (You'll get a prompt to save any workbooks that haven't been saved since their last edits.) Press the Shift key as you click the File menu, and you'll notice that the Close command has changed to Close All. Click that command, and each workbook will be closed in turn. If a prompt appears asking if you want to save changes, click Yes to save them or No to close the workbook in question without saving changes. (To abandon the group closing process, click Cancel.)

Tip

If there are any problems printing any of the workbooks you've selected, appropriate print error messages will appear. If, for example, one of the workbooks is empty, a "Nothing to print" message will appear. If one of the workbooks contains worksheets set to Landscape orientation, a prompt will appear asking if you want the printer to change its orientation automatically. Respond to these prompts so that the print process can continue for the remaining workbooks with printable content.

Warning

If any of the workbooks you want to open are already open, when you try to open them again in the Open dialog box, a prompt appears, warning you that if you choose to reopen the file, all changes made since the file was previously opened will be lost. Click Yes to reopen the workbook and lose the changes, or No to leave the currently open copy intact—that is, to ignore your instruction to reopen the file.

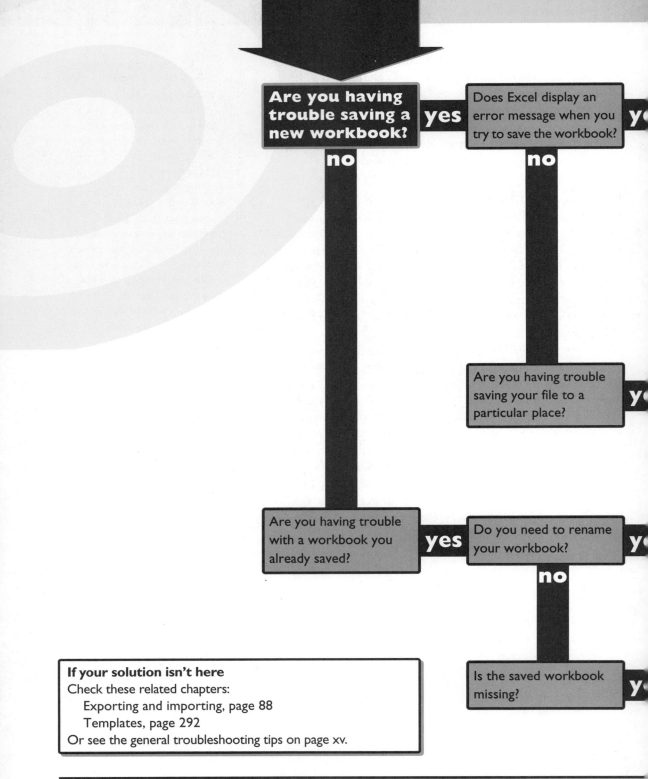

Are you having trouble saving a new workbook?

yes → Does Excel display an error message when you try to save the workbook?

yes →

no

Does Excel display an error message when you try to save the workbook?

no

Are you having trouble saving your file to a particular place?

y

Are you having trouble with a workbook you already saved?

yes → Do you need to rename your workbook?

y

no

Is the saved workbook missing?

y

If your solution isn't here
Check these related chapters:
Exporting and importing, page 88
Templates, page 292
Or see the general troubleshooting tips on page xv.

Are you saving it in .xls format?

yes

Go to...
I can't save my workbook, page 246.

no

Are you saving it for use by another application?

yes

Quick fix

1. In the Save As dialog box, click the Save As Type drop-down arrow.

2. If you need to be able to open the file in a word processor, click Tab Delimited Text (.txt).

3. If you'll be sending the file to someone who uses Lotus 1-2-3, click WKS (1-2-3) (.wks).

4. Give the file a name in the File Name box, and click OK to save the file in the selected format.

no

Are you trying to save it as a web page?

yes

Go to...
I can't save my workbook in HTML format, page 252.

Go to...
I'm tired of changing folders every time I save a new workbook, page 248.

Quick fix

1. Close the workbook, but keep Excel open.

2. On the File menu, click Open. Navigate to the folder containing the workbook, and right-click the workbook's filename.

3. Click Rename on the shortcut menu, and type a new name for the workbook, including the extension. (Keep the same .xls file extension, or Windows won't know which application to use when opening the file in the future.)

Go to...
I can't find my workbook, page 250.

I can't save my workbook

Source of the problem

If you open an existing workbook file and try to resave it, Excel will stop you if the file is protected from modifications by a password; if the file is open twice on your computer and the copy you're working with is open as read-only; or if the name you're attempting to give the file is already used by another workbook in the same folder.

When Excel refuses to let you save the open workbook, it should explain why. It doesn't merely say "No!" and leave you in the dark—it gives you a message telling you what the problem is. Based on the message you receive, you can act accordingly—provide the password that's required, close the extra version of the file you have open twice, or edit the name you're trying to use so that it isn't the same as the existing file. ▶

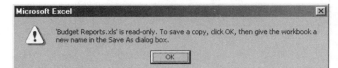

How to fix it

- If you need a password for the file you want to save, you'll have to go to the person who password-protected the file. He or she could have done it using the commands on Excel's Protection submenu or during the saving process. In either case, ask the person for the password, and enter it when you're prompted to do so. If the person won't give you the password or you can't find the person who protected the file, save the file with a different name. You can then bypass the password because the original file won't be overwritten.

- If the file you're trying to save is already open but the copy you're using is read-only, you must either open the Window menu, switch to the other open version of the file, and then close it; or save the read-only version with a different name so that the other open version isn't affected.

- If the file name you want to use for the workbook is already used by another workbook in the folder that you're saving the file to, either give the file you're saving a different name or save it to a different folder.

Tip

Having files with the same name, even if they're in different folders, is risky. It's easy to confuse them and edit or print the wrong file. If you want two or more files to have the same name, consider adding a character to the end of the name, such as Sales Analysis A.xls, Sales Analysis B.xls, and so on. When you have a lot of similarly named files, also remember to check the modified date for the files to make sure you're using the right file. In the Windows Explorer or My Computer window, click Details on the View menu, and check the date the files were last modified.

So how'd they do that password thing?

If the file you tried to save was password-protected to prevent changes, you can use the same feature yourself to protect your files from being opened or modified by people you don't want using them. You can apply a password to a file to prevent people from opening the file without authorization, or force them to supply another password when they try to save changes to the file once it's open. By preventing people from saving the file with the existing name, you force them to save the file with a different name, which leaves your file the same as the last time you saved it.

TIp

The password-protection feature should not be confused with the Protection submenu's commands in Excel—this process is available in all the Office applications, and pertains to the file, not its contents.

To apply a password, click Save As on the File menu. If the file is being saved for the first time (its current name is Book1 or Book2, etc.), you can click Save on the File menu. In the Save As dialog box, navigate to the folder you want to save the file in, and enter a name for it in the File Name box. Click the Tools button, and click General Options on the drop-down menu. (If you're working in Excel 97, click the Options button.) In the Save Options dialog box, enter a password in the Password To Open text box if you want to keep people from opening the file without a password. (Don't worry if your dialog box looks a little different from ours.) ▶

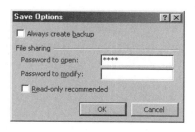

To prevent people from saving the file (with or without any changes) unless they give it a new name (thus creating a new file), type a password in the Password To Modify text box. If you want to further protect the file, select the Read-Only Recommended check box if you want Excel to display a recommendation to users that they open the file as read-only. Click OK. For each password you enter, a Confirm Password dialog box appears, asking you to retype the password you created. Type the password again in each successive box, and click OK. Back in the Save As dialog box, click Save to complete the saving process.

I'm tired of changing folders every time I save a new workbook

Source of the problem

By default, Excel saves new workbooks in the My Documents folder. If you click Save on the File menu or click the Save button and do nothing other than enter a file name for the new workbook, the default file location is applied. Of course it's no problem to choose a different folder for the odd workbooks that don't belong in the My Documents folder, but if every workbook you create belongs in another folder, switching from My Documents to that folder every time you save a new file can certainly be tedious.

The solution to this problem lies in changing Excel's default location for new workbook files. When you choose a new default folder, choose one that's the likely home for the vast majority of your workbooks, not just the one you're dealing with at the time. If you categorize your workbooks by placing them in folders by subject or content, and you aren't sure which one of the folders is the most frequently used, make them subfolders of the My Documents folder and leave that as the default. ▶

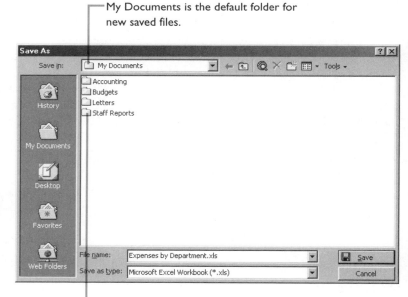

My Documents is the default folder for new saved files.

Double-click a subfolder to select it as the home for your new file.

> **Tip**
> If you decide to create a new folder and make that the default folder for saving workbooks, create one just for workbooks, such as "My Workbooks," which can be a subfolder of My Documents. Give your folders relevant names, and create a folder hierarchy that makes sense according to the relationships between the folders and the files within them.

At the most, you'll have to double-click one of the folders listed in the default folder, adding just one double-click to the process of saving your files.

How to fix it

1. On the Tools menu, click Options.

2. In the Options dialog box, click the General tab.

3. Click to position your insertion point in the Default File Location box. The box should display the name of the default folder to which new files are saved. (Don't worry if your dialog box looks a little different than ours.) ▶

4. Using the arrow keys and the Backspace and Delete keys as needed, edit the contents of the box to show the complete path of the default folder you want to use. The path includes the drive letter (most likely C:\), as well as the full and accurate names of any folders that contain the default folder you want to use.

5. Click OK to put your change into effect and close the dialog box.

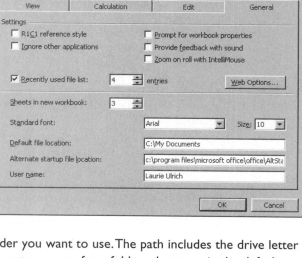

While you're there...

The next time you find yourself on the General tab of the Options dialog box, you can also adjust the number of recently used files displayed at the foot of the File menu. The default is 4, but you can change that to anything from 0 (which turns off the feature altogether) to 9 by clicking the up or down arrows in the Entries box to the right of the Recently Used File List option.

Why bother tinkering with this feature? If you want to make it harder for people who share your computer to tell which files you used last, it's a good idea to display no recently used files on the File menu. Or, if you tend to open the same group of workbooks throughout an average workday, it can be very convenient to have a longer list of files on the File menu. Opening files through this list is a lot faster than clicking Open on the File menu and locating the files in the Open dialog box.

How does this relate to saving files? If the file you click at the bottom of the File menu won't open (indicated by an error message that says the file is not found), it's because the file no longer exists where it was saved the last time you had it open. You might have renamed the file, or you might have moved the file to a different folder. In this case, you'll have to press Ctrl+O, and open the workbook from the Open dialog box. The File menu will be updated the next time you save and close the workbook.

> **Tip**
> Before opening a file from the recently used file list on the File menu, check the Window menu to make sure the file isn't already open. If you open a file that's already open, you'll be surprised when you're unable to save the file without giving it a new name.

I can't find my workbook

Source of the problem

We've all experienced that sinking feeling when we go to open a file from the folder where we just *know* we saved it, and it isn't there. Panic sets in, and perhaps a feeling that you're losing your memory. Where could the file be? How did it get lost?

Unless you deleted or moved the file since saving it, it's right where you left it. The problem lies in your memory of where it was saved. While it's possible that you or someone else did rename, move, or delete it since you saved it, if you're the only person using your computer, and you don't experience loss of memory on a regular basis, the file is simply saved in a different folder than the one you remember.

The solution? Find it. Before you say, "Well, duh!" what I mean is, let Excel find it for you. In the Open dialog box (where you might already be, if you're trying to open a file and can't find it), use the Find command to search your entire computer or perhaps just a specific group of folders for the file that's not where you thought you left it.

Tip
If you recently worked on the file you're looking for, use the list of recently used files at the foot of the File menu to reopen it. No matter where you really saved it, this list will point to the file in its current location, and clicking the file will open it. You can then click Save As on the File menu to see where the file is stored. If the file isn't in the list of recently used files but was used in the last day or so, try the Start menu's Documents menu. (Click Start, and then point to Documents.) If the file is listed on the Documents menu, you can open it from that shortcut, and again, you can click Save As on the File menu to see where it is stored.

How to fix it

1. If the Open dialog box isn't already open, click Open on the File menu to display it.

2. Click the Tools button, and click Find on the drop-down menu. (If you're working in Excel 97, click the Advanced button.)

Tip
If more than one file meets your Find criteria, look in the Size, Type, and Modified columns in the Open dialog box to determine which file is the one you want.

3. In the resulting dialog box, click the Look In drop-down arrow, and click your local hard drive on the drop-down list—it's better to look everywhere on your local drive than to try to guess where the file is. Make sure the Search Subfolders check box is selected.

4. In the Define More Criteria section, click a condition (Includes, Begins With, or Ends With) in the Condition drop-down list.

5. Enter at least part of the missing file's name in the Value box. Bear in mind the condition you've selected when entering a portion of the file name. ▶

6. Click the Find Now button.

7. Click Yes to add the file name search criteria to the Find dialog box, so you can use it again the next time you perform a search in the Open dialog box. Excel will search the local hard drive and all of its subfolders (or whatever drive or folder path you chose to search) and will display a list of the folders and files that meet the criteria you just set. ▶

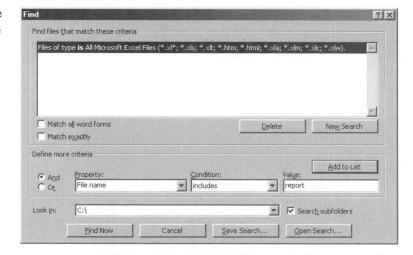

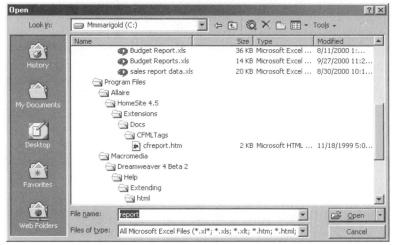

And what if I still can't find it?

There's always the possibility that your file has been deleted. Before leaping to that upsetting conclusion, however, there are other search features in the Find (or Advanced Find, if you're working in Excel 97) dialog box that can help you find a file that's been renamed or whose name you don't remember. You can search for your file based on its contents, creation date, last modification date, size, the template used to create it, or virtually any field you might have filled in (such as Author or Title) in the file's Properties dialog box. (For more information about the Properties dialog box, see "I don't want my name to appear in the comment box" on page 28.)

To make use of these tools, click an option in the Property drop-down list in the Find dialog box. The default is File Name, but the Property list contains 35 other items that you can use instead. Then select a condition option, and enter the appropriate text in the Value box.

I can't save my workbook in HTML format

Source of the problem

You want to use the global reach of the web so that clients and colleagues can view and interact with your worksheet data. Excel gives you the tools to do it. You can save your entire workbook, a single worksheet within the workbook, or even a section of a worksheet in HTML format, and post it as a page on the web. You can add interactivity, which means people can click the worksheet content and use Excel tools to edit and use the data. Those changes won't affect the actual data stored on the web, but your visitors can save the content they edit to their local computers, or copy your content to their own locally stored workbook for their own use. But saving your Excel data in HTML format can have problems. When you try to save a workbook, a worksheet, or a section thereof in HTML format, you might get an error message indicating that the file name you're trying to apply is not accessible. If this occurs, one of the following situations must exist:

- You're trying to use a name that's already being used for an HTML file in the same folder.

- You're trying to save the file to a location on the network that's not available, or to a nonexistent local drive or folder.

- You're trying to save too much data. If the amount of data exceeds the limit that can be accurately saved in HTML format, Excel won't let you complete the process.

The solutions to the first two problems require that you use a different name, location, or both for the HTML version of your content. In the last case, you must save a smaller section of your worksheet.

How to fix it

To save your file with a different name or to another folder, follow these steps:

1. Click Save As on the File menu.

2. To save the file with a different name, type the new name in the File Name box of the Save As dialog box. If you need to save the file to a different location (because the one you've selected is unavailable), click a different folder in the Save In drop-down list.

If you're trying to save too much data in HTML format, and you're working in Excel 2000, follow these steps to reduce the amount of data you're saving:

1. Select the range of cells on a single worksheet that contains the data you want to publish on the Internet.

2. On the File menu, click Save As Web Page.

3. In the Save As dialog box, click the Selection option, which is defined as the range of cells you selected. (If you selected the entire sheet, the word *Sheet* appears next to this option.) If you want, select the Add Interactivity check box so that you will be able to modify the new web page on the Internet. ▶

4. Designate a file location for the new web page in the Save In drop-down list, and then type a name for your page in the File Name box.

5. Click the Save button. The page is created, and the dialog box closes, leaving your worksheet open in Excel format.

Tip

Want to see what your new web page looks like after you create it? Instead of clicking Save in the Save As dialog box, click Publish. In the Publish As Web Page dialog box, you can confirm selections you might have already made. In addition, you have the opportunity to view the new web page in your default browser right after it is created. In the Publish As Web Page dialog box, select the Open Published Web Page In Browser check box, and then click Publish again to launch your default browser and display the new web page as it would appear on the Internet.

You can open your new web page by pressing Ctrl+O, making sure All Files (*.*) appears in the Files Of Type box, and then double-clicking the name of the file you just saved. (The page name should appear with an .htm file extension.)

This solution is continued on the next page.

I can't save my workbook in HTML format

(continued from page 253)

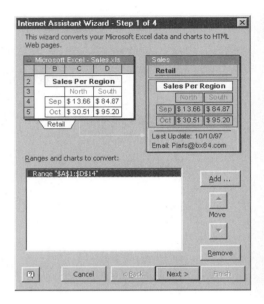

If you're working in Excel 97, you'll need to follow these steps to save a range of cells, or all of the cells on a worksheet, in HTML format:

1. Select the range of cells on a single worksheet that contains the data you want to publish on the web, and then click Save As HTML on the File menu.

2. The Internet Assistant Wizard appears, displaying the wizard's first step, with the range you selected in the Ranges And Charts To Convert section. Click Next. ▶

3. In the next step, accept the default option of creating a new HTML file, and then click Next.

4. In the wizard's third step, enter any header and footer information you want in the boxes provided, and then click Next.

5. In the wizard's fourth and final step, make sure the Save The Result As An HTML File option is selected, and then designate a file name and location for your new web page in the File Path box.

6. Click Finish to save the new web page.

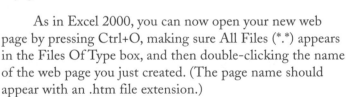

When you name your file, don't use spaces. Although Excel won't prevent you from using them, most web browsing software doesn't support file names with spaces in them, and your page might not be displayed properly if you include spaces in the file name. If you want the appearance of a space, use the underscore character. (Hold down the Shift key, and then press the hyphen [-] key.)

As in Excel 2000, you can now open your new web page by pressing Ctrl+O, making sure All Files (*.*) appears in the Files Of Type box, and then double-clicking the name of the web page you just created. (The page name should appear with an .htm file extension.)

When you publish your content to the web, whatever formatting you've applied—text and numeric formatting, cell shading, text colors—will appear on the web as it appeared in your worksheet. It's a good idea, therefore, to take a look at the rest of the web site to which your Excel-based page will be added. If you or your company employed a designer to create your site (or if you took the time to design it yourself), you don't want to add content that will clash with your color scheme or overall tone.

Don't just sit there, do something!

Excel 2000 Your Excel data can be a handy addition to any web site, but you can increase its usefulness by adding interactivity to the published content. Interactivity lets you work with the data on the web page, making changes to the data and editing or adding formulas. ▶

Of course you're interacting with only your copy of the content, not the data as it is stored on the web server that provides the web site content—when you close the page or hit the Back button in your browser, all changes are lost.

If you want to keep the data and your changes, you have to save the page to your local drive, which will create an .html file from the data including any edits you've made. This file can be reopened in any browser window (even if you're offline), in Excel, or even in Microsoft Word.

You can make changes to content on a web page.

	A	B	C	D
1	Application	Course #	Course Name	Course Date
2	Access	MSA1	Access level 1	10/12/2000
3	Access	MSA2	Access level 2	10/25/2000
4	Access	MSA3	Access level 3	10/30/2000
5	Excel	MSE3	Excel level 3	11/5/2000
6	Windows	MSWU	Windows 98 User	11/2/2000
7	Excel	MSE2	Excel level 2	10/20/2000
8	Windows	MSNTA	Windows NT Admin	11/8/2000
9	Excel	MSE1	Excel level 1	10/8/2000
10	FrontPage	FPWD1	Web Design w/Fron	11/5/2000
11	FrontPage	FPWD2	Web Design w/Fron	11/15/2000
12	Word	MSW2	Word level 2	10/15/2000
13	Publisher	MSPUB	Publisher Basics	11/13/2000
14	Word	MSW3	Word level 3	11/1/2000
15	Access	MSAD1	Access Application	11/10/2000
16	PowerPoint	MSP1	PowerPoint level 1	10/15/2000
17	PowerPoint	MSP2	PowerPoint level 2	10/30/2000
18	Word	MSW1	Word level 1	10/5/2000

Tip
You can also copy the web content to the clipboard, paste it in an open workbook on your local computer, and then play with the data there.

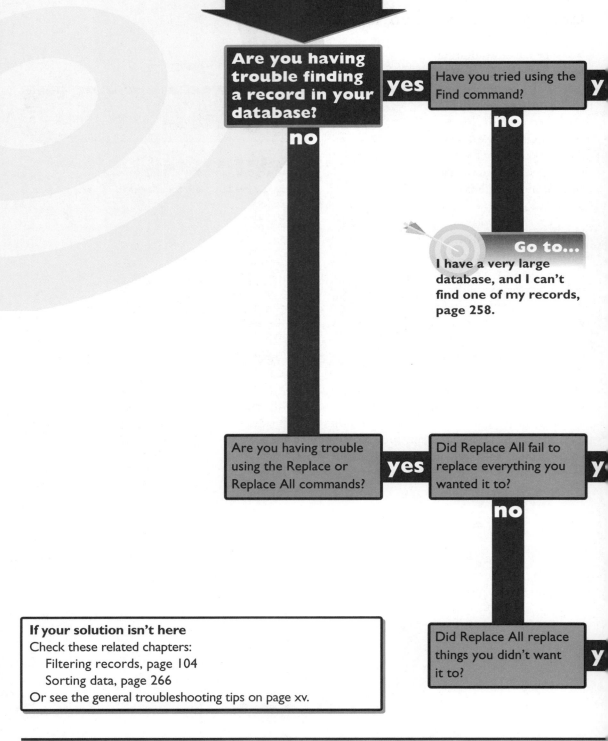

Are you having trouble finding a record in your database?

yes → Have you tried using the Find command?

→ **y**

no ↓

no ↓

Go to...
I have a very large database, and I can't find one of my records, page 258.

Are you having trouble using the Replace or Replace All commands?

yes → Did Replace All fail to replace everything you wanted it to?

→ **y**

no ↓

If your solution isn't here
Check these related chapters:
Filtering records, page 104
Sorting data, page 266
Or see the general troubleshooting tips on page xv.

Did Replace All replace things you didn't want it to?

→ **y**

arching for data

Did the Find command result in an error message? **yes**

Go to...
When I use the Find command, I get an error message, page 260.

no

Do you need to search in more than one field in your database? **yes**

Go to...
The Find command doesn't allow me to search by example, page 264.

no

Are you unsure which worksheet contains the content you need to find? **yes**

Quick fix
1. Group your sheets by clicking the first sheet tab in the workbook, holding down the Shift key, and then clicking the last sheet tab.
2. Release the Shift key.
3. Click Find on the Edit menu.
4. Enter the content you're looking for in the Find What box of the Find dialog box.
5. Click Find Next to find and highlight each occurrance of the Find What content on any sheet in your workbook. If necessary, click Find Next again until you locate the specific instance of the content you are looking for.
6. To ungroup your sheets, right-click a sheet tab, and click Ungroup Sheets on the shortcut menu.

Quick fix
If you used Replace All and not all of the changes you expected happened, the problem lies with your Find What value. Check it for typos, and make sure the Match Case and/or Find Entire Cells Only check boxes are selected only if they're appropriate for the situation.

Go to...
I used Replace All, and now I wish I hadn't, page 262.

I have a very large database, and I can't find one of my records

Source of the problem

Any Excel worksheet can have thousands of rows, each one a record in a database. The more records you have, the more likely you are to have to rely on Excel to find one of them when you can't seem to locate it by scrolling through the list. Imagine you have a contacts database, and you need to find the guy who installed the skylight in the office last year so you can call him about a leak that's developed. You don't remember his name, and it's unlikely that his company name is Skylights, Inc. How do you find him?

Excel has a variety of tools that you can put into service to help you find records in your database. Depending on the columns, or fields, in your database, you might or might not be able to use all of them. For example, if you have a column with *Contact Type* as the label, you might be able to find the skylight installer if you have entered *Contractor* in the Contact Type field of his record. You could find him by using AutoFilter to filter that field for *Contractor*. If you have a Date Of Last Contact field, you could sort the records by that field and look for records dated around the time you called him last year to install the skylight. If your database contains a Memo field into which you typed notes about each contact, you could select that column, click Find on the Edit menu, and search on the word *skylight*, which should be in that field for this person's record.

So, you have three options for finding your missing record: use AutoFilter, Sort, and/or Find. Why "and/or"? Because if you try one and come up dry, you can always try another option. At least one of the tools described here will find a missing record in virtually any database, unless that record has been deleted.

"Filtering records" on page 104 and "Sorting data" on page 266 cover the use of AutoFilter and sorting, respectively, and you can refer to those chapters to use those tools to locate your missing data. But the Find feature is probably the most effective of the tools you can use to locate a missing record, provided you know a word (or portion thereof) or a number in that record that you can use for the search.

> **Tip**
> You don't need to type a whole word or phrase to find the text you're looking for. If, for example, you wanted to find the guy who installed the skylight, you could type *sky* in the Find What box, and aside from stopping at skywriters or Skye Terrier breeders, you're likely to turn up the missing skylight installer in no time.

How to fix it

1. If you're sure which column contains the word or number you're searching for, select that entire column by clicking the letter in the column heading. If you're not sure which column contains the word or number you're searching for and you're willing to look through the entire list, hopping from each incident of the word or number as it occurs in any field, click any cell within the database.

2. Click Find on the Edit menu to open the Find dialog box. ▶

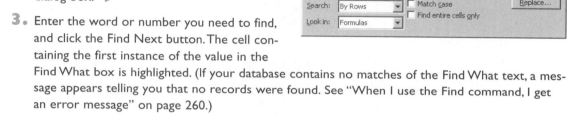

3. Enter the word or number you need to find, and click the Find Next button. The cell containing the first instance of the value in the Find What box is highlighted. (If your database contains no matches of the Find What text, a message appears telling you that no records were found. See "When I use the Find command, I get an error message" on page 260.)

4. If the first result of the search isn't the record you were looking for, click Find Next again, and continue to do so until the data you're looking for is highlighted.

5. Click Close to close the dialog box and end the Find session.

Hide and seek

You can use the Find dialog box's Match Case and Find Entire Cells Only options to refine your search and eliminate stopping on cells that don't really match your criteria. Selecting the Match Case check box allows you to enter a value in the Find What box in lower, upper, title, or sentence case so that only those cells containing your entry in that same case will be found. ▶

This cell met the Find criteria. ⌐

This cell didn't meet the Find criteria because it's in the wrong case.

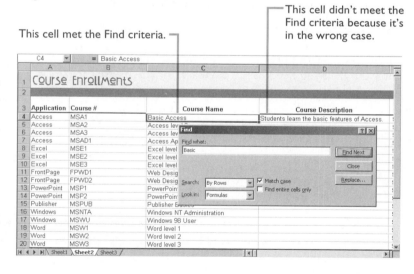

Select the Find Entire Cells Only check box to restrict your results to cells containing the exact entry—no more, no less—that you typed in the Find What box. For example, if you're looking for the year 1998, you'd want to select the Find Entire Cells Only check box to avoid finding cells containing entries such as "$51,998.62."

When I use the Find command, I get an error message

Source of the problem

You use the Find command to search for a record, and when you click Find Next in the Find dialog box, a error message tells you that none of the records meet your search criteria. If the Office Assistant is displayed, it gives you the bad news; otherwise, the error appears in a message box. You can click OK to make either one of them go away, but that solves only the "don't kill the messenger" part of your problem. You still haven't bee able to find the record you were looking for. ▶

The problem stems from one of two situations:

- The data you seek simply isn't in the database.

- Your Find criteria are faulty.

In the first situation, the problem is not solvable, unless you enter the data you need in the database, in which case the data is not only back in the database, but you know precisely where it is! In the second situation, the solution is to check your critria and fix typos or turn the Find options on or off, depending on whether or not you're using them and whether they're appropriate.

Microsoft Excel	✕
Microsoft Excel cannot find the data you're searching for. If you are certain the data exists in the current sheet, check what you typed and try again.	
OK	

Tip

Make sure that you don't have a section of your worksheet selected while your search is going on. If you select one or more columns or rows before issuing the Find command, the search will be restricted to those cells. If you want to search the whole database, make sure you don't have a range selected when you try to find your data.

How to fix it

1. Press Ctrl+F to display the Find dialog box, and then clear the check boxes for any Find options (such as Match Case and Find Entire Cells Only) that you might have selected during your first Find attempt.

2. Check the spelling of the text you entered in the Find What box. If you entered a number, make sure there is no transposition or other typo.

3. After correcting any errors, click Find Next again.

4. If the desired data is still not found, try entering a likely error in the Find What box. For example, if you're looking for the city of Phoenix, type *Pheonix*, a common misspelling of the word.

5. If that doesn't work, try making the Find What entry less specific. This will increase the number of unwanted hits as you click Find Next, but if you're looking for *Phoenix* and can't find it with the correct spelling (*Phoenix*) or the common misspelling (*Pheonix*), typing a simple *Ph* in the Find What box will flush out the data if it has been incorrectly entered as, say, *Phenix*.

Keep your comments to yourself

Another Find dialog box feature that can unintentionally sabotage your search is the Look In drop-down list. Make sure it displays Formulas or Values, but not Comments. If Comments appears in the Look In box, Excel will look for your Find What entry only in any comments you've inserted in the worksheet.

If you do want to search your worksheet's comments, click Comments in the Look In list, and click Find Next. When the content you're looking for is found in a comment, the cell that contains the comment is selected, but the comment text itself will not be displayed—this is the primary reason people don't think to check if the Look In box is set to Comments when their search doesn't work. The search appears to select the wrong cell, and other than the red comment triangle in the cell, there's no indication that the comment is involved.

Look everywhere

By default, Excel's Find command works only in the active worksheet. If the data you're looking for is in another sheet, you won't find it until you run the Find command in that sheet. If you want to search an entire workbook or several sheets at once, group the sheets in the workbook before commencing the search.

To group the sheets you need to search, click the tab for one of the sheets you want to group, hold down the Ctrl key, and continue to click the other sheet tabs until all the sheets you want to group are selected. (When the sheets are grouped, their tabs will all be white.) Then click any cell on any of the grouped sheets, click Find on the Edit menu, and begin your search. When the desired data is found, you can ungroup the sheets by right-clicking any one of the sheet tabs and clicking Ungroup Sheets on the shortcut menu.

> **Tip**
> Don't forget to ungroup your sheets after you've finished working with them as a group. A significant number of commands are unavailable while sheets are grouped, including the Sort command, and the submenu of the Filter command, both of which are located on the Data menu.

I used Replace All, and now I wish I hadn't

Source of the problem

Replace All is a very powerful feature. It's great for making sweeping changes to a large worksheet, saving time and reducing the margin for error. You shouldn't expect to spot every incident of X and replace it with Y on your own, as it's very likely you'll miss at least one of the Xs. Imagine needing to edit your worksheet so that all of the serial numbers that currently start with B change to begin with R. You could sort the list of products by serial number, and then with all the Bs together, edit them manually, or you could let Excel do the work.

Wait a minute. What's that? You say you let Excel do the work with Replace All, and now your worksheet is a mess? ▶

Well, I'm not surprised. Many people use Replace All and end up regretting it. Why? Either because the entries in the Find What or Replace With boxes were wrong, and the wrong stuff ended up being replaced (or was replaced

with the wrong stuff); or because some of the cells that met the Find What criteria should have been left alone. What do you do when you've clicked the Replace All button and now you wish you hadn't?

The first thing to try is clicking Undo. If Replace All was your last action, Undo will revert the worksheet to its status prior to the Replace command being issued. If Undo doesn't work—maybe because there have been too many changes since you made your mistake, and the Replace All command is too far back in the worksheet's history—you can retrace your steps to reverse your replacement. If you replaced X with Y, and now you want the Xs back, use the Find Next and Replace buttons to replace the Ys with Xs. By using Replace rather than Replace All, you avoid creating additional problems if some of the Ys were already there (before the original Replace All fiasco) and you want to keep them.

How to fix it

1. If you applied the Replace All command to an entire workbook (with grouped sheets) or to a specific area of a worksheet, recreate that situation by grouping the sheets or selecting the range in which the reversal should occur.

2. On the Edit menu, click Replace. The Replace dialog box opens. ▶

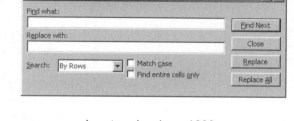

3. In the Find What box, enter the content that replaced your original content.

4. In the Replace With box, type the original entry that the Replace All replaced. For example, if you accidentally replaced every instance of the number 1998 with 2000, and you meant to replace it only where 1998 represented the year 1998, type *2000* in the Find What box and *1998* in the Replace With box.

5. Be sure to select the check boxes for any Find options (such as Match Case or Find Entire Cells Only) that you might have selected originally, or that will help your reversal take place. For example, if the Find Entire Cells Only check box was not selected the first time the Replace All command was used, selecting this check box for the reversal will narrow its results, and fail to fix the cells that shouldn't have been originally replaced.

6. Use the Find Next and Replace (rather than Replace All) buttons to move through your worksheet and edit the cells that need fixing.

How WOULD you change all the Bs to Rs?

Replace All can be used safely if you set up your Find What and Replace With entries properly. To use the serial number change as an example, imagine that all serial numbers starting with B have to change so that they start with R due to changes in product labeling. The thought of changing every B manually and perhaps missing at least one is daunting, so you decide to use Replace All—but you need to set it up to work properly.

To set up Replace All, start by selecting the column (for example, the Serial Number column) so that no other entries that start with the letter B are edited. On the Edit menu, click Replace, and in the Find What box, type the letter *B*. In the Replace With box, type the letter *R*. Select the Match Case check box so that capital or lowercase letters in the middle of words aren't affected, and then click Replace All. The replacements will be made only in the column you selected.

The Find command doesn't allow me to search by example

Source of the problem

You used a data entry form to build your database, and now you'd like to use it to scroll through your records, looking (or rather, allowing Excel to look) for records that have one or more common elements. Although you can group all worksheets and use Find to search through an entire workbook for a specific letter, word, or number, Excel might find lots of cells that don't contain what you're looking for if the Find What value is too broad, or if it's searching everywhere and not just in certain fields (or columns) in your database. If you focus the Find command on a particular field, you will find only those records with that entry in that par-ticular field—you can't search for multiple entries in multiple fields in one Find session. Although I might sound like I'm saying the Find tool isn't terribly useful, that's not my goal—Find is a very useful tool. It's just a little limiting if you want to find one particular record that has very specific entries in two or more fields.

For a more sophisticated level of searching, known in database terminology as *searching by example*, you really need to use a form. Even if you didn't use a form to enter your list's records, a form exists for your data-base, listing all the fields (your column labels) and al-lowing you to view each record individually in a Form dialog box. The form also allows you to set search cri-teria and view only the records that meet those criteria. It's a rather handy little device! ▶

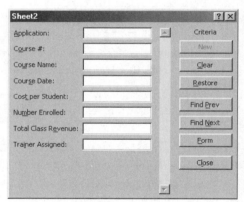

Enter example data into specific fields, and click Find Next or Find Prev to see records that match the example field-for-field.

How to fix it

1. Click any cell that contains data in your list.

2. On the Data menu, click Form. The Form dialog box opens, displaying boxes for all of your database fields.

3. Click the Criteria button. The boxes for the fields are cleared so you can enter example data for each field on which you wish to search.

4. Enter the example data in the fields you want to use for the search. Using a database of courses as an example, you could enter the name of an application in the Application field, and a price in the Cost Per Student field to list all the classes about a certain topic that have a certain cost. ▶

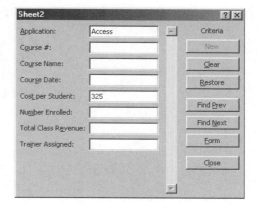

5. Click either the Find Next or Find Prev button to view the first record that meets your criteria.

6. Click either the Find Next or Find Prev button to view the rest of the records that meet your criteria, one click at a time. When you've seen them all, your computer will beep (if a sound is turned on) to indicate that there are no more records that meet your criteria.

Tip
There is one problem with using a form to look for records. It's a tiny problem, not to be confused with a huge, unacceptably horrible problem. If none of your records meet the criteria you've set, the first record in the database will appear in the form as soon as you click the Find Next or Find Prev button. If you're not paying attention, you might think that the displayed record is the right result of your search.

My criteria are greater than your criteria

When you use the form to search for records, you can enter search operators, such as > for greater than, < for less than, and = for equals. This obviously works well for numbers, dates, and times. If you use it for fields that contain text, it works alphabetically, so >A means words starting with the letters B, C, D, and so on, but not A; and >M means words starting with the letters N, O, P, and so on, but not M. Got it?

You can also use the asterisk to indicate "anything." Using the course database as an example, to find all the classes pertaining to Excel, you could type *E** in the Application or Course Name box and click Find Next or Find Prev to see all the records for classes starting with the letter E. What good is this? It saves you typing the whole word *Excel*, and for fields with long, possibly hard-to-spell names or terms in them, it's very convenient.

Tip
When searching fields that contain currency-formatted numbers, there is no need to type the dollar signs or commas. For example, to see all the courses with Total Class Revenue in excess of $1,800, you'd type >1800 in the field's box.

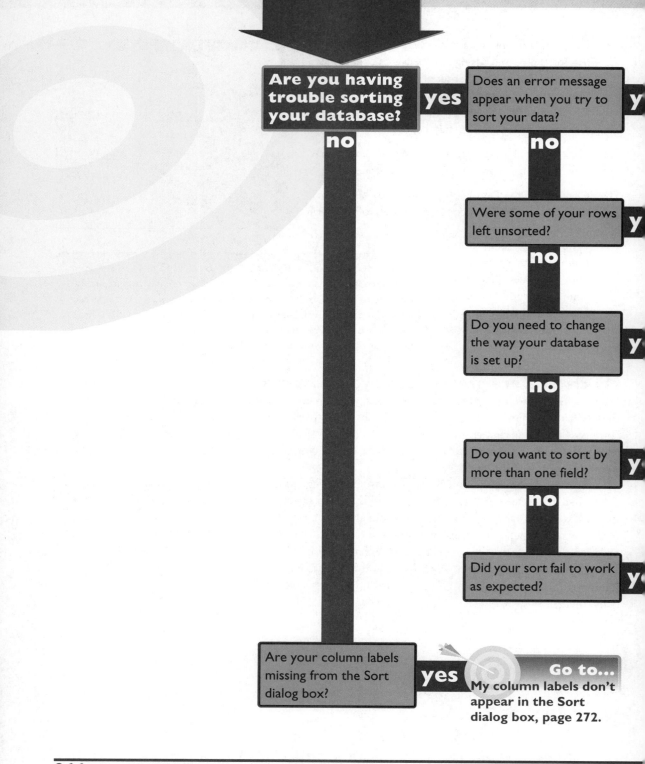

Are you having trouble sorting your database?

yes → Does an error message appear when you try to sort your data? → **y**

no

Were some of your rows left unsorted? → **y**

no

Do you need to change the way your database is set up? → **y**

no

Do you want to sort by more than one field? → **y**

no

Did your sort fail to work as expected? → **y**

Are your column labels missing from the Sort dialog box? → **yes**

Go to...
My column labels don't appear in the Sort dialog box, page 272.

Sorting data

Quick fix

If you get an error message when you try to sort your data, it's often because Excel doesn't detect an actual database—two or more rows with common content in a series of columns. Check to make sure that you have a database in your worksheet, and that the active cell is within the database you want to sort.

Quick fix

When only a portion of your database sorts, it's either because there is a blank row between two rows of data, or because you selected a series of rows before clicking the Sort command. Delete any blank rows (blank cells in rows are OK), and make sure that there aren't rows or ranges of cells selected. Then click Sort on the Data menu, or use the Sort buttons on the Standard toolbar.

Go to...

I didn't set up my database properly, and now I can't sort it, page 274.

Go to...

I'm not sure how to sort my database by more than one field, page 268.

Go to...

The sort I applied didn't work as I expected, page 270.

If your solution isn't here
Check these related chapters:
   Filtering records, page 104
   Searching for data, page 256
Or see the general troubleshooting tips on page xv.

I'm not sure how to sort my database by more than one field

Source of the problem

A quick sort of your database by a single field (a column) is very simple—click any cell in that field, and click the Sort Ascending or Sort Descending button. Done. But what if you want to do a more complex sort? One that puts the database in order by two or more fields so that you can, for example, see a list of upcoming courses by topic, and then within those topic groups, by date? You can't do it with the Sort buttons on the toolbar, because after you've sorted by one field, sorting by another throws out the first sort in favor of the second. If, for example, you sort by course topic and then by date, the database ends up in date order, with no regard for the topic.

What can you do? Excel offers a Sort dialog box that allows you to sort your database by up to three fields. Only three? Yes, only three. That might sound limiting, but for the type of databases that are stored in Excel (or that should be stored in Excel), three is generally plenty. If your database is so complex that you wish you could sort by five or six different fields, you probably want to use Microsoft Access, if only for the sorting capabilities.

> **Tip**
> Sort an Excel database in Access? Absolutely. Check out "Exporting and importing" on page 88. You can paste your Excel database in an empty Access data table and then use the Access tools to sort by as many fields as you have in the database.

How to fix it

1. Click any single cell in the database.

2. On the Data menu, click Sort. The Sort dialog box appears, showing three possible sorting levels: Sort By, Then By, and another Then By. ▶

3. Click the Sort By drop-down arrow, and select the field (column) you want to sort by first. (By default, Excel selects the database's first field, but you can change this if you want.)

4. Click either Ascending or Descending for the sort order.

5. Click the second field you want to sort by in the first Then By drop-down list, and click either Ascending or Descending for this field.

6. If you need to, click a third field in the last Then By drop-down list, and click either Ascending or Descending.

7. Click OK to perform the sort. The dialog box closes, and your database is sorted by the fields you chose, in the order you selected them. ▶

	A	B	C	D	E	F	G	H	I
1				Course Enrollments					
2									
3	Application	Course #	Course Name	Course Date	Cost per Student	Number Enrolled	Total Class Revenue	Trainer Assigned	
4	Word	MSW2	Word level 2	10/15/2000	$ 325.00	8	$ 2,600.00	Fuller	
5	Word	MSW3	Word level 3	11/1/2000	$ 350.00	12	$ 4,200.00	Kline	
6	Word	MSW1	Word level 1	10/5/2000	$ 300.00	9	$ 2,700.00	Talbot	
7	Windows	MSWU	Windows 98 User	11/2/2000	$ 300.00	10	$ 3,000.00	Corson	
8	Windows	MSNTA	Windows NT Admi	11/8/2000	$ 500.00	5	$ 2,500.00	Elmaleh	
9	Publisher	MSPUB	Publisher Basics	11/13/2000	$ 350.00	8	$ 2,800.00	Kline	
10	PowerPoint	MSP1	PowerPoint level 1	10/15/2000	$ 300.00	6	$ 1,800.00	Talbot	
11	PowerPoint	MSP2	PowerPoint level 2	10/30/2000	$ 350.00	8	$ 2,800.00	Talbot	
12	FrontPage	FPWD1	Web Design w/Fro	11/5/2000	$ 400.00	12	$ 4,800.00	Fuller	
13	FrontPage	FPWD2	Web Design w/Fro	11/15/2000	$ 500.00	12	$ 6,000.00	Fuller	
14	Excel	MSE3	Excel level 3	11/5/2000	$ 350.00	9	$ 3,150.00	Corson	
15	Excel	MSE2	Excel level 2	10/20/2000	$ 325.00	7	$ 2,275.00	Elmaleh	
16	Excel	MSE1	Excel level 1	10/8/2000	$ 300.00	10	$ 3,000.00	Fuller	
17	Access	MSA1	Access level 1	10/12/2000	$ 300.00	6	$ 1,800.00	Cook	
18	Access	MSA2	Access level 2	10/25/2000	$ 325.00	8	$ 2,600.00	Cook	
19	Access	MSA3	Access level 3	10/30/2000	$ 350.00	8	$ 2,800.00	Cook	
20	Access	MSAD1	Access Application	11/10/2000	$ 400.00	4	$ 1,600.00	Moore	
21					Total Revenue	142	$ 50,425.00		
22									
23									

So what are those Options about?

The Sort dialog box's Options button is used most often to allow you to do case-sensitive sorts. When placing items in order, items in lowercase should precede those in uppercase, if you're doing an ascending sort. The case of your worksheet content is ignored if you don't turn on this option, but if you need to take case into account as you perform the sort, click the Options button in the Sort dialog box, and select the Case Sensitive check box. ▶

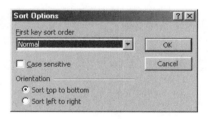

To proceed, click OK, and then in the Sort dialog box, set up your sort as needed. Click OK to perform the sort, and you'll see your lowercase items (if they're in a sorted field) appear first if you're sorting in ascending order, or last if you're sorting in descending order.

The sort I applied didn't work as I expected

Source of the problem

This raises the question, "What were you expecting?" If you were expecting the database to be placed in some alphabetical or numerical order and it didn't end up that way, the source of the problem could be that you were sorting on a single field (a column) in your database using the Sort Ascending or Sort Descending button on the toolbar, and you accidentally sorted a different field than the one you thought you had. Or perhaps you meant to sort in ascending order and clicked the Sort Descending button instead. If you were using the Sort command, you might have chosen a different field to sort by than you'd intended to use. And if you were sorting by more than one field, you might have chosen to sort them in the wrong order.

With this many variables, it makes sense to sit back and review exactly what it is you wanted to accomplish with your sort, which tools are the best to use to achieve that result, and how those tools are meant to be used. Then you can try again. If the sort you just did made a real mess of your records, click Undo to reverse whatever happened. You can also close the file without saving, if that won't lose any entries or edits you've made since you last saved. Once you've decided what you want and have thought about how to get it, try your sort again.

How to fix it

1. Click any cell in the field you want to sort by. ▶

2. Click the Sort Ascending button on the Standard toolbar. The database should be placed in order by the

	A	B	C	D	E	F	G	H	I
1				Course Enrollments					
2									
3	Application	Course #	Course Name	Course Date	Cost per Student	Number Enrolled	Total Class Revenue	Trainer Assigned	
4	Word	MSW1	Word level 1	10/5/2000	$ 300.00	9	$ 2,700.00	Talbot	
5	Excel	MSE1	Excel level 1	10/8/2000	$ 300.00	10	$ 3,000.00	Fuller	
6	Access	MSA1	Access level 1	10/12/2000	$ 300.00	6	$ 1,800.00	Cook	
7	Word	MSW2	Word level 2	10/15/2000	$ 325.00	8	$ 2,600.00	Fuller	
8	PowerPoint	MSP1	PowerPoint level 1	10/15/2000	$ 300.00	6	$ 1,800.00	Talbot	
9	Excel	MSE2	Excel level 2	10/20/2000	$ 325.00	7	$ 2,275.00	Elmaleh	
10	Access	MSA2	Access level 2	10/25/2000	$ 325.00	8	$ 2,600.00	Cook	
11	PowerPoint	MSP2	PowerPoint level 2	10/30/2000	$ 350.00	8	$ 2,800.00	Talbot	
12	Access	MSA3	Access level 3	10/30/2000	$ 350.00	8	$ 2,800.00	Cook	
13	Word	MSW3	Word level 3	11/1/2000	$ 350.00	12	$ 4,200.00	Kline	
14	Windows	MSWU	Windows 98 User	11/2/2000	$ 300.00	10	$ 3,000.00	Corson	
15	FrontPage	FPWD1	Web Design w/Fro	11/5/2000	$ 400.00	12	$ 4,800.00	Fuller	
16	Excel	MSE3	Excel level 3	11/5/2000	$ 350.00	9	$ 3,150.00	Corson	
17	Windows	MSNTA	Windows NT Admi	11/8/2000	$ 500.00	5	$ 2,500.00	Elmaleh	
18	Access	MSAD1	Access Application	11/10/2000	$ 400.00	4	$ 1,600.00	Moore	
19	Publisher	MSPUB	Publisher Basics	11/13/2000	$ 350.00	8	$ 2,800.00	Kline	
20	FrontPage	FPWD2	Web Design w/Fro	11/15/2000	$ 500.00	12	$ 6,000.00	Fuller	
21					Total Revenue	142	$50,425.00		
22									

This cell is active, so the database will be sorted by the Number Enrolled field.

field containing the active cell, in A–Z order if the content is text. If the field contains numerical content, or if the database is in numerical order, lowest numbers will appear first.

If the problem arose from a multiple-field sort, you need to think about your fields and what data they contain, and let that guide your sort order. Here are some guidelines:

- For the first sorted field, choose a field that has the most duplicate entries in it. In a list of computer course offerings, the Application field would contain a lot of duplicates. Why are duplicates important? Because sorting by a field with few unique entries turns the database into a series of groups, and then the next fields you sort by will put the records in those groups in order. ▶

Tip
If your numeric data contains negative numbers, an ascending sort will put those numbers first in the database, followed by records with a zero in the sorted field, followed by positive numbers. If the field by which you're sorting has blank cells, those records will appear last in an ascending sort.

	A	B	C	D	E	F	G	H	I
1				Course Enrollments					
2									
3	Application	Course #	Course Name	Course Date	Cost per Student	Number Enrolled	Total Class Revenue	Trainer Assigned	
4	Access	MSA1	Access level 1	10/12/2000	$ 300.00	6	$ 1,800.00	Cook	
5	Access	MSA2	Access level 2	10/25/2000	$ 325.00	8	$ 2,600.00	Cook	
6	Access	MSA3	Access level 3	10/30/2000	$ 350.00	8	$ 2,800.00	Cook	
7	Access	MSAD1	Access Application	11/10/2000	$ 400.00	4	$ 1,600.00	Moore	
8	Excel	MSE1	Excel level 1	10/8/2000	$ 300.00	10	$ 3,000.00	Fuller	
9	Excel	MSE2	Excel level 2	10/20/2000	$ 325.00	7	$ 2,275.00	Elmaleh	
10	Excel	MSE3	Excel level 3	11/5/2000	$ 350.00	9	$ 3,150.00	Corson	
11	FrontPage	FPWD1	Web Design w/Fro	11/5/2000	$ 400.00	12	$ 4,800.00	Fuller	
12	FrontPage	FPWD2	Web Design w/Fro	11/15/2000	$ 500.00	12	$ 6,000.00	Fuller	
13	PowerPoint	MSP1	PowerPoint level 1	10/15/2000	$ 300.00	6	$ 1,800.00	Talbot	
14	PowerPoint	MSP2	PowerPoint level 2	10/30/2000	$ 350.00	8	$ 2,800.00	Talbot	
15	Publisher	MSPUB	Publisher Basics	11/13/2000	$ 350.00	8	$ 2,800.00	Kline	
16	Windows	MSWU	Windows 98 User	11/2/2000	$ 300.00	10	$ 3,000.00	Corson	
17	Windows	MSNTA	Windows NT Admi	11/8/2000	$ 500.00	5	$ 2,500.00	Elmaleh	
18	Word	MSW1	Word level 1	10/5/2000	$ 300.00	9	$ 2,700.00	Talbot	
19	Word	MSW2	Word level 2	10/15/2000	$ 325.00	8	$ 2,600.00	Fuller	
20	Word	MSW3	Word level 3	11/1/2000	$ 350.00	12	$ 4,200.00	Kline	
21					Total Revenue	142	$50,425.00		
22									

This database is sorted by the Application field, creating alphabetized groups.

- For the second sorted field, choose a field with fewer possible duplicates. Again, think of the course enrollment database. After sorting by the Application field, sorting by the Trainer Assigned field would be good, because there could be some duplicate trainers per application, but there might not be.

- For the third sorted field, choose a field that's likely to be all unique entries, such as Course Number for the course enrollment list shown, or Last Name for an employee database.

When performing a multiple-field sort, click any cell in your database, click Sort on the Data menu, select your fields as just described, and then examine your selections in the Sort dialog box to make sure you've selected them in the right order—first field in the Sort By box, second in the first Then By box, and third in the last Then By box. After doing this check, click OK to perform the sort.

Tip
Be careful not to select any cell ranges before opening the Sort dialog box. If you select a series of rows, only those rows will be sorted. If you select a block of cells that is outside the range of cells that actually contain your data, Excel might not see your column labels, and they won't appear in the dialog box. In short, before a sort, click carefully in the database so that you're not misdirecting Excel as to which records or database you want to sort.

My column labels don't appear in the Sort dialog box

Source of the problem

By default, Excel recognizes the first row in a database (the column labels) as the field names—the names that identify the pieces of each record in the database. When you click Sort on the Data menu, those field names show up in the Sort dialog box so that you can choose which fields to sort your database by. There are situations, however, where Excel doesn't see the first row as your field names, and instead offers Column A, Column B, and so on, as the field names. ▶

Why does this happen? If in your zeal to tell Excel which cells contain your database, you select a column that's not part of the database—such as column G when your database resides in only columns A through F—Excel won't see a field name in that column and therefore won't see your other field labels.

This is sort of a case of "Doctor, it hurts when I go like that." The doctor responds, "Don't go like that." The key to letting Excel see your column labels is in not selecting any of the database prior to issuing the Sort command.

How to fix it

1. Click any cell in your database. Do not select any range of cells, and don't click an empty cell outside of the range of records occupied by the data you want to sort.

2. On the Data menu, click Sort. The Sort dialog box appears, with one of your field names in the Sort box.

3. Click the Sort By drop-down arrow, and click a field name to sort by a different field (if desired) and then click the Ascending or Descending option.

4. As needed, select sort fields in the two Then By drop-down lists. For both options, don't forget to click either the Ascending or Descending option.

5. Click OK to perform the sort.

> **Tip**
> If you sort your database while the generic field names (Column A, Column B, for example) are in the Sort By drop-down list, when your database is sorted, the real field names will be sorted in with the data. If you don't see your field names in the drop-down list, click Cancel.

A field by any other name

When you build your database, it's important to have field names for all of the columns that will contain data—don't leave any out. If you do, you'll run into a modified version of the problem of no field names appearing in the Sort dialog box. When one or more of your fields has no name (no column label), the Sort dialog box will list Column A, Column B, and so on, in the Sort By and Then By drop-down lists. If you click the Header Row option, Excel will say, "Ah ha! There they are!" and list the field names it sees in the top row. Except for the blank fields. Those will continue to appear in the list of field names as their column letters. ▶

If you select the Header Row option, you'll be able to sort your database without your field names being sorted in with the data, so you can complete the sorting process if this situation exists. However, it will be difficult to sort by any of the unnamed fields because you can't easily tell what kind of data the unnamed columns contain.

Tip

Clicking the Header Row option in the My List Has section of the Sort dialog box won't always make Excel see the field names in your database. If you click it and your field names don't appear in the Sort By drop-down list, click Cancel to get out of the dialog box, and then click a single database cell before clicking Sort on the Data menu again.

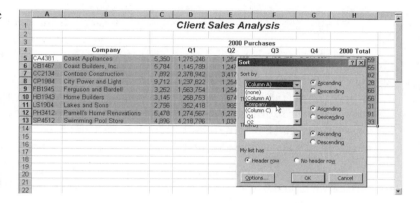

Tip

The Sort dialog box is a big part of the reason it's a good idea to keep your field names short. The Sort By and Then By drop-down lists don't show the full name of the field if the name exceeds 16 characters. Keep the names short and to the point so that no matter where you're seeing them, you can read most or all of the field names.

I didn't set up my database properly, and now I can't sort it

Source of the problem

You know the old saying, "Anything worth doing, is worth doing right." Annoying when someone says this after you've done something wrong, isn't it? In this case, though, it's not so much that you've done something wrong, but that you weren't aware of Excel's requirements for database structure and content, and you're paying the price by being limited in how you can use and manipulate the database. Some problems you might run into:

- Your database won't sort at all—Excel throws an error message at you when you use the Sort buttons or issue the Sort command. The simple reason is likely that you're not in your database when you try to sort, and Excel can't see the database. So the simple solution is to click a cell within the database before trying to sort. If a single database cell is already selected, then the structure of your database is the culprit—a more complex problem.

- You're able to sort, but the sort comes out wrong. The problem lies either with your sort setup (maybe you asked Excel to sort by the wrong fields (or columns) or by the right fields but in the wrong order), or with the way your database is structured. Again, I'm using the S word—STRUCTURE. The way you set up your Excel database is key to it working properly. "Working properly" means that you are able to sort it, filter it, and use things like subtotal reports and PivotTables with it. (See "Filtering records" on page 104, "Subtotal reports" on page 284, and "PivotTables" on page 220.)

The solution to your sorting problem lies in fully understanding what Excel needs from you in terms of database layout and content. Once you have a sense of this, you can edit your database accordingly. Your future databases will fall together quickly and work seamlessly with whichever data command you choose to apply.

How to fix it

Excel databases have some very basic structural requirements—in fact, there are only two:

- There can be no blank rows between your column labels and the last record in your database. Don't skip a row, add visual space with blank rows, or manually insert a subtotal row at any point in the database. Blank rows throw off sorts and filters.

- There can be no blank columns between the first and the last columns in a database. If the first column in your database is B, and your database has seven fields, H has to be the last column—don't skip any columns, for any reason. To delete a blank column, select the column by clicking its heading. Then right-click the selected column, and click Delete on the shortcut menu. ▶

Don't leave blank columns unless you want Excel to think your database ends here.

	A	B		C	D	E	F	G	H	I
1						Client Sales Analysis				
2										
3							2000 Purchases			
4				Company		Q1	Q2	Q3	Q4	2000 Tot
5	CA4381			ices	5,350	1,275,246	1,254,975	2,135,476	2,514,962	7,180,
6	CB1467			s, Inc.	5,784	1,145,789	1,247,325	1,357,952	1,342,189	5,093,
7	CC2134			struction	7,892	2,378,942	3,417,895	1,002,456	1,342,189	8,141,
8	CP1984			nd Light	9,712	1,237,822	1,254,975	2,319,876	2,257,955	7,070,
9	FB1945			Bardell	3,252	1,563,754	1,254,975	2,135,476	2,514,961	7,469,
10	HB1943			s	3,145	258,753	674,926	759,183	241,894	1,934,
11	LS1904			ns	2,756	352,418	985,476		988,637	2,326,
12	PH3412			e Renovations	5,478	1,274,567	1,278,964	1,578,962	1,127,898	5,260,
13	SP4512			ol Store	4,896	4,218,796	1,037,564	987,526	852,147	7,096,

In addition to the structural requirements just listed, Excel also has some database requirements pertaining to content:

Delete blank columns to avoid sorting problems.

- Don't leave any column labels blank. Every column in your database is a field, and every field must have a name.

- Don't leave any rows blank. Although you can have blank fields in a record, you can have no blank records. This includes deleting the content from a row in order to edit the record, and accidentally leaving it blank. If you want to delete a record, select the row, right-click the selected row, and click Delete on the shortcut menu. The entire row will go away, and you can properly sort the data as you want.

- Use consistent terminology. If you're listing a series of departments in an employee database, decide on the abbreviations you'll use right up front. Don't type "Mktg." in one record, and "Marketing" in another. Why? Because if you filter by department, the Marketing people will come before the Mktg. people, and if you're going to go on and do a subtotal report, that will be a problem.

If you stick to these very simple rules, you'll be able to easily sort your database, filter it, subtotal it, and turn it into a PivotTable as needed. If your database is in violation of any of these rules, you can fix it—add column labels where any are missing, delete blank rows, and delete blank columns. Go through and edit inconsistent spellings and abbreviations. After you've cleaned up the structure and content of your worksheet, you'll be able to sort it properly and any problems that do occur should be solved by the other solutions in this chapter!

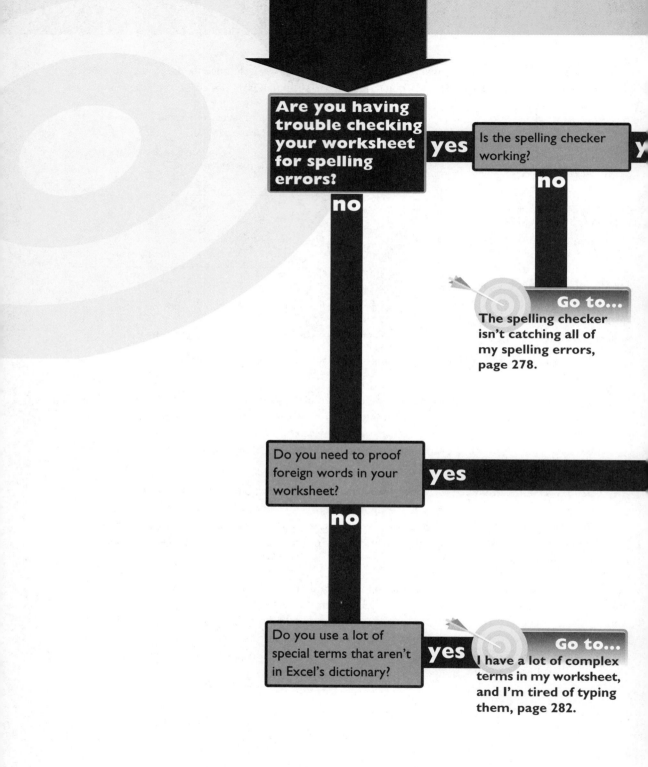

Are you having trouble checking your worksheet for spelling errors?

yes → Is the spelling checker working? → **y**

no ↓

no ↓

Is the spelling checker working?

no ↓

Go to...
The spelling checker isn't catching all of my spelling errors, page 278.

Do you need to proof foreign words in your worksheet?

yes →

no ↓

Do you use a lot of special terms that aren't in Excel's dictionary?

yes →

Go to...
I have a lot of complex terms in my worksheet, and I'm tired of typing them, page 282.

Do you need to customize the way Excel checks your spelling?

yes

Quick fix

To make Excel skip over words in capital letters (such as acronyms and product or serial numbers), click Spelling on the Tools menu. In the Spelling dialog box, select the Ignore UPPERCASE check box, and proceed with your spelling check.

no

Do you want to stop Excel from correcting your spelling automatically?

yes

Quick fix

If you notice that words you type change as soon as you have typed them, that's AutoCorrect at work. On the Tools menu, click Auto-Correct to see a list of the corrections Excel makes automatically. You can clear the check boxes for the preset options, delete the entries in the Replace and With boxes if you don't want the corrections made, or add your own entries to the list. Click OK when you are finished making adjustments.

Go to...

I'm not sure how to check the spelling of foreign words, page 280.

If your solution isn't here

Check these related chapters:

Entering data, page 78

Naming cells, page 200

Or see the general troubleshooting tips on page xv.

The spelling checker isn't catching all of my spelling errors

Source of the problem

Unlike Microsoft Word, where your spelling errors are marked as soon as you make them, in Excel you have to wait until you use the spelling checker to find out where your errors are. So you click Spelling on the Tools menu (or click the Spelling button), and the Spelling dialog box appears. A few errors are presented, one by one, and you choose to change a spelling to a suggested alternative, ignore a perceived error (because it's an esoteric term or name, and you know it's spelled correctly), or add a word to the dictionary so that it won't be flagged as misspelled the next time you type it. Then, just when you think that your worksheet must be free of errors, you happen to spot some. Why didn't Excel catch them? There are a few possibilities:

- The misspelled word is in all capital letters, and you have your spelling checker set to ignore words in uppercase. ▶

- A word that was spelled incorrectly was added to the dictionary, so now Excel thinks it's correct as is.

- The misspelled words were on another worksheet, and Excel checks the spelling on only the active sheet.

The spelling checker did not stop on this entry because the spelling checker is set to ignore words in all uppercase letters.

These are all fixable problems. You can turn off the option to ignore words in caps, and you can remove a misspelled word from the dictionary so that an accurate dictionary is being used to check your spelling. If your spelling errors are in another sheet, you can use the spelling checker on that sheet, or group the sheets before checking your spelling.

How to fix it

To adjust the way Excel checks the spelling in your active sheet (or in a group of sheets in the open workbook) so that words in uppercase are not ignored, follow these steps:

1. On the Tools menu, click Spelling.

2. In the Spelling dialog box, clear the Ignore UPPERCASE check box. As you continue to check your spelling, words in all capital letters will not be skipped.

To remove a misspelled word from the dictionary, follow these steps:

1. Open Microsoft Word to display a blank document.

2. On the Tools menu, click Options, and then click the Spelling & Grammar tab.

3. Click the Dictionaries button.

4. Without clearing its check mark, select the CUSTOM.DIC dictionary. If you know your word was added to a different dictionary, select that one instead. ▶

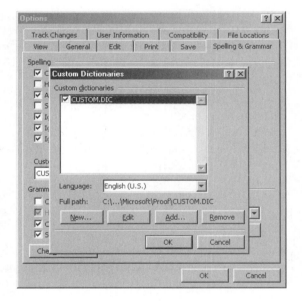

5. Click the Edit button, and then click OK when a message warns you that automatic spell checking in Word will stop until you reactivate it again in the Options dialog box. A list of words, in a single column, opens in Word.

6. Find the word you want to remove from the dictionary. Select it, and press the Delete key. Be sure to delete any blank line that remains after the word itself is deleted.

7. Click the Save button on the Standard toolbar to save the dictionary document with your word omitted.

8. Click Close on the File menu. To restore automatic spell checking in Word, click Options on the Tools menu, and on the Spelling & Grammar tab, select the Check Spelling As You Type check box. Click OK.

9. Exit Word by clicking Exit on the File menu, and then return to Excel.

I'm not sure how to check the spelling of foreign words

Source of the problem

Suppose you work for a multinational company, or belong to an organization that has members all over the world. Or suppose you run an international export/import business. Regardless, your worksheets contain information provided or intended for use by people who don't speak your native language. You don't want to offend anyone by leaving misspellings in the worksheet, and you don't want the spelling checker to stop on the foreign words every time you check the spelling of the portions of the worksheet that are in your own language. What to do? ▶

In a standard installation of Excel 2000 (or Office 2000, if you installed the whole suite), English, Spanish, and French dictionaries are installed. You can install other dictionaries by making selections during installation. Once these dictionaries are installed, you can switch to them to check individual words, cell ranges, entire worksheets, or groups

of sheets in a workbook. After checking the words, you can switch back to the dictionary of your native language, and continue using that dictionary to check the spelling in the rest of your documents.

Tip

There are subtle differences in the same language as it is used in different countries. When choosing a French dictionary, for example, be sure to select the right one—for France, Canada, or whichever French-speaking region your material is targeted to. When using an English dictionary, remember that English in Australia, Canada, the United Kingdom, and so on is different than English in the United States. Choose the version of the language that matches the origin of the people who will be using your worksheet so as not to offend anyone with an inappropriate use or spelling of a word.

Tip

If the dictionary you need to use is not installed, insert your Office CD-ROM, and use the Add/Remove programs option in the Windows Control Panel to install the dictionary you need. The installation process will vary depending on the version of Office you're using.

How to fix it

Excel 2000 If you are using Excel 2000 and you want to check your spelling using a different language dictionary, try this technique:

1. In the worksheet containing the words you want to check, click Spelling on the Tools menu.

2. In the Spelling dialog box, click the Dictionary Language drop-down arrow and choose the language of the words you want to check. ▶

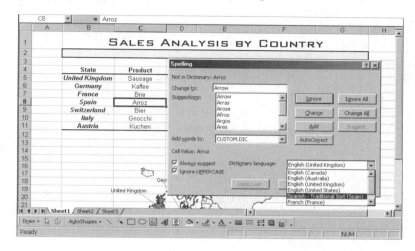

3. A prompt appears, indicating that you have to restart the spelling checker in order for the dictionary change to take effect. Click OK to close the prompt.

4. Close the Spelling dialog box so that you can restart the spelling checker.

5. On the Tools menu, click Spelling again. Because you're checking spelling in a different language, words in your native language will probably be flagged as misspelled. Click Ignore to go past them—you can always check spelling in your own language later.

6. If foreign words come up as misspelled, use the Change or Change All commands to apply a suggested correction to the text, or type the correction if you know it.

7. Move through the text, dealing with any other errors. Click OK when Excel tells you that the spelling checker has finished.

8. When all the words have been checked and corrected as needed, return to the dictionary of your own language by repeating steps 1 through 4.

I have a lot of complex terms in my worksheet, and I'm tired of typing them

Source of the problem

If your worksheets are loaded with legal, political, medical, scientific, or other types of specialized terminology, you probably do get very tired of typing the often complex words. Aside from the spelling checker flagging such words as misspelled (simply because they're not in Excel's very basic dictionary), there's the tedium of typing them over and over, and dealing with the increased margin of error for typos that long or complex words present. I feel your pain.

What can you do? You can add these terms to Excel's list of AutoCorrect entries, turning them into automatic entries that you can trigger with an abbreviation. For example, if you need to type *gerrymandering* (a legal and political term), you could turn it into an AutoCorrect entry that is triggered by your typing *grym* whenever you want to insert the entire term. As soon as you type *grym*, Excel will turn it into *gerrymandering*. Need to type *pseudoephedrine*? Create an AutoCorrect entry that will turn *psud* into *pseudoephedrine* every time. As long as the trigger (the characters you type that get changed into the term you want to appear in the worksheet) isn't a real word, which you'd want to be able to type without it turning into something else, the list of entries is as unlimited as the list of terms you're tired of typing.

How to fix it

1. In any open worksheet, click AutoCorrect on the Tools menu to display the AutoCorrect dialog box. ▶

Tip

When you create AutoCorrect entries, the entries are available and functional in all the applications that support AutoCorrect. So, if you create an entry in Excel, you'll be able to use it in Word as well. This doubles the usefulness of your entries.

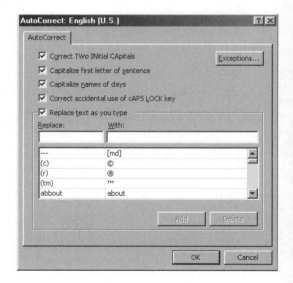

2. In the Replace box, type the trigger that you want to turn into another word when you type it.

3. Press Tab to move your insertion point to the With box.

4. Type the replacement—the text that the trigger should turn into.

5. Click the Add button.

6. Repeat steps 2 through 5 for as many entries as you want to create.

7. Click OK to close the dialog box.

Tip

Another great use for Auto-Correct is for inserting names. Do you create reports that refer to various personnel within your organization? Store AutoCorrect entries for each person and have their initials turn into their name when inserted in a cell. For example, if you need to type *Alexander Nicodopolous* every week, store AJN (if his middle name is John), or AxN (if you don't know his middle name or he doesn't have one) as an AutoCorrect entry. Storing AN would be a bad idea, as it's a real word.

Pulling the trigger

AutoCorrect entries can outlive their usefulness. If a term, name, or phrase becomes unnecessary, you can get rid of it. When you want to remove an AutoCorrect entry you created, simply click AutoCorrect on the Tools menu, and type the trigger in the Replace box. The entry automatically appears in the With box. Click the Delete button in the dialog box, and the entry is deleted. Repeat these steps for any other entries you want to get rid of, and then click OK to exit AutoCorrect.

If you make a mistake when creating an AutoCorrect entry, you can edit entries instead of deleting them. Click AutoCorrect on the Tools menu to open the AutoCorrect dialog box, and type the trigger for the entry in question in the Replace box. When the With box content appears for that entry, make your edits to the trigger, the replacement text, or both. Click the Replace button to store the entry with the changes you've made, and then click OK to close the AutoCorrect dialog box.

I hit the darn Caps Lock key again

If you've ever pressed the Caps Lock key by mistake, only to look up and see that what you've typed looks like a ransom note (with uppercase and lowercase text all jumbled up) you're not alone. I always hit Caps Lock when I'm reaching for the A key with my little finger. But I never end up with that ransom note look. Why? Because AutoCorrect fixes it.

Among other things, AutoCorrect fixes accidental Caps Lock use by changing all uppercase to lowercase (and vice versa) as soon as you type a word with a lowercase first letter and caps for the rest of the word. On the Tools menu, click AutoCorrect, and in the AutoCorrect dialog box, select the Correct Accidental Use Of Caps Lock Key check box, and then click OK.

AutoCorrect's fixes can save you from looking like you were typing with mittens on. For example, it can capitalize the names of days of the week and the first letters of sentences, and fix the kind of typo that occurs when you hold down the Shift key too long and end up with two initial capitals.

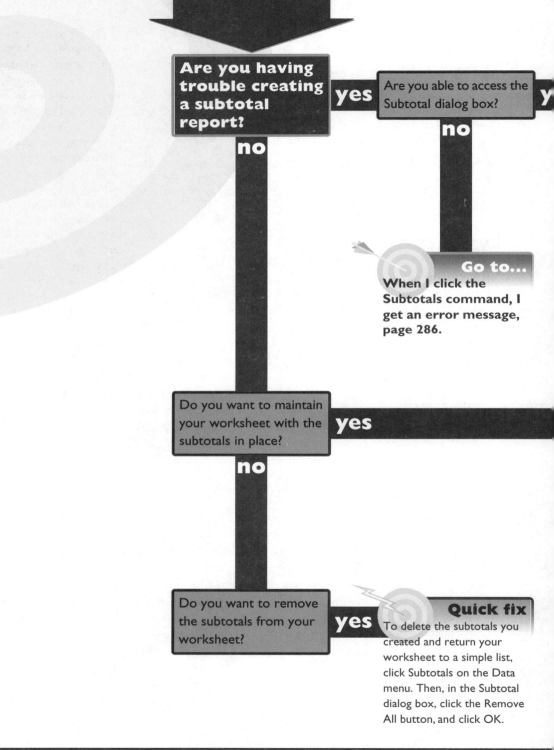

Are you having trouble creating a subtotal report?

yes → Are you able to access the Subtotal dialog box?

y

no

no

Go to...
When I click the Subtotals command, I get an error message, page 286.

Do you want to maintain your worksheet with the subtotals in place?

yes

no

Do you want to remove the subtotals from your worksheet?

yes

Quick fix
To delete the subtotals you created and return your worksheet to a simple list, click Subtotals on the Data menu. Then, in the Subtotal dialog box, click the Remove All button, and click OK.

Are you having trouble with the order of your subtotals?

yes → **Go to...** My subtotals are in the wrong places, page 288.

no

Are you having trouble with the calculations in your subtotal report?

yes → **Go to...** The wrong function is applied to my subtotaled records, page 290.

Quick fix

Your subtotal report can remain in place indefinitely. If you want to edit the worksheet (adding, changing, or deleting data), first be sure that the report detail is showing. You can then insert rows and columns as needed and edit existing data as you would in any other worksheet. Be careful, however, not to delete the rows that contain your subtotals. Other than that, you should have no trouble maintaining a subtotaled worksheet for as long as you want to.

If your solution isn't here
Check these related chapters:
Functions, page 158
Sorting data, page 266
Or see the general troubleshooting tips on page xv.

When I click the Subtotals command, I get an error message

Source of the problem

In order to use Excel's Subtotals feature, you need a list of records, called a *database*. If you have such a database, you need to select a single cell within it, not a range of cells, when you click Subtotals on the Data menu. If the selected cell is not in your database, or if you have a range of cells or a series of rows or columns within the database selected at the time you click the command, you'll receive one of three error messages:

- If you have a range (as few as two cells) selected, Excel will tell you that it can't detect which row in your database contains column labels.

- If you have a series of rows (not including row 1) selected, Excel will tell you that it found a row of cells above the selection and ask you to verify that they are your column labels. ▶

- If you are in a cell outside of the database, Excel will tell you that no database was found. This error will also appear if your worksheet contains no database at all.

So, the cause of your error message is either that no database exists (because you don't have a database of identically structured rows in your worksheet), or that you had a range of cells or rows selected before you issued the Subtotals command. The solution? Make sure your worksheet contains the right kind of database to be subtotaled, and that only a single cell within that data is active when you click Subtotals on the Data menu.

How to fix it

To make sure your worksheet has the kind of content that lends itself to the process of creating a subtotal report, keep in mind this list of requirements:

- Your database should contain at least three rows—one that contains your column labels, and at least two rows of data.

- Your database shouldn't contain blank rows, either between the column labels and the data, or between rows of data.

- Your database shouldn't contain blank columns between the first column in the database and the last. For example, if your database uses columns A through H, columns B, C, D, E, F, G, and H must contain labels. There can be blank cells in the columns in each of your rows, but the columns must have labels. ▶

	A	B	C	D	E	F	G	H
A1		= Employee List						
1			EMPLOYEE LIST					
2								
3	Last Name	First Name	Date Hired	Department	Current Salary	Bonus %	Insurance Y/N	Insurance Carrier
4	Maurone	Richard	6/13/1999	Sales	$ 76,000.00	6.5%	Y	BCBS
5	Lambert	Harry	2/15/1998	Administration	$ 62,500.00	7.0%	Y	BCBS
6	Talbot	Ann	6/7/1997	Marketing	$ 65,000.00	5.0%	Y	BCBS
7	Kline	Desiree	3/15/1997	Marketing	$ 68,500.00	7.2%	Y	BCBS
8	Balsamo	Anthony	2/27/1997	Administration	$ 74,325.00	6.7%	N	None
9	Chambers	Rosemary	11/15/1996	Accounting	$ 65,500.00	5.7%	Y	HMO
10	Fuller	Robert	11/18/1995	Sales	$ 78,500.00	6.0%	Y	HMO
11	Miller	David	9/24/1995	Marketing	$ 62,500.00	5.0%	N	None
12	Patrick	Kaitlin	9/23/1995	Accounting	$ 62,500.00	5.8%	N	None
13	Elmaleh	Miriam	8/24/1995	Human Resources	$ 72,250.00	5.0%	N	None
14	Shuster	Merrick	4/30/1995	Sales	$ 75,500.00	6.5%	N	None
15	Pederzani	Bruce	1/3/1995	Sales	$ 75,000.00	6.2%	Y	BCBS
16	Zerbe	Robert	11/27/1994	Human Resources	$ 75,650.00	6.3%	Y	BCBS
17	Mermelstein	David	10/4/1993	Sales	$ 76,500.00	6.2%	Y	BCBS
18	Freifeld	Iris	8/3/1993	Accounting	$ 78,500.00	6.2%	Y	HMO
19	Fox	Seymour	7/15/1993	Marketing	$ 65,500.00	6.0%	Y	BCBS
20	Ulrich	Lillie	12/15/1992	Human Resources	$ 73,000.00	5.5%	Y	HMO
21	Frankenfield	Daniel	5/25/1992	Sales	$ 78,500.00	6.8%	Y	HMO
22	Geiger	Mary	4/30/1992	Administration	$ 63,250.00	6.5%	Y	HMO
23	Balinski	Joseph	9/2/1989	Sales	$ 68,500.00	6.8%	Y	HMO
24								

A properly set up database has column labels and rows of data.

That's a rather short list. And it's the same list of requirements that a database must meet in order to be sorted or filtered using either the AutoFilter or the Advanced Filter feature. (You access both features by pointing to Filter on the Data menu.) If you adhere to these requirements, you should have no problem creating a subtotal report for your database.

Tip
In order for a subtotal report to have some value, there must be some numeric data included—preferably data that can be summed or averaged to derive some useful information. Otherwise, all you can do is perform a count of items in subtotaled groups, and although that can be useful, it's just the tip of the iceberg in terms of what subtotal reports can tell you about your data.

Be a data pack rat

The power of your database is in the data you choose to store in it. The more information you store, the more data you can use, and the more uses you'll have for your data. This is certainly true when it comes to using the Subtotals feature—the more data you maintain in your database, the more sorting options you have for placing the database in ordered groups, and the more analysis you can do with subtotals. For example, if you're keeping an employee database, don't just keep their names and social security numbers—keep track of which department they're in, when they were hired, how many vacation days they have. You'll have that much more information to sort by and subtotal to show how many people are in each department, which departments maintain employees for the longest time, and, if you're keeping salary information, what the cost is of running each department.

My subtotals are in the wrong places

Source of the problem

When you create a subtotal report, you can choose where the subtotals will appear by choosing which fields to subtotal. Typically, these are points in the worksheet where groups have been created by sorting data by fields that contain a lot of common content, such as a list of employees sorted by their departments. The sorting you do prior to creating the subtotals (or having Excel create them for you) controls the effective placement of your subtotals, and can make or break your subtotal report's usefulness. If you're finding that the subtotals in your report aren't where you want them, the problem lies with the setup procedure you used. ▶

To solve the problem, simply remove the subtotals and start again, paying close attention to the fields you choose to subtotal. Do you have to remove the current subtotals? Well strictly speaking, no, but if the ones that are there are in the wrong place, adding more subtotals won't solve that problem. Better to wipe the slate clean and start over.

A subtotal report is applied to the Department field, but it should have been applied to the Current Salary field for a more useful report.

How to fix it

1. Click any cell in the data, and then click Subtotals on the Data menu.

2. In the Subtotal dialog box, make sure the Replace Current Subtotals check box is selected.

3. Verify the field selected in the At Each Change In list. This should show the field (the column label) that your database was sorted by prior to creating the subtotal report.

4. Click a function in the Use Function list that will be appropriate for the fields you intend to subtotal. If, for example, you're subtotaling a field containing dollar amounts, SUM is a good choice. If

you're subtotaling the number of people belonging to a particular organization or the number of products in a particular warehouse, use COUNT.

5. Scroll through the Add Subtotal To list, selecting the check boxes for the fields you want to subtotal, and clearing the check boxes for the fields you don't want to subtotal. ▶

6. Click OK to create the subtotal report.

Now what do I do with it?

When the subtotal report appears, you'll notice small buttons numbered 1, 2, and 3 on the left side of the worksheet, to the left of your row numbers. As you click these small buttons, you'll discover that:

- Clicking the 1 reduces your database to the grand totals for the field or fields you chose to subtotal. All detail for each sorted group disappears.

- Clicking 2 reduces your database to just the subtotals, followed by a grand total. ▶

- Clicking 3 displays the entire database, showing all detail lines from each subtotaled group of rows.

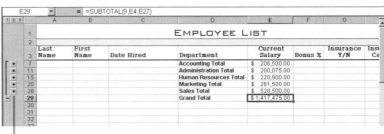

Click these plus signs individually to display (expand) specific sections of the report.

You'll also notice that as soon as a section of the worksheet is collapsed (hidden), a plus sign appears to the left of the worksheet. You can click any plus sign to expand particular subtotals, displaying their details.

What else can you do with a subtotal report? You can print it. You can copy the subtotals to other worksheets and workbooks (but you have to keep your subtotal report in force in the active sheet or the other worksheet or workbook that uses the subtotals will no longer work properly). You can also refer to the subtotals in other reports, such as departmental budgets, referencing the subtotals through formulas.

The wrong function is applied to my subtotaled records

Source of the problem

Excel is an intuitive product, but not intuitive enough to apply the correct function to your subtotals. For that, it relies upon you. If you're subtotaling a numeric field (a column containing numbers), you might want to total all the numbers in the field using the SUM function, or you might want to average them. If you're subtotaling a text field (a column containing letters as well as numbers), you probably want to count the items in the field using the COUNT function. These are just assumptions, however. The choice of which function to apply to your subtotals is yours. One thing to remember: you can choose only one function per subtotal operation, so if you're subtotaling an assortment of both text and numeric fields all at once, chances are one of the subtotals will be less than useful because the same function probably won't be appropriate for all of your subtotaled fields. ▶

To solve this problem, remove the existing subtotals and then apply the subtotals again, being careful to choose the appropriate function and *only* the fields for which that function would make sense. You can then perform multiple subtotals on the same database of information, selecting a different function and different fields for each successive use of the Subtotals command.

The COUNT function works well for the Department field, but isn't very useful for the Current Salary field.

How to fix it

1. Click any cell in the report, and then click Subtotals on the Data menu.

2. In the Subtotal dialog box, click Remove All to return your database to a non-subtotaled state.

3. Review your fields and choose the ones you want to subtotal. Thinking of each one and the type of data it contains, decide which function will be most appropriate for each field. (It's best to make these decisions while you're examining your database, rather than when you're working in the Subtotal dialog box.)

4. On the Data menu, click Subtotals to reopen the Subtotal dialog box.

5. Click a field name (a column label) in the At Each Change In list. The field name you click in this list should be the field by which you sorted or organized the entire database. If you sorted the database by more than one field (by clicking Sort on the Data menu to access the Sort dialog box—see "Sorting data" on page 266), this is normally the first field by which you sorted.

6. Scroll through the Use Function list, and click the function you want to use for the fields you intend to subtotal. Remember that you can use only one function per subtotal operation, so the one you choose has to be appropriate for all of the fields you want to subtotal.

7. In the Add Subtotal To list, select the check boxes for the fields you want to subtotal, and clear any check boxes for fields you don't want to subtotal or that won't work with the chosen function.

8. Click OK to create the subtotal report.

9. Leaving the first subtotal process intact, repeat steps 4 through 8 for each successive subtotal operation. Select a different function for each one, and select only the fields that will make sense with that function. ▶

The SUM function has been applied to the Current Salary field, and the COUNT function has been applied to the Department field.

Tip

It's a good idea to duplicate your database and subtotal just one or two fields on each copy rather than have too many fields subtotaled on any one version of your database. If too many fields are subtotaled, you create visual chaos, and limit the report's effectiveness.

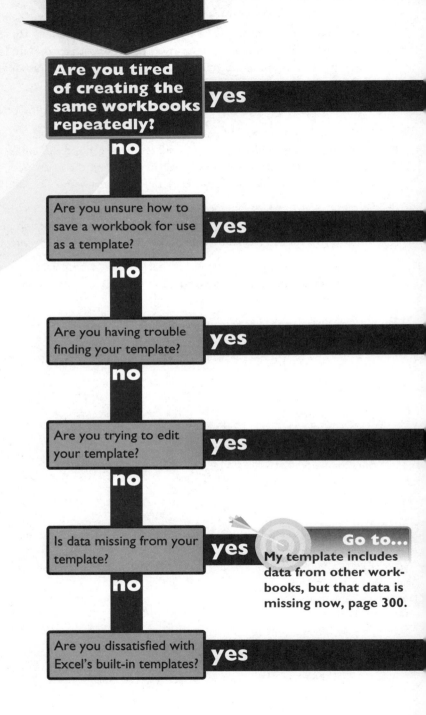

Are you tired of creating the same workbooks repeatedly? → **yes**

no

Are you unsure how to save a workbook for use as a template? → **yes**

no

Are you having trouble finding your template? → **yes**

no

Are you trying to edit your template? → **yes**

no

Is data missing from your template? → **yes**

Go to...
My template includes data from other workbooks, but that data is missing now, page 300.

no

Are you dissatisfied with Excel's built-in templates? → **yes**

Go to...
I don't want to keep creating the same workbook over and over, page 294.

Quick fix

To make new templates available in the New dialog box, save them in Excel's Templates folder. In the Save As dialog box, click Template (.xlt) in the Save As Type list. If you save them anywhere else, they won't appear in the New dialog box and you won't be able to base new workbooks on them.

Go to...
My template doesn't appear in the New dialog box, page 298.

Quick fix

If you need to edit a template, click Open on the File menu, and navigate to the Templates folder. (The path to the Templates folder is C:\Windows\Application Data\Microsoft\Templates in Excel 2000, or C:\Program Files\MSOffice\Templates in Excel 97.) Double-click the template you want to edit, make your changes, and then save and close the template.

Go to...
I'm tired of inserting my logo every time I use the Invoice template, page 302.

If your solution isn't here
Check these related chapters:
   Formatting worksheets, page 136
   Saving, page 244
Or see the general troubleshooting tips on page xv.

I don't want to keep creating the same workbook over and over

Source of the problem

Every week, every month, or at some other all-too-frequent interval, you create a workbook. Its design is the same as the one before it—what changes is the specific data that you customize for particular companies, departments, employees, and so on. The title is the same, the layout is the same, the column and row labels are the same, and the sheets within the workbook are named and ordered in the same manner. The formulas are the same, even the text and border formatting is the same. Yet you're re-creating the darn thing every time. This has caused you problems beyond simply wasting your time and contributing to your carpal tunnel syndrome—each version of the workbook is a little different than the previous one. Some of the formatting is lost, column labels are slightly reworded. Once you even forgot an entire section or worksheet within the workbook. You tried opening an old workbook and editing it to reflect new data, but then you accidentally saved the file, overwriting the older workbook, and now that's lost. You can't risk that happening again, but you need each new workbook to be the same as the old ones.

What can you do? Isn't there a way to create the same workbook over and over again, with the same content and formatting, whenever you need it? Yes! You can turn a workbook into a template, and use it over and over again to create similar workbooks, with no risk to the original workbook. The content, formatting, layout, names and order of individual worksheets within the workbook—everything—will be the same every time you use the workbook template. ▶

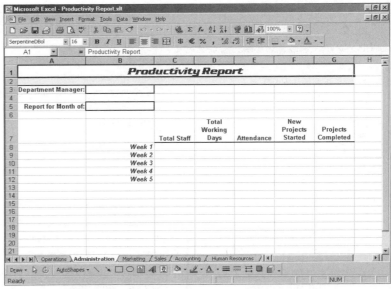

You can create a template based on a workbook that you use over and over.

How to fix it

To turn an existing workbook into a template, follow these steps:

1. Open the existing workbook that you want to use as your template.

2. Delete any specific data that you don't want in every new workbook that's created from this template. (You can keep formulas, labels, titles, and formatting; just be sure to delete any data that was specific to this existing workbook.)

3. Make any formatting or content changes you want reflected in the new workbooks created from this template. Check your spelling and your formulas, and clean up inconsistencies in formatting. Also make sure the individual worksheets in the workbook are named and ordered the way you want them to be.

4. When the file is cleaned up and ready, click Save As on the File menu. Be very careful not to click Save, because doing so will overwrite the existing file, and you'll lose the original.

> **Tip**
>
> Creating templates is different from creating and formatting multiple worksheets in the same workbook. (For more information, see "Entering data" on page 78.) The problem you're trying to solve here is creating the same set of worksheets in separate workbooks.

> **Tip**
>
> Don't confuse the templates you create with the Invoice and Purchase Order templates that come with Excel. Those templates are automated and filled with features you must edit or tweak for your own needs (and some of the features can't be altered). The templates you create yourself can be molded over time as your needs change. The only thing these two types of templates have in common is the way you access them. To access these templates, click New on the File menu. Templates that you create will be on the General tab; the Invoice and Purchase Order templates that come with Excel will be on the Spreadsheet Solutions tab. Click the tab that houses the template you want, and then double-click the name of the template. If you double-clicked either the Invoice or Purchase Order template, click Enable Macros to open a workbook based on whichever one you chose.

> **Warning**
>
> If you accidentally click Save after editing your existing workbook for use as a template, you will overwrite the original file—something you probably don't want to do. Be sure you always choose Save As rather than Save from the File menu, so that you get the Save As dialog box, through which you can give the file a new name and designate it as a template by choosing Template (.xlt) from the Save As Type list.

This solution is continued on the next page.

I don't want to keep creating the same workbook over and over

(continued from page 295)

5. In the Save As dialog box, click Template (.xlt) in the Save As Type drop-down list. As soon as you do so, the Save In location will change to the Templates folder. (Don't worry if your dialog box looks a little different from ours.) ▶

6. Type a file name for the template. (Don't type any extension; let Excel add the .xlt extension that designates the file as a template.)

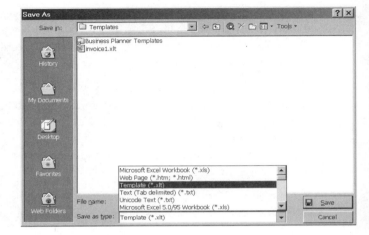

7. Click Save to create the template. Excel closes the workbook that you used as a basis for the template, preserving it in its original state.

8. Close the template.

To use the template, follow these steps:

1. On the File menu, click New. The New dialog box opens, displaying tabs for all of the installed Office templates, as well as any user-created templates, such as the one you created in the previous set of steps. (The templates you create should appear on the General tab.) ▶

2. On the General tab, double-click the template you created to open a new workbook. (The name of the template is followed by a number. The number depends on how many other new workbooks you've opened based

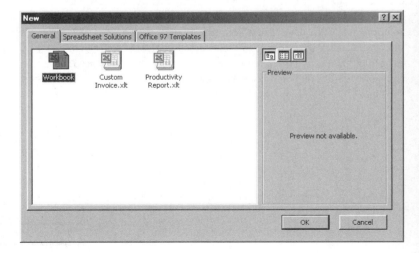

on that template in the current Excel session.) The new workbook contains the title, labels, formulas, and formatting you saved in the template.

3. Enter the data that is specific to this new workbook, and click the Save button. In the Save As dialog box, note that you can save the new workbook with the standard workbook (.xls) format in My Documents or any other folder, just as you would any new workbook. (The template itself is used only as the basis of this new workbook.) Give the workbook a unique name, make sure that Microsoft Excel Workbook (.xls) appears in the Save As Type box, and then click Save.

Cookie cutter ideas

Templates give you the ability to create instant expense reports, invoices, sales reports, payroll workbooks—anything you create repeatedly that varies only in the situational content. Each time you use the template, you start out with a new workbook containing only the basic stuff that was part of the template at the time you created it. Think about any workbooks you create more than once or twice a year, and consider creating templates for them. Templates also make it easy to have standardized forms and reports throughout an office or company. Share your templates with coworkers so everyone can have quick and easy consistency in their workbooks. ▶

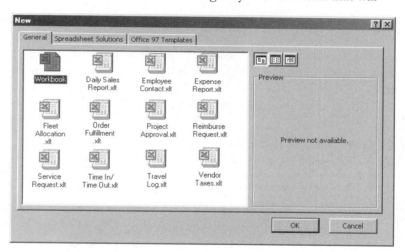

My template doesn't appear in the New dialog box

Source of the problem

You created a template, and now you're ready to use it. You click New on the File menu, and you're looking around in the New dialog box, clicking the tabs (such as General or Spreadsheet Solutions), and you don't see a template with the name you gave it. What gives?

The fact that your template doesn't appear in the New dialog box is due to the fact that it's not stored in the Templates folder, or in a direct subfolder of that folder. That one step in the template-creation process is key to the accessibility of templates, yet it's the one that people ignore most often. Excel tries to make it easy to do it right, by switching automatically to the Templates folder as soon as you choose Template (.xlt) for your file type. People feel compelled, however, to change folders, and to save the template with other workbook files, thinking that they should be stored together. An understandable mistake, but a mistake just the same.

To solve the problem, you have to find the file and then move it to the Templates folder.

How to fix it

To find your file, follow these steps:

1. On the File menu, click Open.

2. In the Open dialog box, click the Tools button, and then click Find on the drop-down menu to open the Find dialog box. (If you're working in Excel 97, click Advanced in the Open dialog box to display the Advanced Find dialog box, which is virtually identical to the Excel 2000 Find dialog box.)

3. The Find dialog box is set to find the .xlt format, but you need to direct it to look on the drive where you saved your file. Using the Look In box, navigate to the drive you want to search.

4. In the Define More Criteria section of the dialog box, click the Value box, and type whatever you know of the file's name.

5. Make sure the Search Subfolders check box is selected. ▶

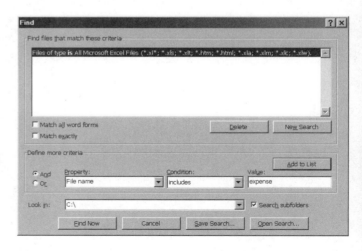

6. Click Find Now.

7. Click Yes to add your file name to the property search criteria. The search begins, and when the template you want to move is found, it appears in the View pane in the center of the dialog box.

Now you're ready to move the template file to the right folder so that it will be available through the New dialog box. Following these steps:

1. Right-click the found file, and click Cut.

2. Click Cancel to close the Open dialog box.

3. On the File menu, click Open to display the Open dialog box again.

4. If necessary, display your local drive (C:) in the Look In list of the Open dialog box so that you can navigate to the proper folder in which to paste your template.

Tip

Of course all of the file cutting and pasting described in this section can be done through Windows Explorer or My Computer, if you're more comfortable using them.

5. If you're working in Excel 2000 and you installed the templates to the default folder, double-click the following folders, in the order listed: Windows, Application Data, Microsoft, and Templates. If you're working in Excel 97 and you installed the templates to the default folder, double-click the following folders in the order listed: Program Files, MSOffice, and Templates. (If you didn't install the templates to the default folder, you'll have to enter the path to the folder you installed the templates in.)

6. In the Templates folder, right-click an empty spot in the list of files and folders, and click Paste on the shortcut menu. ▶

The template file you cut from its previous location now resides in the Templates folder, and it will appear on the General tab of the New dialog box when you click New on the File menu.

My template includes data from other workbooks, but that data is missing now

Source of the problem

This is a very frustrating problem, especially if the workbooks from which your template draws data are not entirely under your control. If your template worked the last time you used it, and if you've done nothing to edit it in any way since then, the reason that some of the external data (particularly in a formula with links to another workbook) is missing can only be that the source of that data—the other workbook—has been moved or deleted, or its contents have been edited so that the data you're looking for is not where it was when you set up your template. If others can edit and delete data within the source workbook, or move or delete the workbook files that contain the data, your template isn't safe. ▶

What can you do? That depends. If you have no control over access to the other workbook, you're stuck dealing with your template's vulnerability, unless you can make and maintain a copy of the other workbook and make that the source of your template's external data. If that's not feasible (perhaps the other workbook requires ongoing updates by another person in order to remain useful), you might have to live with the fact that your template relies on data that is not under your careful control.

The solution then becomes fixing your template by relocating the source of the external data and updating the references to those external

The error in this cell indicates that source data is missing or has been changed.

| G2 | ▼ | = | ='[Monthly Expense Record.xls]Sheet1'!$H$4+'[Monthly Expense Record.xls]Sheet1'!$G$4 |

	A	B					
1	Expense Report						
2						Previous Month's Expense Total:	#VALUE!
3	Date	Expense Description	Amount	Amount to be Paid	Remainder		
4					0		
5							
6							

Tip

Depending on your work environment, you can try asking the person or persons responsible for maintaining your template's external source to be more aware of your dependency on their workbook. If they're willing, you can apply protection and passwords so that only a select few careful users have access to the file on which your template depends. See "People keep changing my text formatting, and I don't want them to" on page 134 for more about protecting your files from unwanted changes.

cells. This requires verifying the location of the other workbook, and checking to see what happened to the cells that your template refers to. To verify the location of your template's external data, you use the Trace Precedents command. Once you've verified the location, you can update your template so that it finds the data it needs. (See "When I edit the cells referenced in my formula, the result doesn't change" on page 152 for more about the Trace Precedents tool.)

How to fix it

1. If you haven't done so already, create a new document based on the template from which data is missing. You'll use this new document to find the source of your template's external data.

2. Click once on the cell that should contain data from another workbook. The cell you click can contain a formula or simply display the content of a cell in the other workbook.

3. On the Tools menu, point to Auditing, and then click Trace Precedents. Precedent arrows appear, and one should point from a workbook icon. ▶

4. Point to the external precedent reference (the icon), and double-click. The Go To dialog box opens, and the external reference is displayed. Click the

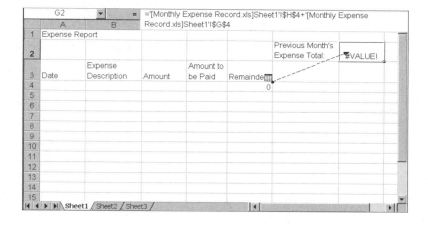

external reference in the Go To list, and then click OK. The source workbook, if it's still where it was when you created the template, opens with the cell referenced in your template displayed.

If the workbook is where it was when you set up your template's reference to it, all you have to do is reenter the data that's missing or edit the data so that it works with your template. For example, if a formula in your template references this cell, and now the cell contains text or something that won't work in the formula, edit the cell to contain what it should. After this adjustment, the template should work, because it will find what it needs where it expects to find it.

If the workbook is missing, you have to find out where it is or if it's been deleted. The fastest way to do that is probably to ask the person who works with it. If that's not possible, find the missing workbook by using the Find feature, which is described in "My template doesn't appear in the New dialog box" on page 298. If the file is missing (perhaps it's been deleted or has a new file name), you might have to redesign your template to find the needed data elsewhere or to use data from within itself.

I'm tired of inserting my logo every time I use the Invoice template

Source of the problem

Excel's Invoice, Expense Statement, and Purchase Order templates are handy if you don't have any of these workbooks of your own, or if you don't use a separate accounting application that provides such forms for you to use when sending someone a bill, expense statement, or purchase order. The templates are functionally (if not visually) well designed, and many users swear by them. They contain generic information and place-holders for things specific to your organization such as your company logo, your company name and address, the date, and in the case of the Invoice template, a unique invoice number, and a space for payment terms—so they're quite customizable. ▶

Suppose you think it's important that your logo be on these forms, but you are tired of doing it every time you use one of the templates. Your problem with the logo is common. It

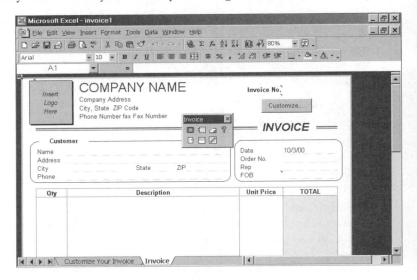

comes from not fully understanding how the templates work. The solution requires you to do some customization, after which the template will offer a completely customized version of itself each time you base a new workbook on it. (By the way, you'll have to keep your logo small enough to fit in the space allocated; otherwise, you'll have to retool the entire top of the template, and that's more trouble than it's worth, believe you me.)

To customize the template, you don't need to open it, but rather to simply open a new workbook based on it, and then use the built-in customization options to make it look the way you want it to. You have to do this only once. (The Invoice template is used as the example in this section; you can apply the steps to the other two templates in Excel as you want.)

How to fix it

1. On the File menu, click New.

2. In the New dialog box, click the Spreadsheet Solutions tab, and double-click one of the template icons, such as that for the Invoice template. A new workbook appears, based on the template.

3. Click the Customize Your Invoice tab at the bottom of the invoice. A series of fields that you can fill in with your own information appears.

4. Scroll down to the bottom of the Customize Your Invoice tab, and find the Formatted Information section, which includes the Select Logo button. ▶

5. Click the Select Logo button to open the Insert Picture dialog box.

6. In the Look In list, navigate to the drive and folder that contains your logo file. When you've found your logo, double-click its icon to replace the Insert Logo Here placeholder.

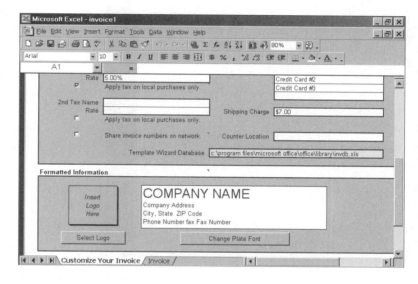

7. Enter your company name and address by right-clicking the COMPANY NAME placeholder to the right of the logo, and then clicking Edit Text on the shortcut menu. Replace the sample text by selecting each line of placeholder text and typing your correct company name and address.

8. Scroll to the top of the Customize Your Invoice tab, and click the Lock/Save Sheet button. When the Lock/Save Sheet dialog box appears, click Lock And Save Template, and then click OK.

9. The Save Template dialog box opens where you can save a customized version of the Invoice template. You'll use this new version each time you create an invoice in the future. Give the file a name, but DON'T change the Save In location—allow Excel to save the template to the Templates folder. Click Save, and click OK when Excel notifies you that the new template has been saved.

Once you've created a customized version of the Invoice template, you can use it any time by clicking New on the File menu, and then double-clicking the icon for the new template on the General tab of the New dialog box. Each time you use the new template, a new invoice workbook will be created, already bearing your logo and company specifics.

Works

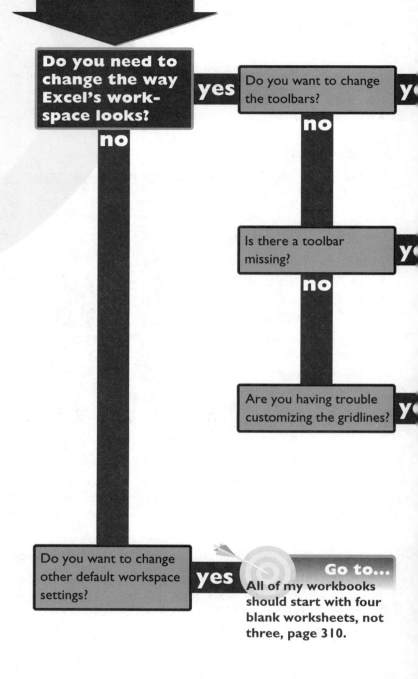

Do you need to change the way Excel's work-space looks?

yes → Do you want to change the toolbars? **y**

no ↓

Is there a toolbar missing? **y**

no ↓

Are you having trouble customizing the gridlines? **y**

Do you want to change other default workspace settings? **yes**

Go to...
All of my workbooks should start with four blank worksheets, not three, page 310.

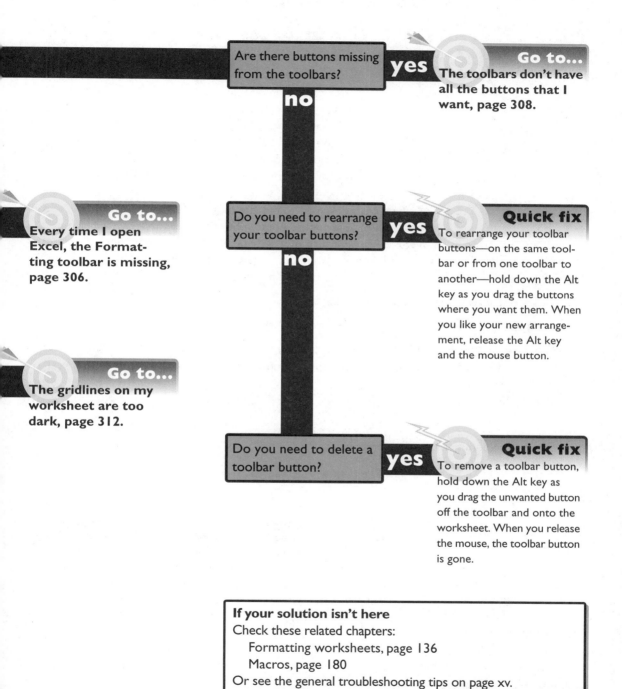

Are there buttons missing from the toolbars?

yes

Go to...
The toolbars don't have all the buttons that I want, page 308.

no

Go to...
Every time I open Excel, the Formatting toolbar is missing, page 306.

Do you need to rearrange your toolbar buttons?

yes

Quick fix
To rearrange your toolbar buttons—on the same toolbar or from one toolbar to another—hold down the Alt key as you drag the buttons where you want them. When you like your new arrangement, release the Alt key and the mouse button.

no

Go to...
The gridlines on my worksheet are too dark, page 312.

Do you need to delete a toolbar button?

yes

Quick fix
To remove a toolbar button, hold down the Alt key as you drag the unwanted button off the toolbar and onto the worksheet. When you release the mouse, the toolbar button is gone.

If your solution isn't here
Check these related chapters:
Formatting worksheets, page 136
Macros, page 180
Or see the general troubleshooting tips on page xv.

Every time I open Excel, the Formatting toolbar is missing

Source of the problem

Don't you just hate that? Your Excel workspace should look the same every time you open the application, with all the tools you know and love right where you left them. It can be aggravating—and for many users, disorienting—to not find a toolbar where you're used to seeing it. You can't blame this one on the gremlins that haunt your office, despite the fact that people like to blame them for everything. Excel's toolbars were designed to put the most commonly used features within easy reach of your mouse pointer, but the placement of toolbars and toolbar buttons isn't carved in stone. You can turn off toolbars quite easily, and you can even move and remove toolbar buttons (see "The toolbars don't have all the buttons that I want" on page 308). Nope, it wasn't the gremlins. The problem was created in one of three ways:

● You accidentally turned off the Formatting toolbar.

● Someone else who uses your computer turned off the toolbar.

● You have the Standard and Formatting toolbars set to share one row (an Office 2000 feature), and the Formatting toolbar is getting the short shrift in terms of toolbar buttons that appear on the visible portion of the toolbar combination. ▶

If your problem is the result of either of the first two reasons, it's easy to fix. Simply redisplay the toolbar, and make sure it's there when you exit Excel. Barring someone else using Excel on your computer and turning it off, the Formatting toolbar will be there the next time you start the software.

If your problem is the result of the toolbars sharing one row, that feature can be turned off. In fact, it's a feature I recommend turning off the minute Office 2000 is installed!

The Standard and Formatting toolbars are sharing one row, but the Standard toolbar is taking up most of the room.

Tip

What if the toolbar you want to display is already selected in the Toolbars list (indicating that it's already displayed), but you just can't see it? Perhaps the toolbar you're looking for is displayed as a floating toolbar and has been positioned so far to one side of the workspace that you can't see it. Or perhaps it's already docked down a side of the workspace where you wouldn't normally expect to see it, and you've simply overlooked it.

How to fix it

To display a missing toolbar, follow these steps:

1. Right-click any toolbar or the menu bar to display a list of toolbars.

2. Click the name of the toolbar you want to display.

3. If the toolbar appears as a floating toolbar, drag it to the top of the workspace to dock it there.

Excel 2000 To make the Standard and Formatting toolbars appear on two separate rows (with all of their respective buttons showing) rather than share one row, follow these steps:

1. On the Tools menu, click Customize to display the Customize dialog box.

2. Click the Options tab, and clear the Standard And Formatting Toolbars Share One Row check box. ▶

3. Click Close to put the toolbars on separate rows.

Tip

If you'd like to see a menu in its entirety as soon as you select it, you can clear the Menus Show Recently Used Commands First check box on the Options tab of the Customize dialog box. With this option turned off, your menus are fully displayed right away, and none of the menu commands appear on the menus with a lighter background, no matter when they were last used.

Float like a toolbar, sting like a bee

If you prefer to use floating toolbars, you can drag the docked toolbars away from the edges of the workspace. Simply point to a toolbar's handle (the vertical bar on the far left end of the toolbar), and when (and only when) your mouse pointer turns to a four-headed arrow, drag the toolbar away from the workspace edge. When you release the mouse button, your toolbar will be converted to a floating toolbar that you can drag around as needed while you work. To dock a floating toolbar, grab it by its title bar, and drag it back to any edge of the workspace. When the title bar disappears, the toolbar is docked.

The toolbars don't have all the buttons that I want

Source of the problem

When they selected the commands to go on the toolbars, Microsoft's software engineers and designers did their best to choose the commands that are used most often by most users. Of course, they didn't call you, so the ones you want aren't there. Isn't that always the way? Don't feel bad though. They didn't call me, either!

The solution to this problem is to stock the toolbars with the buttons you want to see—the ones that represent the commands you use often enough to warrant taking up valuable toolbar real estate.

How to fix it

1. Right-click any of the displayed toolbars, and click Customize at the bottom of the list of toolbars.

2. In the Customize dialog box, click the Commands tab.

3. In the Categories list, click the name of the menu that contains the command you want to add to the toolbar.

4. In the corresponding Commands list (on the right side of the dialog box), locate the command you want to add. (You might need to scroll to find it.)

5. Drag the command to the toolbar, releasing the mouse button when the I-beam pointer is where you want to place the button. ▶

6. If the button appears as text (rather than a picture) and you

The I-beam mouse pointer indicates where the command will appear on the toolbar.

want a picture, click the Modify Selection button in the Customize dialog box, and click Text Only (In Menus) on the drop-down menu.

7. Click Modify Selection again, and then click Change Button Image. A palette of button images appears.

8. Click the button image you want for your new button.

9. Repeat steps 3 through 8 for as many buttons as you want to add. Some of them will have their own default pictures; in that case, you can skip steps 6 through 8.

10. Click Close when you have finished adding and modifying all the buttons you want.

Tip

If you regret the way you positioned your new button, hold down the Alt key, drag the new button to a new position on the toolbar, and then release the mouse button. You can move all the buttons, not just your new one, and you can move them between toolbars. Be careful, though, because you will remove a button if you drag it off the toolbar entirely.

Gimme a shiny, new toolbar

If you have a batch of toolbar buttons that you want to see on the screen together, and you don't want to clutter up your existing toolbars with them, you can create a brand new toolbar. On the Toolbars tab of the Customize dialog box, click New. In the Toolbar Name box of the New Toolbar dialog box, type a name for the new toolbar, and click OK. An empty floating toolbar appears. To add buttons to it, click the Commands tab, and then drag the commands that you want to add to the new toolbar from the Commands list to the new toolbar. ▶

Continue dragging commands onto the new toolbar until you've created the quintessential toolbar for your needs. Click Close to close the Customize dialog box. You can leave your new toolbar in a floating state, or you can dock it along an edge of the workspace. You close it and then reopen it by right-clicking any displayed toolbar, and clicking the new toolbar's name on the toolbar list.

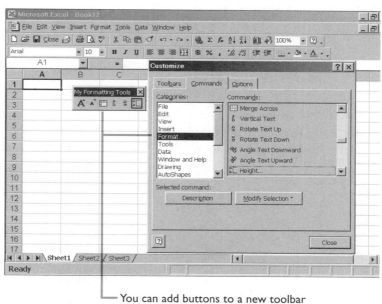

You can add buttons to a new toolbar by dragging commands to it.

All of my workbooks should start with four blank worksheets, not three

Source of the problem

It's a minor issue, and certainly adding an extra sheet to the default three that appear when you start a new, blank workbook isn't a lot of work, but if you want four sheets (or five, or six, or twenty-three) in every new workbook, by golly, you should have 'em. The fact that three is the default number is based on the needs of the average user—many of whom started using spreadsheet programs when there was only one sheet per file and who don't need more than that one for their average workbook now. As more people become more adept in the use of Excel, the more complex and the larger the "average" user's workbooks will become. Perhaps future versions of the software will have a greater number of sheets as the default in new workbooks as a result.

In the meantime, Excel gives you the ability to easily adjust this default (among others) using the Options dialog box.

How to fix it

1. On the Tools menu, click Options to display the Options dialog box.

2. Click the General tab. (Don't worry if your General tab doesn't look exactly the same as ours.) ▶

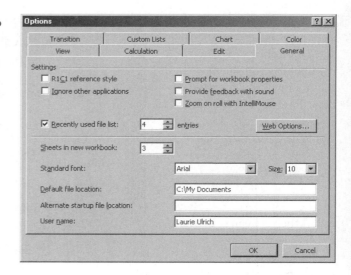

3. In the Settings section of the dialog box, increase or decrease the number of sheets to appear in a new workbook by clicking the up or down arrows on the Sheets In New Workbook box. (The default is 3; you can display as few as 1 or as many as 255 sheets in a new workbook.)

4. Click OK to save this setting and close the dialog box.

The defaults, they are a-changin'

Excel gives you the ability to change twelve different defaults on the Options dialog box's General tab alone. Here are a few you might be interested in changing:

- R1C1 Reference Style. Clear by default, this check box, when selected, numbers the columns instead of labeling them alphabetically. For example, if you're in cell B2 now, under the R1C1 style, that cell would be called R2C2. If you have trouble remembering that column G is the seventh column (in cases where that's an important perspective), you might like R1C1 Reference Style.

- Recently Used File List. If you would like quick access to a greater number of the files you've had open in your previous Excel sessions, increase this setting from the default of 4 to as many as 9.

- Standard Font. Arial is a highly legible, visually clean font. If, however, you would prefer another font for your default in all worksheets, change this setting. You can also change the size for whichever font you choose by clicking a size in the Size list. (The default size is 10 points.)

- User Name. This default is set by the information provided when Excel (or Office) was installed. If you're not the person listed in this field, or if your name has changed (or if you don't want your name to appear at all), edit the box accordingly.

Tip
If you type a number rather than use the up and down arrows to increment the Sheets In New Workbook setting, you can type any number you want. However, if the number you typed is zero, if it isn't a whole number (3.5), or if it is higher than 255, an error prompt will appear when you click OK.

Tip
Whenever you change default settings, make sure they'll be the best settings for the vast majority of your workbooks, not just for the one you're working on at the time or for a small number of your files.

Tip
The General tab's Default File Location option is covered thoroughly in "Saving" on page 244.

The gridlines on my worksheet are too dark

Source of the problem

By default, the color of your gridlines is set to Automatic. What color is that, you might ask? Even if you had the 64-color box of crayons as a kid, you probably don't have a clue what color "Automatic" is. This "color" comes from the Display properties for your computer and, specifically, from the Window text color you chose there. If, for example, your Window text is set to a shade of blue, that same shade would be the color of your gridlines. For most people—those who have kept the default Windows Standard scheme—the color of the gridlines is gray. ▶

If you want your gridlines setting to follow something other than the Window text color, you can change their color for the active worksheet in your current workbook, or for all workbooks in Excel. If you want to change the color of gridlines for all workbooks in Excel, you must change the Window text color on the Appearance tab of the Display Properties dialog box and leave the gridline color set to Automatic in Excel. If you want to change the color of gridlines for the active worksheet, you need to make some adjustments on the View tab of the Options dialog box.

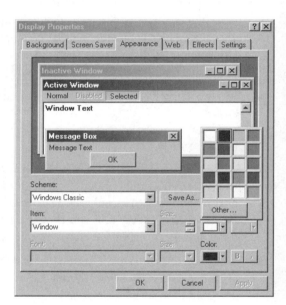

Tip
If you want to change the Window text color, thus changing the Automatic color applied to gridlines, right-click an empty spot on your Windows desktop, and click Properties on the shortcut menu. Click the Appearance tab in the Display Properties dialog box, and click Window in the Item list. Click a color in the Color palette, and then click OK to apply the change and close the dialog box. As long as the gridline color in Excel is set to Automatic, the gridlines in all your workbooks will follow this new Window text color setting.

How to fix it

1. Make sure the worksheet in which you want to change the gridlines' color is visible (or that the group of sheets you want to change are grouped), and then click Options on the Tools menu.

2. Click the View tab.

3. Make sure the Gridlines check box is selected, and then click a color on the Color palette. ▶

4. Click OK to close the dialog box and apply the change to your gridlines.

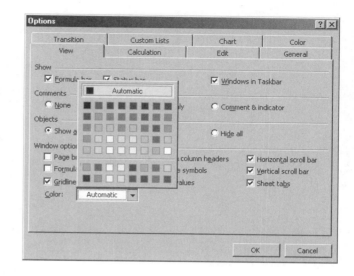

A worksheet with a view

You can change a lot of things about your Excel workspace, but do so with care. The View tab has many options that are turned on by default, meaning that to change them, you'd turn them off. Two options that are turned off by default are:

● Page Breaks. By default, you can see your page breaks only in page break preview. If you select this check box, they'll be shown as dashed lines in normal view. (To insert a page break, click Page Break on the Insert menu.)

● Formulas. If you'd like to see your formulas rather than their results in your worksheet cells, select this check box. This can be a helpful feature if you're doing an overhaul or review of your worksheet's formulas.

Tip

If you insert a page break while the check box for Page Breaks is cleared on the View tab of the Options dialog box, the feature is automatically activated, but only for the active workbook.

Squinting gives you wrinkles

If you find your worksheet gridlines too dark (or too light, or too bright, or too dim), you might also want to change the size of your toolbar icons—either making them smaller or making them larger, depending on your preference and eyesight. To change the size of your toolbar icons, click Customize on the Tools menu, and then click the Options tab. Select the Large Icons check box, and then click Close to magnify the toolbar icons to a larger size.

Index

hyperlinks, *continued*
  removing, 179
  ScreenTips, 173
  self-referential, 176
  targets, 173
  targets, entering, 177
  targets, moving or deleting, 171, 176
  renaming, 171
  testing, 172, 175
  text, underlined, 176
  types, 172, 174–5, 177, 178–79
  web, finding addresses, 174, 175, 177
  to web sites, 174, 178
  to worksheets, 172, 178–79

icons. *See* buttons on toolbars
identical
  files, naming, 246
  worksheets, 142
identifying active cells, 80
illegible
  charts, 10
  text, 126
image size, 145
Import command, 85
imported objects, editing, 89
importing tables from Word, 93
Import List From Cells box, 85
inactive hyperlinks, 176
inconsistencies, finding/fixing, 110
inconsistent formatting, fixing, 128, 129
Increase Decimal button, 117
Increase Indent button, 119
increasing
  decimals, 117
  font size, 127
  indent, 119
  text size, 127
increments, moving in, 71
indent, applying/adjusting, 119
ineffective displays, 12
input messages, creating, 111
Insert Comment command, 27, 121
Insert Hyperlink command, 171, 172, 174, 179
Insert Hyperlink dialog box, 172, 174, 178
inserting
  comments, 27, 31, 63, 121
  euro symbol, 51

inserting, *continued*
  hyperlinks, 171, 172
  hyperlinks to e-mail windows, 178
  hyperlinks to files, 178
  hyperlinks to intranets, 175
  hyperlinks to web sites, 174, 178
  hyperlinks to worksheets, 178–79
  logos in automated templates, 302
  objects, 90–91
  page breaks, 313
  source data in PivotTables, 230
  text boxes, 53
  .wav files, 90
Insert Name command, 206, 207, 209
Insert Object dialog box, 90
Insert Picture dialog box, 303
Insert Table command, 92
installing
  Euro currency button, 50
  foreign language dictionaries, 280
  Microsoft Map, 191
  printer drivers, 11
  printers, 11
insufficient memory, 89
  to create PivotTable, 221
  for printers, 11
intercept, setting in charts, 13
Internet Assistant Wizard, 254
interpreting ScreenTips, 179
intersecting ranges, 165
intranets, hyperlinks to, 175
Invoice template
  customizing, 303
  inserting logo, 302
  opening, 295
items with no data. *See* blank, records

keeping. *See* maintaining
keyboard shortcuts
  adding Shift key, 183
  available characters, 182
  euro symbol, 47
  for long terms, 282
  macros, 181, 182, 185
  Replace dialog box, 110
  reusing, 184
  saving, 111, 187
  selecting entire worksheet, 134

macros, *continued*
  recording, 182–83, 185–87
  replacing, 184
  reusing names, 184
  running, 185
  security, 189
  Stop Recording button, 183, 185
  storing, 183–85
  testing, 187
  viewing code, 183
  viruses, 189
Macros command, 181, 182, 185–86, 188
maintaining chart links, 99
making. *See* creating
Map button, 191, 193
Map Features command, 194
Map Features dialog box, 194–95
Map Labels button, 195
Map Labels dialog box, 195
maps
  adding features, 193–99
  applying, 192
  changed content, 198
  creating, 192
  deactivating, 198
  error messages, 191
  features unrecognized by Microsoft Map, 195, 197
  focal points, 198
  grouping with other graphics, 199
  labels, 195–97
  legends, 193
  moving, 199
  plotting, 192
  resizing, 198–99
  selecting data for, 192
  using, 192
margins in AutoShapes, 75
marking rounded numbers, 53
Match Case check box, 260
Match Case option, 263
matching
  case, when searching, 259
  column width, Excel vs. Word, 93
  conditional formatting, 43
  criteria, 112
  Word formatting, 93
measuring text, 93
memory
  checking, 221
  insufficient, 89, 221
  printer, 11

menus
  displaying full, 306, 310
  highlighting, 306
Merge And Center command, 93, 132–33
merged cells, 133, 217
Microsoft Access
  converting column labels into field names, 102
  converting Excel workbooks into, 102
  field names, changing, 103
  sorting Excel lists in, 268
  tables, 103
Microsoft Excel
  lists, soring in Access, 268
  versions, saving as older, 89
Microsoft Excel 97, applying euro symbol in, 51
Microsoft Map, installing, 191. *See also* maps
Microsoft Map dialog box, 193
Microsoft Visual Basic, 186
Microsoft Visual Basic editor, 183, 187
Microsoft Word, 93
missing
  AutoFilter entries, 108
  buttons, 308
  comments, 25
  data in templates, 300
  files, 250
  Formatting toolbar, 306
  labels, 3
  macros, 184
  records, 106
  rows, 22
Modified date, 246
modifying date/time formatting, 63
monetary symbols, 54
monitor resolution, 126–27
months, displaying entire name, 63. *See also* dates
mouse pointers, 70
moving
  AutoShapes, 70
  between cells, 79
  buttons, 49, 309
  callout lines/subjects, 72
  cell data, 138
  columns, 18–19, 133
  data, 19, 138–39
  formatting, 138
  hyperlinks, 176 (*see also* hyperlinks, targets)
  in increments, 71
  maps, 199
  named cells, 207
  named ranges, 207
  pushpin labels, 197
  objects, 71

quotation marks in formulas, 149

R1C1 reference style, 311
random width and height cells, 92
range references, 5
ranges, annotating, 121
ranges, cell. *See* cell ranges
range statement. *See* data, range
read-only files, 246
read-only status, 65
realigning text in AutoShapes, 77
reapplying functions in subtotal reports, 290
rearranging
　buttons, 305
　columns, 18
　rows, 19
　toolbars, 305, 307
recently used files, 249, 311
recognizing software, 90–91
recording macros, 182–83, 185–87
Record Macro dialog box, 182, 187
Record New Macro command, 182, 185
records
　blank, 275
　deleting, 275
　disappearing, 106
　excluded by filtering, 106
　filtering, 106
　lists of, 23, 286
　missing, 106
　in PivotTables, 226–27
　searching, 258–59
recycling data, 84
redisplaying
　columns, 20
　comments, 27
redoing PivotTables, 222
reducing
　decimal places, 47
　print areas, 239
　subtotal reports, 289
references, cell. *See* cell references
Refresh Data command, 230

refreshing
　PivotTables, 221, 230–31
　problems with, 225, 227
regional settings, 54–55
Regional Settings Properties dialog box, 55
reinstalling printer drivers, 11
Reject All command, 33
rejecting changes, 31–33
relocating
　hyperlink targets, 171
　template source data, 300
Remove All button, 215
removing. *See also* deleting; uninstalling
　Author name, 28–29
　comments, 26
　conditional formatting, 44
　decimal places, 47, 52–54
　filtering criteria, 107
　filters, 109
　hyperlinks, 179
　outlines, 211, 215
　rounding, 52–53
　subtotals, 215
　user names, 28
　words from spelling checker dictionary, 279
renaming
　files, 100, 251
　hyperlinks, 171
　trendlines, 12
　workbooks, 245
reordering
　columns, 18
　formulas, 150
　rows, 19
　worksheets, 143
repeating data, 84
Replace All command, 111, 257, 262–63
　failure, 257
　reversing, 262
　setting up correctly, 263
　undoing, 262
Replace dialog box, 110, 263
replacing, 110
　cells, 149, 257
　macros, 184
　matching case and, 257
　print areas, 239
　subtotals in subtotal reports, 288
reports
　creating based on filtering results, 113
　subtotal (*see* subtotal reports)
rerunning Pivot Table Wizard, 230

About the author

Laurie Ann Ulrich started her professional life planning to be an artist, but she discovered computers in 1981 and has been hooked on them ever since. Moving from computer systems management to managing computer training centers, Laurie formed her own computer training and consulting firm, Limehat & Company, Inc. in 1990, and she's been helping businesses and individuals make effective use of computers ever since. She has trained thousands of students, written hundreds of computer training manuals, and in the last three years has sole-authored, co-written, and contributed to more than 15 nationally published computer books on topics ranging from Microsoft Office to using the Internet to plan a vacation. For a complete list of Laurie's publications and services, and for links to support and creative solutions for users of Microsoft Office, check out *www.planetlaurie.com*.

The manuscript for this book was prepared and galleyed using Microsoft Word 2000. Pages were composed by Online Training Solutions, Inc. (OTSI) using Adobe PageMaker 6.52 for Windows, with text in ACaslon Regular and display type in Gill Sans. Composed pages were delivered to the printer as electronic prepress files.

Cover designer

Landor Associates

Interior graphic designer

James D. Kramer

OTSI Editorial Team

Jan Bednarczuk
Joyce Cox
Nancy Depper
Michelle Kenoyer
Gabrielle Nonast

OTSI Production Team

R.J. Cadranell
Leslie Eliel

Contact OTSI at:
E-mail: info@otsiweb.com
Web site: *www.otsiweb.com*

Target your
solution and fix it
yourself—fast!

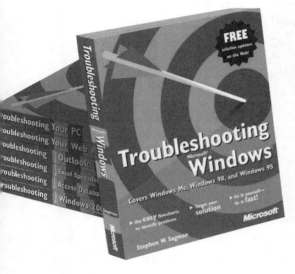

When you're stuck with a computer problem, you need answers right now. *Troubleshooting* books can help. They'll guide you to the source of the problem and show you how to solve it right away. Use easy diagnostic flowcharts to identify problems. Get ready solutions with clear, step-by-step instructions. Go to quick-access charts with *Top 20 Problems* and *Prevention Tips*. Find even more solutions with handy *Tips* and *Quick Fixes.* Walk through the remedy with plenty of screen shots to keep you on track. Find what you need fast with the extensive, easy-reference index. And keep trouble at bay with the Troubleshooting Web site—updated every month with new FREE problem-solving information. Get the answers you need to get back to business fast with *Troubleshooting* books.

ibleshooting Microsoft® Access Databases
(Covers Access 97 and Access 2000)
ISBN 0-7356-1160-2
U.S.A. $19.99
U.K.   £14.99
Canada $28.99

ubleshooting Microsoft Excel Spreadsheets
(Covers Excel 97 and Excel 2000)
ISBN 0-7356-1161-0
U.S.A. $19.99
U.K.   £14.99
Canada $28.99

ibleshooting Microsoft® Outlook®
(Covers Microsoft Outlook 2000 and Outlook Express)
ISBN 0-7356-1162-9
U.S.A. $19.99
U.K. £14.99
Canada $28.99

Troubleshooting Microsoft Windows®
(Covers Windows Me, Windows 98, and Windows 95)
ISBN 0-7356-1166-1
U.S.A. $19.99
U.K.   £14.99
Canada $28.99

Troubleshooting Microsoft Windows 2000 Professional
ISBN 0-7356-1165-3
U.S.A. $19.99
U.K.   £14.99
Canada $28.99

Troubleshooting Your Web Page
(Covers Microsoft FrontPage® 2000)
ISBN 0-7356-1164-5
U.S.A. $19.99
U.K.   £14.99
Canada $28.99

Troubleshooting Your PC
ISBN 0-7356-1163-7
U.S.A. $19.99
U.K.   £14.99
Canada $28.99

osoft Press® products are available worldwide wherever quality computer books are
For more information, contact your book or computer retailer, software reseller, or
Microsoft Sales Office, or visit our Web site at mspress.microsoft.com. To locate your
est source for Microsoft Press products, or to order directly, call 1-800-MSPRESS in
J.S. (in Canada, call 1-800-268-2222).

s and availability dates are subject to change.

Microsoft®

mspress.microsoft.com

Target your
solution
and fix it
yourself—
fast!

FREE solution updates on the Web!

Troubleshooting
Microsoft®
Access Databases
Covers Access 97 and Access 2000

▶ Use *easy* flowcharts to identify problems ▶ Target your *solution* ▶ Fix it yourself— fix it *fast!*

Virginia Andersen

Microsoft

U.S.A.	**$19.99**
U.K.	£14.99
Canada	$28.99
ISBN: 0-7356-1160-2	

Trouble with your database? Troubleshooting Microsoft® Access Databases can help you fix it. This plain-language book will guide you to the source of your problem—and show you how to solve it. Use easy flowcharts to identify your database problems. Get ready solutions full of clear, step-by-step instructions. Go to the quick-access chart for *Top 20 Problems*. Discover even more solutions with handy *Tips* and *Quick Fixes*. Walk through the remedy with plenty of screen shots. Find what you need fast with the extensive, easy-reference index. And keep trouble at bay with the Troubleshooting Web site—updated every month with new FREE solutions.

Microsoft Press® products are available worldwide wherever quality computer books are sold. For more information, contact your book or computer retailer, software reseller, or local Microsoft Sales Office, or visit our Web site at mspress.microsoft.com. To locate your nearest source for Microsoft Press products, or to order directly, call 1-800-MSPRESS in the U.S. (in Canada, call 1-800-268-2222).

Prices and availability dates are subject to change.

mspress.microsoft.com

Target your solution and fix it yourself—fast!

FREE solution updates on the Web!

Troubleshooting Your PC

► Use **easy** flowcharts to identify problems ► Target your **solution** ► Fix it yourself— fix it **fast!**

M. David Stone & Alfred Poor   *Microsoft*

Trouble with your hardware? TROUBLESHOOTING YOUR PC can help you fix it. This plain-language book will guide you to the source of your problem—and show you how to solve it right away. Use easy diagnostic flowcharts to identify your PC problems. Get ready solutions full of clear, step-by-step instructions. Go to quick-access charts with *Top 20 Problems* and *Prevention Tips*. Discover even more solutions with handy *Tips* and *Quick Fixes*. Walk through the remedy with plenty of screen shots to keep you on track. Find what you need fast with the extensive, easy-reference index. And keep trouble at bay with the Troubleshooting Web site— updated every month with new FREE solutions.

U.S.A.	**$19.99**
U.K.	£14.99
Canada	$28.99
ISBN: 0-7356-1163-7	

Microsoft Press® products are available worldwide wherever quality computer books are sold. For more information, contact your book or computer retailer, software reseller, or local Microsoft® Sales Office, or visit our Web site at mspress.microsoft.com. To locate your nearest source for Microsoft Press products, or to order directly, call 1-800-MSPRESS in the U.S. (in Canada, call 1-800-268-2222).

Prices and availability dates are subject to change.

Microsoft®

mspress.microsoft.com

The
practical,
portable
guide to
Microsoft
SQL Server 2000!

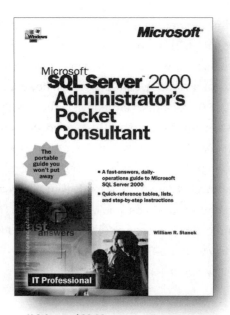

MICROSOFT® SQL SERVER™ 2000 ADMINISTRATOR'S POCK
CONSULTANT is the ideal concise, immediate reference
you'll want with you at all times as you deal with the
details of Microsoft SQL Server 2000 database
administration. Whether you handle administration f
50 users or 5000, this hands-on, fast-answers guide
focuses on what you need to do to get the job done
quickly. With extensive easy-to-read tables, lists, and
step-by-step instructions, it's the portable, readable
guide that will consistently save you time and minim
system downtime by giving you the right information
right now.

U.S.A.	**$29.99**
U.K.	£20.99 [V.A.T. included]
Canada	$43.99
ISBN: 0-7356-1129-7	

Microsoft Press® products are available worldwide wherever quality
computer books are sold. For more information, contact your book or
computer retailer, software reseller, or local Microsoft Sales Office, or visit
our Web site at mspress.microsoft.com. To locate your nearest source for
Microsoft Press products, or to order directly, call 1-800-MSPRESS in the
U.S. (in Canada, call 1-800-268-2222).

Prices and availability dates are subject to change.

mspress.microsoft.com

Proof of Purchase

0-7356-1161-0

Do not send this card with your registration.
Use this card as proof of purchase if participating in a promotion or
rebate offer on *Troubleshooting Microsoft® Excel Spreadsheets*. Card must be used in
conjunction with other proof(s) of payment such as your dated sales receipt—see offer details.

Troubleshooting Microsoft® Excel Spreadsheets

WHERE DID YOU PURCHASE THIS PRODUCT?

CUSTOMER NAME

Microsoft®

mspress.microsoft.com

Microsoft Press, PO Box 97017, Redmond, WA 98073-9830

OWNER REGISTRATION CARD

Register Today!

0-7356-1161-0

Return the bottom portion of this card to register today.

Troubleshooting Microsoft® Excel Spreadsheets

FIRST NAME   **MIDDLE INITIAL**   **LAST NAME**

INSTITUTION OR COMPANY NAME

ADDRESS

CITY   **STATE**   **ZIP**

( )

E-MAIL ADDRESS   **PHONE NUMBER**

U.S. and Canada addresses only. Fill in information above and mail postage-free.
Please mail only the bottom half of this page.

For information about Microsoft Press®
products, visit our Web site at
mspress.microsoft.com

||||

NO POSTAGE
NECESSARY
IF MAILED
IN THE
UNITED STATES

BUSINESS REPLY MAIL
FIRST-CLASS MAIL   PERMIT NO. 108   REDMOND WA

POSTAGE WILL BE PAID BY ADDRESSEE

MICROSOFT PRESS
PO BOX 97017
REDMOND, WA 98073-9830